MALAY

R. W. Dodds is Chief Examiner in 'O' level Malay at London University. A member of the Institute of Linguists, he worked for many years as a lecturer in Singapore and has an extensive knowledge of Malay and its idioms.

D1453359

TEACH YOURSELF BOOKS

To my mother

MALAY

R. W. Dodds

TEACH YOURSELF BOOKS
Hodder and Stoughton

First printed 1977

Copyright © 1977
R. W. Dodds

ISBN 0 340 222352

Printed and bound in Great Britain for
Hodder and Stoughton Paperbacks,
a division of Hodder and Stoughton Ltd,
Mill Road, Dunton Green, Sevenoaks, Kent
(Editorial Office: 47 Bedford Square, London WC1 3DP)
by Hazell Watson & Viney Ltd, Aylesbury, Bucks

Contents

Introduction

Most language courses adopt a position somewhere between the two extremes of the old grammatical method and the total-immersion method, as this one does. The grammatical method is concerned with analysis and it uses sample sentences to illustrate grammatical points. It can be quite useful when the native and the target languages are closely related in structure; but all too often it has qualified students only to talk in the native language about the target language. The total-immersion method recognises fully the semantic basis of language and the need for continual repetition; but, by forbidding all use of the native language, it denies that there is any value in drawing parallels, as aids to understanding, between native and target languages. It is also inappropriate for students studying alone from a book.

For several reasons I am very reluctant to use English grammatical terms in the book, not least because the terms are rarely taught in schools nowadays but mainly because they do not fit Malay and can give false impressions of the language. When I do use them, it is because they are appropriate in those particular contexts and are aids to explanation.

However, I have restricted explanation in English to those points which, I have learnt from teaching experience, perplex students. Other explanations are implicit in the translation exercises. There is, for example, no need for a special note on the imperatives of verbs. There are no inflexional changes to form the imperative and this is soon apparent in the exercises. Similarly, the contents-guide for each standard lesson mentions only the salient features of the lesson and does not summarise the many small points which can be adequately dealt with only by illustration in sentences.

The course progresses gradually from simple utterances through most of the intricacies of spoken Malay to the affix-loaded sentences of modern written Malay. The order of the subdivisions of each standard lesson is: vocabulary and associated phrases, lesson notes, translation exercises, then substitution drills. The weak English synonyms of the vocabulary lists acquire more precise meanings as we see the Malay words working in phrases then in a variety of sentences. Then, because it is essential for spontaneity of speech to learn sentence patterns, as well as words, by heart, the substitution drills are included. The exercises are concerned with Malay usage; and those seeking practice in translating from English can go to the Keys for Exercises and turn them back into Malay.

I have tried hard to ensure that no word or sentence structure is used in the exercises before it has been properly introduced. For any lapses in this respect, I apologise. On the other hand, I have deliberately introduced in the guise of stem words some **běr** and **mě** prefixed verbs before the lessons dealing with those prefixes, so that familiarity with known examples may instil confidence and facilitate the work of the later lessons. Bearing in mind the early introduction of words like **habis** and **rosak**, which are in the active voice in Malay but usually rendered in the passive in English, a glance at the Table of Contents will show the gradual progress towards the standard passive form in Malay. In such ways is the course structured.

I regret that due to the limitations on the size of the book, it was impossible to write narrative situations or conversations to illustrate the teaching points of every lesson; but in early lessons such pieces tend to be stilted and inane, and in later lessons it was felt that the space could be more usefully employed by including sentences to jog the memory regarding the work of earlier lessons.

SUGGESTIONS ON USING THIS BOOK

First, work repeatedly through the pronunciation exercises until you are sure that you can recognise the sounds of words from their spelling; then examine the vocabulary of the first few lessons, bearing in mind all you have learnt so far.

Students should work through each lesson systematically. It is essential to have a light grasp of the new words before attempting to go on; but the words will be fixed in the memory by working through the exercises.

1. Say each word in the vocabulary list aloud after checking its pronunciation. Spend about 30 minutes memorising the words and meanings.

2. Memorise the phrases and notice how the words are employed in them.
3. Read the lesson notes, go back to the vocabulary and check your grasp of the meanings, then read the lesson notes again.
4. Go to the translation exercises. One by one, translate each sentence and check for correctness in the Keys for Exercises. If you find the process easy, translate groups of sentences before checking. Mark the sentences where you have made mistakes, and refer to the notes again if the reasons for your mistakes are not immediately apparent.
5. When you have finished, read every sentence again aloud. Repeat this until you recognise the meaning of each sentence as soon as you see it.
6. Translate the specimen sentences of the substitution drills and check your work. Read each sentence again and again, interposing the words given for substitution. This process should be repeated until every sentence pattern is very familiar to you. Always read aloud.
7. Go to the Keys for Exercises and translate the sentences back into Malay.
8. When you feel you have mastered each lesson, go to the next; but remember that as you go further into the course, the need for short periods of revision becomes greater.

If you wish to refer to a note in a previous lesson but cannot remember its position, look up the word associated with that note in the Malay-English Index. There the numbers used beside words refer to notes associated with those words. Alternatively, you may find a clue to the position of a particular note by looking through the Table of Contents.

Finally, remember that the study of Malay demands a certain humility in students. It is so easy to make rapid initial progress in Malay that false and rather arrogant assumptions about it are easily formed. The language is deceptively and frustratingly simple; attempts to enmesh it in a system of definitive terms never succeed. That is why a complete grammar of Malay has never been written, and why generalisations in this book are qualified with words like 'usually', 'mostly' and 'tends to'. Don't fight the language; accept it as it is. When you start to see the world through Malay eyes, you will know that you are making significant progress.

Pronunciation

Almost all publications in Malay are now in *Rumi*, romanised script; and *Jawi*, the Arabic-related script, is confined almost solely to use in religious texts.

All of our letters are used except '*q*', '*x*' and '*v*', which appear only in borrowed foreign words. The letter '*c*' has the '*ch*' sound used in *chair*, and the '*g*' is hard as in *get*. Malays tend to use '*f*' and '*p*' interchangeably in some words but the '*p*' sound is much more natural to the Malay tongue.

The following exercises have been arranged to ensure systematic progress so you should follow them in the order that they appear.

1. 'B', 'd', 'p' and 't' as final letters   When these are the final letters on English words, we allow an escape of air from the mouth; but Malays do not. Practise saying the following English words without this explosive sound. (You can exaggerate at first by closing the mouth and swallowing immediately after the last consonant is formed.)

> sick, but, rub, cup, pack, lick, hot, fit, bed, lid, top, cap, neck, sit, cub, tap.

You may notice that the preceding vowel tends to be shortened and hardened by clipping the last letter short. Do not forget these letters in subsequent exercises.

2. The hard 'a'   This sound is heard more often in the north than in the south of England. Contract the long '*ar*' sound of *bard* to *bad*, making sure that you are not producing a combination of *bared* and *bed*. This is the sound for all *a*'s except for those employed as final letters. The reading list begins with three words borrowed from English:

> bas (*bus*), kad (*card*), pam (*pump*), dan, bab, had, lat, Mat, nak, hal, jam, tas.

3. The final 'a'   This is the final '*a*' of *data*, *Dora* and *phenomena*. In Malay, word-stress is never placed on this sound. Practise the two different '*a*' sounds in these words and put the stress on the first syllable:

> ada, apa, lada, jaga, tanda, bapa, dada, kata, lama, mana, raja, rata, raya, sama.

4. The pepet 'ĕ' This is shorter than the final '*a*'. It is the brief indeterminate sound in consonantal clusters, as can be seen in the Malayanised spelling of *screw* as **sĕkĕru**, where the pepet ĕ is only very slightly longer than the sounds between the English '*s*', '*c*' and '*r*'. The pepet ĕ carries stress only when found in the company of no other vowel but another pepet ĕ or a final **a**. In this practice-list, stress is indicated in the words of more than two syllables:

> ĕnam, dĕmam, bĕras, bĕkas, tĕbal, tĕbang, sĕnang, lĕkas sĕbab, rĕtak, ĕmpat, gĕlap, pĕta, bĕlákang, sĕkárang, bĕrĕnáng, sĕbĕráng, bĕlánja, pĕnjára, jé'ntĕra, tĕ'ntĕra.

5. The complete 'e' This is the '*e*' of *cafe* or, to put it another way, the severely shortened '*ay*' of *way*.

> ela, eja, beta, desa, bena, beres, gentel, dewan, deret, meja.

6. Stress Students should not worry too much about syllabic stress. Except in the instances already referred to (pepet ĕ and final **a**), the stress on the syllables of other words is so nearly even as to make close examination unnecessary.

7. The vowel 'i' This is near to the '*e*' of *return*, not the longer sound of '*ee*' as in *feed*. It is harder (nearer to the '*i*' of *thin*) when it is followed by two consonants, and also when, in its particular syllable, it appears between two consonants (that is, in a closed syllable). Two groups of words are given; in the second the sound of '*i*' is slightly harder.

> di, dia, bisa, bĕri, tiga, bila, kilat, silap, mandi, ini, isi, sini, lihat, gigi, pagi, tidak, jiwa;

> baring, lintang, kĕring, rakit, sakit, simpan, nasib, parit, minta, miskin, minyak, habis, dinding, keliling, dingin.

8. The vowel 'o' In terms of English this sound is between the '*o*' of *go* and the '*u*' of *shut* but it is best described as the French '*eau*' sound. As with the '*i*' the sound is very slightly harder (coming nearer to the '*o*' of *got*) in closed syllables and when preceding two consonants. The second group has this harder sound.

> otak, orang, kota, roda, rotan, roti, belok, tolak, rosak, pĕdoman, modal, oleh, topeng, boleh, kotak;

> bomba, ombak, rompak, ronda, dongeng, sombong, rombong, tongkat, lompat, bongkar.

9. The vowel 'u' Under similar conditions this sound ranges from the 'oo' of *root* to the 'u' of *butcher*; but, in addition to the circumstances of open and closed syllables, the sound of 'u' is affected by the letter that follows it. The hardening effect of 'k' is particularly noticeable in this respect, just as the 'oo' of *cook* differs from that of *cool*.

> bumi, guna, budi, tipu, batu, mula, tulis, pulang, suku, suka, kuning, sĕru, guling, baru, dunia, kutu;

> hukum, sumbat, gunting, bĕtul, bungkus, bĕlum, lanjut, jumpa, hidup, minum, sĕmut, tumpul, rumput.

10. 'Ng' and 'ngg' The letters 'ng' are represented in Jawi script as a single letter and students will find it advantageous to consider them as such. Their sound is that of 'ng' in *singer* but, unlike English words, some Malay words begin with ng, though they are few in number. A difficult word like nganga is more easily pronounced if seen as nga+nga, the second a, of course, having a final-a sound.

As one might expect, 'ng' followed immediately by another 'g' then takes the sound of 'ng' in *linger* because, as was said previously, a single 'g' has a hard sound as in *get*.

> yang, tong, barang, tukang, bunga, pangkal, pangkat, burung, bungkus, tangki, tukang, sĕngaja, tengok, mĕngapa, ngĕri;

> tinggal, meninggal, tinggi, ringgit, pinggang, panggung, ganggu, panggil, mĕngganti, tanggung, tunggang.

11. 'H' and 'r' To Malay ears, English speakers often seem lazy in pronouncing these sounds, the 'r' generally and the 'h' in particular at the end of words and when immediately followed by another consonant. First, it is necessary to distinguish between two h sounds. The explosive h, as in *house*, is found when the same vowel precedes and follows the 'h'; and though the Malays themselves sometimes ignore **h** as the initial letter of some words (like **hulu/ulu**), you are advised to pronounce it clearly until you are familiar with common practice. The breathed **h** requires no sudden expulsion of air from the mouth, and at times it is so light as to be indiscernible to the beginner's ear. It is found between unlike vowels, at the end of words, and immediately before another consonant.

The **r** should be rolled very slightly. Beginners often forget to do so when it is a final letter.

The first group of words employs the explosive **h**. Sometimes you will see the letter between unlike vowels because an explosive **h** has been borrowed in these words from Arabic or because emphasis is needed to distinguish one word from another, as with **Tuhan** and **tuan**.

> paham, jahat, mahal, dahan, bohong, lohor, Johor, bahan, bahu, nahu, lihat, leher, pihak, lahir;

> tanah, patah, bĕlah, boleh, bodoh, bunuh, musuh, masih, kasih, jahit, tahi, pahit, mahu, ahli, tahu, pĕrahu, mahkamah;

> askar, sabar, bĕsar, bĕlajar, ekor, fikir, pasir, mĕngalir, umur, ukur, dapur, ĕrti, harga, tĕrjun, sĕrbu.

12. The consonant 'c' As previously mentioned, this has the 'ch' sound of *chair*.

> cat, cacat, baca, suci, cuci, laci, pucat, cakap, cantik, bocor, cĕpat, cĕrmin, cĕrdik, cĕrita.

13. The combination 'sy' This is the equivalent of '*sh*' in English.

> syarat, syarikat, masyhur, syukur, syak, syor, syurga.

14. The combination 'ny' This is the '*ny*' of *canyon*. As with **ng**, it is better to consider the two letters together as one.

> banyak, bunyi, tanya, punya, monyet, sunyi, kunyah, kunyit, nyaris, nyamuk, nyawa, nyanyi.

15. The combination 'kh' This is the '*ch*' of *loch* when it is not over-emphasised.

> khabar, khas, khemah, khidmat, akhir, akhlak, makhluk, Khamis, tarikh, tawarikh.

16. The combination 'gh' The influence of h on the g here is the same as on the h in the previous **kh** combination. There are only a few words that contain gh.

> **ghaib, mubaligh, masyghul, maghrib, ghafur, ghalib.**

17. The glottal stop The glottal stop, as heard in the cockney for *bottle* (*bo'ol*), is usually represented by **k** because it is so close to the final-k sound. Less obvious at times is the break between two vowels as they come together in some words.

> **rakyat, makna, rukyah, saat, taat, masaalah.**

18. Diphthongs and vowel combinations

ai: This is the vowel sound of *sign*. It also becomes the sound of an **a** that is followed by a **y**, as in saya (*sigh-yer*):

> **lain, main, baik, air, cair, gadai, hĕlai, sungai, ramai, capai, sĕlĕsai, sampai;**
>
> **dayang, wayang, layang, paya, payah, payung, gaya, ayam, kaya.**

ia: At the end of a word this combination has the sound of '*ia*' in *Indonesia* but elsewhere in words it is the '*ea*' of *meander* in a northern English voice.

> **dia, mulia, dunia, sĕdia, bahagia, diam, biasa, liat, siapa, siasat, siang, biar, liar.**

au: This is the '*ow*' sound of *cow*. An **a** followed by a **w** also takes on the sound of this diphthong.

> **bau, lampau, gurau, harimau, jauh, sauh, daun, kaum, saudara, laut, kalau;**
>
> **awal, kawal, kawan, cawan, kawad, lawat, awak, bawa, bawah.**

ua: As used in many words, this combination has a **wa** sound. In other words the **u** is heard more clearly, as in the second of these groups:

> **buat, kuat, kuala, muat, puak, buang, tuang, suami, buaya, kuali, kuasa, puas;**
>
> **jual, tua, kĕtua, cuaca, sĕluar, suara.**

Note

The diacritic mark used over the e for pepet ĕ is no longer employed in Malay printing. It would, in fact, have been easier in this book to distinguish the complete e (since it is less common) by a mark, but because students are expected to meet the previous conventional mark in older books, and in some dictionaries, it is retained here.

Lesson One (Introductory)

Simple greetings; literal and figurative meaning; titles and names; introducing substitution-drill exercises.

Vocabulary

apa what
bagus excellent
baik good, well
ĕncik sir, Mr.
ĕrtinya meaning, it means
duduk sit, live, stay
jalan road, walk, travel
kasih love, affection
khaber news
mari come, here
masuk enter

pagi morning
pĕtang afternoon, evening
sama-sama thank you (in return)
saya I, me, my
sĕlamat safe, secure
sila please (in invitations)
sini here
tĕrima receive
tinggal live, reside, remain
tuan Mr., sir

Phrases

apa ĕrtinya what is the meaning of
apa khabar how are you, how do you do
khabar baik I am very well, fine
sĕlamat pagi good morning
sĕlamat pĕtang good afternoon, good evening
tĕrima kasih thank you

sila masuk please enter
sila duduk please sit down
mari sini come here
saya paham I understand, I see
sĕlamat jalan goodbye (*spoken to someone leaving*)
sĕlamat tinggal goodbye (*spoken to someone staying*)

Lesson Notes

The main aims of this lesson are to acquaint you with a few useful phrases and to introduce certain aspects of the language to

1

those students who, because of little experience of language study, may take for granted the intricacies of English and thereby make unwarranted assumptions about Malay. It is necessary to examine and be aware of the true ideas expressed in English phrases and sentences, otherwise haziness, ambiguity and incomprehension will follow in our translations. The first rule for students of a foreign language is: Do not translate words; translate ideas.

1. *Literal and figurative meaning* Hearing the words 'carry out', you may think immediately of the literal meaning of a person bearing an object out of a building or enclosure. Then you may think of the figurative meaning 'execute, accomplish', concerning a task or duty. These ideas are quite different and it is a peculiarity of English that they may be expressed with the same phrase.

The phrases given in this lesson show that words do not always mean what they say literally; though, if examined closely, the Malay often seems to have more basic truth in it than the English.

apa khabar?	what news (of yourself)?
khabar baik	news good
těrima kasih	received (with) affection
sama-sama	same same

2. *Forms of address* The Malays are a very polite and status-conscious people; and, therefore, formal modes of address are commonly used except between very close friends. The word ěncik is nearer to the French *monsieur* than *Mr*. because it can be used with or without a name, thus:

Apa khabar, Ěncik Hassan?
or **Apa khabar, ěncik?**

As well as being used with men's names the abbreviated form Cik is used with a woman's first name for *Miss* or *Mrs*. In Brunei and some other parts of Borneo the equivalent of ěncik is **awang** for males and **dayang** for females.

The word **tuan** is used similarly for male high-ranking civilians, army officers, and male Europeans generally. (The title of Joseph Conrad's book *Lord Jim* appears to be a rather grandiose interpretation of **Tuan Jim**.)

The word **Haji** indicates the person, or the title of the person, who has performed the pilgrimage to Měkah (Mecca).

3. *ĕrtinya* The stem of this word is **ĕrti** and it comes in its lengthened form **mĕngĕrti** as a verb to understand. The particle **nya** you will find attached to many words in later lessons; but, for the present, think of it as 'of it', or simply learn **ĕrtinya** as given in the vocabulary and phrase lists. You cannot use it in 'What do you mean?', where the implication is 'I understand all of your words, but what is your gist?' Here a different Malay word is required.

4. *duduk, tinggal* Notice the overlap of meaning of these two verbs in the sense of 'live, reside'. The difference lies in the inference of permanent residence with **tinggal**, and temporary with **duduk**. So, **duduk** is a little more appropriate for staying in hotels, for example.

5. *jalan* This word can be both noun ('road') and verb ('to travel, walk'). How to distinguish between the two, when it is necessary, is the work of another lesson.

6. *mari* This is the imperative (form of command) of 'come', and so it can be used in 'Come here' and 'Come on, let's', but it is not used in statements such as 'I come from Kuala Lumpur'. Later you will see **mari** used as an alternative for **sini**.

7. *sama-sama* The repetition of words, or 'reduplication', is a common feature of Malay. The words are always separated by a hyphen. The purposes of reduplication will be studied in later lessons. You will also see later that **sama-sama** can mean 'together' in some contexts.

8. *saya* When called, as from another room, a Malay often responds with **saya**, when we might say, 'Here', or 'Yes'.

9. *sila* There are several ways of indicating the politeness of 'please' in Malay. This word is used in very short invitations such as those given in the phrases.

10. *sini* This refers to the place 'here', and not to 'here' meaning 'take', as in 'Here is some money'.

11. *tĕrima kasih* Malays will often smile their thanks without speaking, or use **tĕrima kasih** for 'No, thank you', in which case

the accompanying gesture or the situation will make apparent what is intended. In this lesson we are over-using the expression for the sake of practice.

12. *names of people* Being Moslems, Malays do not have 'Christian' names. After the personal first name you will often find **bin** ('son of'), and **binti** ('daughter of') used as links to the names of their father. In this lesson the following names are used:

Male—**Hassan, Ali, Mohamed,** and **Othman** (and its variant **Osman**);
Female—**Fatimah, Měriam, Azizah,** and **Zuraidah.**

Drill Exercises

(*a*) Use this simple greeting as a pattern for wishing each of the other seven people mentioned above a good morning:

Sělamat pagi, Cik *Hassan.*

(*b*) Repeat the process, bidding them, 'Good afternoon', and asking how they are.

pattern: **Sělamat pětang, Cik *Fatimah.* Apa khabar?**

(*c*) Pair the men with the women in their respective order, and have the ladies call the men.

pattern: **Ěncik *Othman!*—Saya!
Mari sini, ěncik.**

(*d*) Use the same pairs in this invitation to 'Come in' and the grateful response.

pattern: **Sila masuk, Cik *Zuraidah*—Těrima kasih, ěncik.**

(*e*) Repeat this with an invitation to be seated.

pattern: **Sila duduk, Cik *Ali.*—Těrima kasih, Cik *Měriam.***

(*f*) Let them bid each other good-bye, the women staying and the men leaving.

pattern: **Sělamat jalan, Cik *Hassan.*—Sělamat tinggal,
Cik *Fatimah.***

4

(*g*) Translate the following conversation then repeat it four times, substituting in turn **masuk, tĕrima, sĕlamat** and **kasih** for **bagus**:

Apa khabar, ĕncik?	Bagus, tuan.
Ĕncik, apa ĕrtinya 'bagus'?	Ĕrtinya 'excellent'.
Saya paham. Tĕrima kasih.	Sama-sama, tuan.

Lesson Two

Simple sentences; contextual assumption of tense and number; word order and the copula verb 'to be', possession, questions, the demonstratives *ini* and *itu, tidak*; superfluous English words; *kami* and *kita, dia orang* and *mĕreka.*

VOCABULARY

air water, liquid
ambil get, fetch, take (possession of)
askar soldier, military, army
baca read
baju shirt, blouse, jacket
bĕri }
kasi } give
bikin }
buat } do, make
buka open, switch on, take off (clothes)
buku book
dia he, him, his, she, her, it
ini this, these, here's
itu that, those
jangan don't, must not
kami we
kita we
lampu lamp, light

makan eat, food
mĕreka they, them, their
minum to drink
orang man, people, someone
pakai wear, put on (clothes), use
pĕrĕmpuan woman, female
pĕriman civilian (*sometimes* **preman**)
pintu door, gate
roti bread
siapa who?
surat letter, document, note
tidak }
tak } no, not, or not
tolong help, please
topi hat
tulis write
tutup shut, close
ya yes

The following words are easily recognisable:

apol apple
Cina China, Chinese
Inggĕris English, British

kopi coffee
Mĕlayu Malay
pensil pencil

6

rĕkrut   recruit
teh   tea

polis   police

PHRASES

suratkhabar   newspaper
bukutulis   writing book
baju askar   uniform (military)
pagi ini   this morning
kĕrja polis   work as a
  policeman
pĕtang ini   this afternoon/
  evening

orang Mĕlayu   a Malay,
  Malays
orang Cina   a Chinese,
  Chinese people
pintu masuk   entrance, entry-
  door

LESSON NOTES

13. *Simple Malay sentences* Malay sentences typical of normal conversation rely very heavily upon their context for their full meaning. In this lesson it is important that you realise that number (whether singular or plural) and tense (the timing of actions) will usually be apparent to both speakers, either because of their situation or from their previous words. If we contrast 'This is a book' with 'These are books', we see that every word used indicates whether one or more than one object is referred to. However, if we employ a 'Tarzan' type of speech and words which do not change for the plural and say, 'Here sheep', we then need other words to make the meaning precise, or we need to be in the situation and able to observe the number of objects. In the simple Malay sentence

Pĕrĕmpuan tulis surat

pĕrĕmpuan can be 'a woman', 'the woman', 'women', 'some women', 'the women', and the same applies to surat; and tulis could mean 'write', 'writes', 'wrote', 'is writing', 'were writing', etc. This 'telegram' language demands a kind of crossword-puzzle mental agility to relate all the inferences made in several sentences and phrases. By thinking of a variety of possible situations for each sentence in the exercises, you will come to appreciate the economy and elasticity of spoken Malay. Later you will study the various means of expressing ideas with greater precision.

14. *Word order* Word order is important in Malay, due mainly to an almost total absence of a copula verb 'to be'. The words 'am/is/are/was/were', etc., which are omitted in the 'I Tarzan, you Jane' kind of speech, have their functions served by a definite order of words. Notice how alteration of word order changes meaning in these examples:

ini surat   this is a letter; these are letters; (or) here's a letter
surat ini   this letter; these letters
itu buku   that is a book; those are books
buku itu   that book; those books

When a noun immediately precedes a pronoun or noun, the meaning of 'of' is understood between them. Notice again the contrasts in these pairs of examples:

	baju saya my shirt (shirt of me)
but	**saya pĕrimen** I am a civilian
	topi Ahmad Ahmad's hat
but	**Ahmad askar** Ahmad is a serviceman
	buku siapa? whose book? (book of whom?)
but	**siapa dia?** who is he/she?

15. *Questions* Questioning words such as 'what', 'when' and 'why' may be found at the beginning, the end, or in the middle of sentences, as is illustrated here:

Apa ĕncik bikin hari ini?
Hari ini ĕncik bikin apa? } What are you doing today?
Ĕncik buat apa hari ini?

The simplest method of changing statements into questions is by inflexion of the voice. A questioning tone is used in the second of these sentences:

Dia tutup pintu   He shut the door.
Dia tutup pintu?   Did he shut the door?

16. *Superfluous words* When the central ideas are extracted from many English sentences, some words are found to be superfluous for translation purposes. In the following sentences brackets are placed around examples of such words:

Take this letter (and) give (it) to (the) typist.
What (is) that? (It is) a machine.

8

Here you see the 'and' is unnecessary because it is only joining two short sentences. The first 'it' can remain unexpressed because there is nothing else with which it can be confused; and the second 'it' can be translated by repeating 'that', or it can be ignored once again. So the Malay style would be

What that? (That) machine.

Other examples of such words are shown in the next sentences, where 'any' has to be seen as the negative form of 'some'.

I have (some) money.
I haven't (any) money.

Sometimes an English word will be used for such an obvious idea that it seems absurd to have an equivalent Malay word, as in

Take off (your) hat.

At other times blocks of English words seem to be superfluous once a particular situation is known.

The things in this shop are expensive. If (they were on sale) in the market, (they would be) a little cheaper.

17. *Bikin, kasi* Though having the same meaning as **buat** and **běri** respectively, these are very colloquial words which are used in written Malay when conversation is quoted. An odd use of **běri** which a student may meet is the idea of 'let, permit', used with regard to private property. Hence,

Jangan běri dia masuk Don't let him come in.

18. *Baju* Any garment, male or female, that is slipped on over the shoulders is a **baju**. What sort of **baju** it is can be indicated by a following word, as in

baju kot a jacket

Sometimes **baju** has the general meaning of 'clothes', as in

baju askar military uniform

19. *Tidak* The abbreviated form of **tidak** is **tak**, and at the end of a sentence **tak** means 'or not'.

Ěncik tulis surat ini tak? Did you write this letter or not?

9

Notice also that the negative statement can be changed into a question simply by using a questioning tone.

Awak tak tĕrima surat?   Didn't you receive the letter?

20.   *Ini, itu*   Like 'this' and 'that' in English, these words will indicate the nearness of an object to the speaker, but the application of the words can be surprising. One example is sufficient at this stage. Whereas we might say 'here in Kuala Lumpur' and 'there in Singapore', the Malays say 'in this Kuala Lumpur' and 'in that Singapore'.

21.   *Kami, kita*   In standard Malay both of these words mean 'we' but differ in that **kita** includes, whereas **kami** excludes, the listener. The difference is shown in these sentences:

Come with me and *we*'ll look for the shop together. **(kita)**
When my wife and I were in Penang, *we* stayed in Georgetown. **(kami)**

This is more complicated in parts of Borneo, where **kita** is used as a polite 'you', particularly towards elderly people. The inclusive 'we' is then **kita 'ni (kita ini)**.

22.   *Jangan*   This word is used for 'don't' in negative commands and is not the 'don't' of statements such as 'I don't know', where **tidak** would be appropriate. Putting the pronoun 'you' before the English command would necessitate changing the 'don't' to 'must not', but the Malay retains **jangan**.

Jangan buka surat   Don't open the mail
Awak jangan buka surat   You mustn't open letters

23.   *dia orang, mĕreka*   The standard Malay word for 'they' (of people) is **mĕreka**, but in every-day speech **orang** is sometimes added to some pronouns to make them plural, **dia** being such a pronoun in this example. You would differentiate between 'He is a Malay' and 'They are Malays' by using **orang** twice in the latter and pausing slightly where the obliques are shown.

Dia / orang Mĕlayu   He is a Malay
Dia orang / orang Mĕlayu   They are Malays

24. *ya* This word is reminiscent of the American 'yeah'. It is rarely used in isolation; expect it to be supported with other words, as when we say, for example, 'Yes, I did'. Students may see it sometimes written elsewhere as **ia**, but this spelling is avoided here because **ia** is also an abbreviation of **dia** which you will meet later.

EXERCISES

Read and translate:

A. 1. Ini surat. 2. Itu nasi. 3. Ini roti. 4. Ini air. 5. Itu teh? Ya, itu teh. 6. Ini baju? Ya, itu baju. 7. Ini topi dia? Tidak, ini topi dia. 8. Itu pensil ĕncik? Ya, itu pensil saya. 9. Itu buku awak? Tidak, ini buku saya. 10. Ini topi mĕreka? Ya, itu topi mĕreka. 11. Apa itu? Ini pena saya. 12. Apa ini? Itu kopi kita. 13. Ini apa? Itu suratkhabar Tuan Smith. 14. Itu apa? Itu bukutulis mĕreka.

B. 1. Saya orang Inggĕris. 2. Dia orang Cina. 3. Ĕncik orang Mĕlayu? Ya, saya orang Mĕlayu. 4. Awak askar? Tidak, kami periman. 5. Orang India itu orang pĕriman? Tidak, mĕreka askar. 6. Pĕrĕmpuan itu siapa? Dia orang Indonesia. 7. Orang Mĕlayu itu pĕriman? Tidak, mĕreka rĕkrut polis. 8. Siapa orang Cina itu? Itu Ĕncik Lim.

C. 1. Tutup pintu. 2. Tolong tutup lampu. 3. Buka topi. 4. Jangan buka lampu. 5. Baca surat ini. 6. Jangan pakai baju itu. 7. Minum air ini. 8. Jangan makan nasi itu. 9. Apa dia baca? Dia baca suratkhabar. 10. Awak bikin apa? Saya tulis surat. 11. Apa pĕrĕmpuan itu buat? Dia ambil suratkhabar. 12. Askar Inggĕris itu pakai apa? Mĕreka pakai baju askar. 13. Orang polis itu bikin apa? Dia orang tolong kami. 14. Siapa ambil air minum itu? Cik Mĕriam ambil. 15. Tolong bĕri dia baju ini. 16. Tolong kasi saya bukutulis itu.

D. 1. Kami tak tĕrima surat ĕncik. 2. Mĕrĕka tidak baca surat saya. 3. Kita jangan buka pintu itu. 4. Dia tidak tolong kami. 5. Awak jangan bĕri dia masuk. 6. Dia tak masuk askar, masuk polis. 7. Ini baju siapa? Baju Ĕncik Dollah. 8. Buku itu buku siapa? Buku Osman. 9. Itu buku apa? Buku Inggĕris. 10. Baju itu baju apa? Baju polis. 11. Awak kasi dia buku itu tak? 12. Mĕreka ambil suratkhabar itu tak? 13. Saya tidak tĕrima surat pagi ini. 14. Mĕreka tidak makan roti, makan nasi.

Read aloud, substituting the words given below each pattern for the words given in bold type in the pattern.

E. *pattern:* Ini **baju** ĕncik? Tidak, itu **baju** saya.
buku; roti; topi; surat; suratkhaber; bukutulis

F. *pattern:* **Ĕncik** bikin apa pagi ini?
mĕreka; awak; dia; orang Cina itu; askar Mĕlayu itu; pĕrĕmpuan India itu

Repeat this exercise twice, using the following word order (without change of meaning):

Pagi ini ĕncik bikin apa?
Apa ĕncik bikin pagi ini?

G. *pattern:* Jangan **tulis surat** pĕtang ini.
makan nasi; pakai baju kot; buka pintu; buka lampu itu; buat kopi; pakai baju pĕriman

H. *pattern:* Tolong kasi dia **pena** ini.
kopi; baju; bukutulis; surat; air minum; pensil

I. *pattern:* Saya tak **ambil pena, ambil pensil.**
  (*N.B.* **ambil** *is repeated*)
makan nasi, roti; baca surat, buku; pakai pensil, pena; bĕri dia topi, baju; tutup pintu, lampu; tolong Ahmad, Ali

J. *pattern:* Ini **buku** siapa? Itu **buku** saya.
pensil, kami; suratkhabar, dia; topi, mĕreka; kopi, Tuan Husin; baju, pĕrĕmpuan itu; teh, orang India itu

K. *pattern:* **Buku** apa dia **baca**?
pintu, tutup; topi, pakai; surat, buka; baju, ambil; pena, pakai; buku, bĕri

Lesson Three

Further use of *ini/itu*, and the definite article; variety of word order with demonstratives, nouns and adjectives, and word stress; *mana*; *hĕndak* indicating intention and futurity; the suffix *an*; omission of *kĕ*.

VOCABULARY

baru new, newly, recently, only then

bawa carry, bring, lead, drive (vehicle)

bĕli buy

bĕrsih clean

bĕsar large, important, main

bilik room

dapat obtain, succeed in, catch (illness)

datang come

dari ⎱ from (place)
daripada ⎰ (people)

di at, in

hantar send, see off (on journey), accompany

hĕndak ⎱ want to, intend to,
nak ⎰ to be going to

kampung village, home

kĕdai shop

kĕchil small

kĕpada ⎱ to (people)
kĕ ⎰ (place)

kĕrja job, to work

kĕreta vehicle, car

kotor dirty

lama old (of things) long (of time)

makanan food

mana where, which

pakaian clothes

panas hot, heat

pasar market

pĕdas hot (of taste)

pĕjabat office, bureau

pĕrgi go

rumah house, home

sĕjuk cold, cool

⎧ **di mana** where . . . at
⎨ **dari mana** where . . . from
⎩ **kĕ mana** where . . . to

Malayanised English words:

lori lorry

tĕrak truck

opis office

fail file

13

bilik makan	dining-room	**orang běsar**	V.I.P., dignitary
bilik kělas	classroom	**pějabat pos**⎫	
kědai makan	restaurant	**pos opis** ⎭	post office
air minum	drinking-water	**masuk askar**	join the army
bawa jalan	lead the way	**masuk kěrja**	reach work

LESSON NOTES

25. *Ini, itu* One of the functions of the English word 'the' is to
serve as 'that' when it means 'that — referred to previously'.
The change from 'a' in the first of the sentences to 'the' in the
second is shown by italics, and 'the' in these cases would be
translated by **itu**, because 'that' covers the meaning:

> One day *a* boy observed *an* accident from the top of *a*
> hill. *The* boy ran down *the* hill to the nearest telephone to
> report *the* accident to the police.

The examples of 'the' in 'the top', 'the nearest telephone', and
'the police' cannot be replaced by 'that' and it should be assumed,
at least for the time being, that there is no equivalent in Malay.

The Malay use of **itu** is sometimes carried further than 'the'
in English because it can also be used with pronouns and names,
as in

> **dia itu, měreka itu, Ali itu.**

In such cases it would indicate still that the persons had been
mentioned in previous sentences.

There is no equivalent in English of **ini** when used in **awak
ini**, the effect of which is simply to give 'you' a more familiar
tone.

Both **ini** and **itu** are abbreviated in quick speech to **'ni** and **'tu.**

26. *Word order* Notice how English sentences vary according
to the Malay word order. In the following examples an oblique
is used to indicate the very slight pause in Malay where the
English verb 'to be' (am, is, are, was, were, etc.) is understood:

> **Ini / kěreta běsar.** This is a big car.
> **Kěreta ini / běsar.** This car is big.
> **Kěreta běsar ini (/ baru).** This big car (is new).

One of the methods of stressing a word in Malay is to bring it nearer to the beginning of its sentence or, perhaps, half-sentence. The words in italics in these pairs of sentences are stressed in each second sentence because of this change of position:

Dia duduk *lama* di kampung itu. ⎫
Lama dia duduk di kampung itu. ⎬ He stayed a long time in the village.

Dia *baru* masuk kĕrja. ⎫
Baru dia masuk kĕrja. ⎬ He has just arrived at work.

Dia hantar *surat itu.* ⎫
Surat itu dia hantar. ⎬ He sent that letter.

Because of what might be called the 'elastic' qualities of Malay, which allow different translations of a sentence according to its various possible contexts, it is often advisable to state the topic or subject first and allow conjecture or comment to follow. This is one of the reasons why you will often hear a questioning word at the end of a sentence rather than at the beginning in the English fashion.

27. *Mana* When it means 'which?', mana is best placed after the word it relates to, as in buku mana? ('which book?') and kĕdai mana? ('which shop?'). This is to prevent confusion with mana used as an abbreviation of di mana, kĕ mana, or dari mana, or the Malay for 'how' that you will use later.

28. *'ndak, nak* These are abbreviated forms of hĕndak which are very common in conversational speech, the negative form being tak 'ndak only, since tak nak is considered a characteristic of children's talk. In addition, nak can be used for the English 'to' which means 'in order to'. By comparing the following sentences and noting the different positions of nak, you can see its change of function and the effect it has on the tense, or timing, of pĕrgi:

Dia nak pĕrgi kĕdai bĕli baju.   He *is going to* go shopping to buy a shirt.

Dia pĕrgi kĕdai nak bĕli baju.   He went shopping *to* buy a shirt.

29. *Kĕ* In the exercises you will meet pĕrgi kĕdai and pĕrgi kampung, where kĕ has been omitted in these very common expressions, just as we would say 'go home' rather than 'go to home'.

30. . . . *an* This suffix is used often to form a noun from a verb. The examples in this lesson are **pakaian** ('clothes') from **pakai** and **makanan** ('food') from **makan.**

31. *Lama* This word can be used as 'old' of people but it would mean 'for a long time' or 'veteran' rather than 'advanced in years'. It can be used, for example, in 'old friend', 'old soldier' and 'veteran driver'.

32. *Pĕrgi* In 'bazaar Malay', the debased Malay used generally between people of different race, this word is pronounced **pigi**. In dialect it may even be reduced to **pi.**

33. *Kampung* The Malay kampung is a more closely-knit community than the English village, and **kampung** is often used where we would use 'home', as in 'going home' (from outside the village) and 'sending a letter home'.

34. *saya, baru* The spelling of these words formerly was **sahaya** and **baharu,** but the modern pronunciation is best rendered by **saya** and **baru.** In written Malay **baharu** is still quite common. You can see another variant in the place-name **Johor Bahru.**

Exercises

Read and translate:

A. 1. Ini roti lama. 2. Itu makanan pĕdas. 3. Ini makanan panas. 4. Itu rumah baru. 5. Ini pakaian bĕrsih. 6. Ini pasar bĕsar. 7. Itu kĕreta kecil. 8. Itu teh sĕjuk. 9. Itu air kotor. 10. Itu kĕreta kecil. 11. Ini teh panas. 12. Ini pintu masuk? 13. Ini jalan bĕsar? 14. Itu air minum? 15. Itu kem polis? 16. Ini kĕdai baru?

B. 1. Nasi itu pĕdas. 2. Kopi ini sĕjuk. 3. Pĕjabat ini kĕcil. 4. Buku itu kotor. 5. Pasar itu bĕsar. 6. Air ini panas. 7. Kampung itu baru. 8. Bilik ini kĕcil. 9. Kĕreta saya lama. 10. Kĕdai dia baru. 11. Pĕjabat mĕreka bĕsar. 12. Rumah saya panas. 13. Pakaian dia kotor. 14. Kampung ĕncik bĕsar? 15. Baju saya kotor? 16. Bilik dia bĕrsih?

C. 1. Minum air sĕjuk ini. 2. Masuk jalan bĕsar itu. 3. Bawa kĕreta kĕcil ini. 4. Ambil baju bĕrsih itu. 5. Duduk di pĕjabat

16

lama itu. 6. Běli topi běsar itu. 7. Hantar surat kěcil ini.
8. Jangan makan nasi kotor ini. 9. Jangan masuk bilik běrsih
ini. 10. Jangan bawa lori lama itu. 11. Jangan pakai air panas
ini. 12. Awak jangan buka pintu masuk itu. 13. Dia jangan
tutup pintu běsar itu. 14. Měreka jangan pěrgi kě kědai kopi
itu.

D. 1. Dia nak pěrgi kě kědai běli roti. 2. Dia pěrgi kě pasar
nak běli baju. 3. Dia nak pěrgi kědai běli bukutulis. 4. Měreka
pěrgi kě kampung nak běli kěreta lama. 5. Tuan nak bikin apa?
Saya nak běli buku. 6. Di mana ěncik duduk? 7. Měreka
tinggal di mana? 8. Kě mana ěncik nak hantar surat itu?
9. Tuan datang dari mana? Dari London. 10. Daripada siapa
dia běli kěreta lama itu? 11. Kěpada siapa ěncik kasi baju
baru itu? 12. Saya baru dapat surat daripada Ěncik Kadir.
13. Baru měreka masuk kěrja. 14. Kami duduk lama di
kědai makan. 15. Mat nak jalan kě mana? Kě rumah Ěncik
Daud di kampung itu. 16. Lama dia kěrja askar. 17. Di mana
Ěncik Hassan? Di bilik makan. 18. Tidak lama dia kěrja di
sini. 19. Saya běri topi běsar itu kěpada Zainal. 20. Baju
kotor itu saya ambil dari bilik kěcil. 21. Jalan mana pěrgi ke
Muar? 22. Kěreta mana ěncik nak bawa? 23. Saya datang kě
pintu běsar, tak dapat masuk. 24. Dia orang tak dapat pěrgi
kě pasar. 25. Ěncik Ahmad nak buat apa? Dia nak kěrja di
opis. 26. Awak nak apa? Nak makan. 27. Mereka nak
minum, tak 'ndak makan. 28. Saya tak 'ndak masuk askar, nak
masuk polis. 29. Apa ěncik nak? Nak bawa orang kě Labis.
30. Tuan Jones pěrgi kě Kuala Lumpur nak hantar orang kě
London.

E. Insert **di mana, kě mana** or **dari mana,** whichever is appropriate, in the blank spaces in these sentences:

1. — měreka datang? 2. Awak duduk — ? 3. Mat nak bawa
lori ini — ? 4. Orang itu bawa těrak datang — ? 5. Ěncik
kěrja — ? 6. Tuan hantar surat itu — ?

F. Read and translate these sentences, then make them negative
and give them emphasis in the manner of this example:

> **Saya** *lama* **tinggal di Ipoh itu.**
> (*becomes*) **Tidak** *lama* **saya tinggal di Ipoh itu.**

1. Dia lama kěrja di pějabat itu. 2. Měreka lama makan nasi di
kědai itu. 3. Dia lama bawa kěreta. 4. Awak lama tulis surat

17

itu. 5. Kami lama buat kĕrja itu. 6. Dia lama jalan datang sini.

G. Read, translate, then give emphasis in the style of this example:

> **Dia baru bĕli rumah kĕcil itu.**
> (*becomes*) **Rumah kĕcil itu baru dia bĕli.**

1. Saya baru tulis surat bĕsar itu. 2. Dia baru bawa air sĕjuk itu. 3. Kadir baru tutup pintu bĕsar itu. 4. Hassan baru tutup pintu kĕcil itu. 5. Ahmad baru bĕli topi baru itu. 6. Saya baru baca buku baru itu.

Exercises H—L are substitution drills.

H. *pattern:* **Mat** nak kĕ mana? Nak kĕ **Muar.**
ĕncik, Johor Bahru; awak, pĕjabat pos; Cik Mĕriam, pasar; mĕreka, kĕdai makan; dia orang, kampung; tuan, rumah bĕsar itu

I. *pattern:* Ĕncik **kĕrja** lama di **sini?**
duduk, sini; tinggal, kampung ini; kĕrja, pĕjabat itu; duduk, bilik kĕlas; duduk, Kampung Bĕsar; kĕrja, kĕdai makan itu

J. *pattern:* Ini **air bĕrsih.** Air itu kotor. (N.B. **air** is repeated)
pakaian, bĕrsih, kotor; kopi, panas, sĕjuk; roti, baru, lama; kĕreta, bĕsar, kĕcil; pensil, baru, kĕcil; teh, panas, sĕjuk

K. *pattern:* **Bilik** mana? **Bilik kotor** itu. (noun repeated)
pasar, baru; jalan, bĕsar; rumah, lama; baju, bĕrsih; pĕjabat, kĕcil; air, kotor

L. *pattern:* Ĕncik Mat tak dapat **datang kĕrja.**
pĕrgi pasar; bĕli kĕreta baru; buka pintu; bĕli suratkhabar; pĕrgi kampung; datang kĕrja pagi ini

M. Here are four long sentences, containing enough information to make them complete, broken down into conversational question and answer form to show the brevity of such responses in their context:

Ahmad pĕrgi kĕdai nak bĕli suratkhabar.
Ahmad pĕrgi kĕ mana? Pĕrgi kĕdai.
Nak bĕli apa? Nak bĕli suratkhaber.

Husain datang dari pĕjabat nak ambil buku kĕcil itu.
Husain datang dari mana? Dari pĕjabat.

Dia nak apa? Nak ambil buku.
Buku apa? Buku kĕcil itu.

Kopral Osman duduk di bilik kĕlas tulis surat kĕpada Ĕncik Kadir.
Osman itu siapa? Dia kopral polis.
Di mana dia? Duduk di bilik kĕlas.
Buat apa? Tulis surat.
Kĕpada siapa dia nak tulis? Kĕpada Ĕncik Kadir.

Ali pĕrgi kampung nak ambil buku dia daripada Husain.
Ali pĕrgi kĕ mana? Pĕrgi kampung.
Nak bikin apa? Ambil buku.
Daripada siapa? Daripada Husain.
Buku itu buku siapa? Buku Ali.

Lesson Four

Question intonation reinforced by *apa* and *adakah;* uses of *ada;* short affirmative and negative responses; juxtaposition to suggest conditional relation; *bĕlum* and tense indication; the particles *kah* and *lah;* prepositions; the position of quantitative adjectives.

VOCABULARY

ada   to have, possess, to be present/situated
almari   cupboard, locker
anak   the young of, child
atas   top, above, on
bandar   town
banyak   many, much, a lot of
bawah   bottom, under
bĕlakang   back, behind
bĕlum   not yet
besok ⎫
esok ⎬   tomorrow
bukit   hill
cari   seek, look for
dalam   inside, interior, deep
hadapan ⎫   front, in front,
dĕpan ⎬   next (week, year, etc.)
hari   day

istĕri   wife
kasut   shoe
kĕluar   to go out
kĕrusi   chair
laci   drawer
luar   outside
malam   night
pĕti   box, crate
sĕkarang   now
sĕkolah   school
sĕluar   trousers
sĕmalam   yesterday
suami   husband
tadi   just now, last (refers to time within last 24 hrs.)
taruh   put, put away, add (sugar, etc.)
tunggu   to wait (for)

Malayanised English words:

bas   bus
benk   bank

doktor   doctor
gĕlas   glass (for drinking)

20

PHRASES

malam sěmalam } last night
malam tadi
malam ini   tonight
pěti sějuk   refrigerator
pěti surat   post-box
sěluar baju   suit
makan pagi   breakfast
makan malam   (have) dinner
orang kědai   shop-keeper
orang kampung   villager
pintu masuk   entrance
pintu kěluar   exit

kěrusi meja   furniture
anak istěri   wife and children
marilah kita   let's
meja tulis   desk
almari fail   filing cabinet
luar bandar   rural
kědai buku   bookshop
kědai kasut   shoe-shop
baju dalam   vest
hari ini   today

LESSON NOTES

35. *Apa, adakah*   In this lesson **apa** is used in another sense. It serves to introduce a question and can be thought, like the French '*est-ce que*', to signify 'Is it that?' When used in this way it has a rising tone, and there is a very slight pause after the word, though in quick speech this is difficult to detect. It is not used in this way in written Malay, where **adakah** takes its place. When speaking to Europeans many Malays become formal in speech, and so you may hear **adakah** more often.

36. *Ada*   This word has two main uses:

(*a*)   it translates 'have/has/had' when they mean 'possess'—not as in 'has gone', 'have bought', etc.;
(*b*)   it can be used like the verb 'to be' when used in the sense of 'located', 'situated', and 'present'.

Examples:

Dia ada rumah baru.   He has a new house.
Rumah ěncik ada di mana?   Where is your house?
Saya ada di bandar.   I was in the town.
Hashim ada?   Is Hashim in/here/there?

The presence of **di** in a sentence usually indicates the *second* use of **ada**.

21

37. *Short responses* Malays often take the most significant word in a question and use it or its negative form to say 'yes' or 'no'. Examples in English would be as follows:

Do you like living here? Like.
Do you want to buy it? Not want.

In this lesson **ada** is used for short responses in this way:

Hashim ada di pĕjabat? Ada. Is Hashim in the office? Yes.
Ĕncik ada kĕreta? Tak ada. Have you a car? No.

38. *Juxtaposition* By placing sentences or part-sentences together, the comparison of one with another can indicate a meaning which they would not possess when separated. In this way 'if' can be suggested at times, as in,

Ali tak ada di bank, carilah di kampung.
(If) Ali isn't in the bank, look for him in the village.

39. *Bĕlum, tense indication* The timing of actions, or, more accurately, the tenses of verbs, are shown in English by changing the words according to a formal pattern. For example, we know that before 'am watching' will be the word 'I', and that it can indicate an action being continued at the present time, whereas 'has sent' is stressing the completion of a past action. As you have already seen, the timing of Malay verbs is often shown by their context. But when the context alone is not sufficient to indicate tense, Malays use words which can be classed as 'tense-indicators'. Time indications such as **besuk, malam tadi,** and **semalam** come into this category and act like the English word 'tomorrow' added to 'He goes to Labis'. Another of these tense-indicators is **bĕlum,** in which the idea of 'have/has not' is contained.

Dia bĕlum kĕluar rumah. He hasn't come out of the house yet.

40. *Pergi* Movement to or from the speaker can be shown in English by the three different verbs and their prepositions printed in italics below:—

(*a*) He *hasn't come from* Sĕrĕmban yet. (to)
(*b*) He *hasn't gone to* Sĕrĕmban yet. (away)
(*c*) He *hasn't been to* Sĕrĕmban yet. (away and back).

In Malay there is no change of verb as in (c) and only the context will show whether

Dia bĕlum pĕrgi kĕ Sĕrĕmban

is in the sense of (b) or (c), though, of course, **bĕlum datang dari** will be used in (a).

41. *Kah, lah* These two particles are used to stress the words to which they are joined, **kah** being used in questions and **lah** most often in statements. Thus a word may be stressed either by bringing it nearer to the beginning of its sentence (see the note on word order in Lesson Three), or by using **kah** or **lah,** or by both methods together.

When **lah** is used on a command it softens the command. Thus **Janganlah** is less harsh than **Jangan.**

42. *Word order, itu* In this lesson you will see **itu** (and it could apply to **ini**) moving further away from the noun it describes. Notice the development below:

> **buku itu**
> **buku kĕcil itu**
> **buku di atas meja itu**

It can be seen that **itu** gradually moves away from **buku** and that the phrase **di atas meja** is an equivalent of the single word **kĕcil**; and 'the on-the-table book' shows a necessary and logical word arrangement in Malay, because a word order similar to the English—'the book on the table'—would, in fact, say 'the book is on the table' **(buku itu di atas meja).**

43. *Prepositions* The English words usually indicating position or direction, such as under/above/behind, etc., do not have exact equivalents in Malay. It is better to see the Malay words **luar/ dalam/hadapan/bĕlakang/atas/bawah** as nouns translating the outside/the inside/the front/the rear/the top/the bottom; then you will see why **kĕ, di** and **dari** are used with these words to do the work of the English prepositions. For example:

> into **kĕ dalam** (*to the inside of*)
> on **di atas** (*at the top of*)

In Malay conversation **di** and **kĕ** are often dropped in such cases, but until you are certain that no ambiguity will arise, you should retain the full form.

44. *Banyak* Words indicating quantity, such as those meaning 'few', 'many' and 'several', are usually placed in front of the noun they are describing. For example:

banyak orang a lot of people
banyak kĕreta many vehicles

45. *Next, dĕpan* Finding the Malay equivalent of 'next' gives some difficulty to speakers of English. You will find that it depends whether the English word means 'different', 'again', 'one more' and other such nuances in particular contexts as to which Malay word is appropriate. In this lesson **hadapan** and its shortened form **dĕpan** are given as 'next' when applied to 'year', 'month' and 'week', though they are not used in the exercises in this way before Lesson Six.

EXERCISES

Translate.

A. 1. Ĕncik ada kĕreta? Ada. Kĕreta ada di mana? Ada di jalan di luar pĕjabat. 2. Zainal ada anak? Ada. Sĕkarang anak ada di mana? Ada di sĕkolah. 3. Osman tak datang kĕrja hari ini? Tidak, dia hantar istĕri kĕ kampung. Kampung istĕri ada di mana? Ada di Jalan Batu. 4. Tuan ada istĕri? Bĕlum. Tuan ada rumah? Tidak, saya duduk di hotel. 5. Marilah kita pĕrgi kĕ bandar. Saya tak 'ndak pĕrgi sĕkarang. Awak ada kĕrja sĕkarang? Kĕrja saya tak banyak. Tunggulah saya di kĕdai kopi. 6. Sĕjuklah air minum ini. Ya, saya baru ambil dari pĕti sĕjuk. Bĕsarkah pĕti sĕjuk itu? Ya, bĕsar.

B. 1. Malam sĕmalam ada banyak orang di bandar. 2. Taruhlah fail itu di dalam laci meja saya. 3. Ĕncik tunggu siapa di pintu bĕsar itu tadi? Saya tunggu istĕri datang dari kampung. 4. Tolonglah taruh surat ini kĕ dalam pĕti surat. 5. Ada banyak fail di dalam almari. 6. Banyak orang ada di dalam lori. 7. Tak ada makanan di rumah, pĕrgilah bĕli di pasar. 8. Pĕrgilah ambil kĕrusi dari bĕlakang bilik. 9. Pagi tadi saya taruh fail di atas meja tulis. Sĕkarang ada di dalam almari fail. 10. Di hadapan sĕkolah ada banyak kĕreta. 11. Doktor tak ada di rumah, carilah di kampung. 12. Bĕsarlah lori di dĕpan kĕdai itu. 13. Suami dia kĕluar rumah tadi nak cari anak di atas bukit. 14. Ambillah kasut baru itu dari pĕti. 15. Hari ini dia kĕrja di bandar, besuk nak kĕrja di kampung. 16. Surat di dalam fail itu bĕlum banyak. 17. Di bawah rumah ada kĕreta lama. 18. Banyak orang kampung nak pĕrgi kĕ bandar hari ini. 19. Dia pakai kasut tadi nak kĕluar rumah. 20. Apa ĕncik kĕrja lama di pĕjabat malam tadi? 21. Kĕrusi meja di dalam pĕjabat itu barukah? 22. Di manakah anak istĕri dia sĕkarang? 23. Adakah tuan ambil surat dari laci tadi? 24. Kĕ manakah ĕncik nak hantar anak istĕri pĕtang ini? 25. Hari ini anak saya masuk sĕkolah. 26. Saya tak 'ndak pakai pĕti kĕcil itu. Taruhlah di bĕlakang kĕdai. 27. Ĕncik Ali ada? Bĕlum, dia nak kĕ benk pagi ini. 28. Apa ĕncik duduk di luar bandar? 29. Orang kĕdai tak datang pagi ini. 30. Pĕtang sĕmalam dia tak tutup pintu almari fail. 31. Siapakah orang di dalam kĕreta bĕsar itu? 32. Bĕsarkah anak dia sĕkarang? 33. Tak dapatkah dia masuk?

Substitute in the following exercises:

C. *pattern:* Ada banyak **orang** di **dalam kĕdai.**
kĕreta, luar kampung; rumah, bawah bukit; kĕrja, dalam pĕjabat; bas, hadapan sĕkolah; air, atas jalan; lori, bĕlakang benk; sĕluar baju, dalam almari; kĕrusi, luar bilik

D. *pattern:* **Hasan** tak ada di **opis,** carilah di **bilik makan.**
istĕri dia, rumah, pasar; orang kĕdai, kĕdai, kampung; fail itu, atas meja, dalam laci; suami dia, pĕjabat, kĕdai kopi; anak saya, rumah, sĕkolah; baju itu, dalam almari, pĕti itu

E. *pattern:* Apa ĕncik tak 'ndak pĕrgi kĕ **opis pagi ini?**
pasar, pĕtang ini; bandar, malam ini; pĕjabat, besok; kĕdai buku, pagi esok; benk, pagi tadi; sĕkolah, besok pĕtang

F. *pattern:* **Rumah** di **hadapan** sĕkolah itu **baru**kah?
jalan, dĕpan, baik; bilik makan, dalam, bĕsar; kĕdai makan, luar, bĕrsih; orang, dalam, banyak; bilik, dalam, panas; kampung, bĕlakang, kĕcil

G. *pattern:* **Sĕjuk**lah **air** di **dalam gĕlas** itu.
banyak, orang, atas, bukit; kĕcil, kĕreta, dĕpan, pĕjabat; bĕrsih, sĕluar, dalam, almari; kotor, kasut, bawah, meja; bĕsar, lori, bĕlakang, sĕkolah; baru, kĕrusi meja, dalam, bilik

H. *pattern:* **Kĕreta** ada di mana? Ada di **jalan.**
kĕrusi, dalam bilik; meja, dalam pĕjabat; kĕdai, dĕpan benk; pasar, bandar; sĕkolah, bĕlakang benk; rumah, luar bandar

I. *pattern:* Apa awak bĕlum **makan?**
makan pagi; minum pagi ini; hantar surat itu; dapat surat itu; pĕrgi ke benk; hantar istĕri kĕ kampung

Lesson Five

Characteristics of *balik, cukup, dulu, jumpa, pandai,* and *sĕbĕlah*; *sudah* and tense indication; more yes/no responses; balanced words in sentences.

VOCABULARY

balik   return, back
bĕlajar   learn, study
bĕras   rice (uncooked)
bila   when
boleh   can, able to
cakap   speak, say
cukup   enough
dulu ⎱ previously, ago,
dahulu ⎰   first, awhile
habis   finish, completely
jauh   far, a long way
jumpa   meet, find
kanan   right (opp. 'left'),
   senior (of rank)
kapal   ship, boat
kiri   left (opp. 'right')
macam   like, type, sort
mahal   expensive
mahu   want
mĕsti   must, have to, had to
murah   cheap

naik   ascend, by (of
   transport) board, travel by
pandai   clever, good at
pĕgawai   official, officer
pusing   turn, circumvent
sakit   sick, ill
sĕbĕlah   one side, the side of,
   next (door to)
sana   yonder
sĕbab   reason, because
sĕdikit ⎫
sikit ⎭   a few, a little
situ   there (place)
sudah ⎫ have/has, completed,
'dah ⎭   finished, is now
suka   to like, would like to
sungai   river
tahu   know (facts), know
   how to
turun   descend, alight from
bagaimana ⎫
macam mana ⎭   how

Malayanised English words:

Kastam   Customs
teksi   taxi

teket   ticket
fĕri   ferry

PHRASES

sĕbĕlah **kiri**   left side
sĕbĕlah **kanan**   right side
sĕbĕlah **sana**   far side
sĕbĕlah **sini**   this side
di **kiri kanan**   on both sides
pusing **kanan**   turn right
pusing **kiri**   turn left
pĕgawai **kanan**   senior official
pĕgawai **kastam**   customs officer
rumahsakit   hospital
kĕreta ṣakit   ambulance
bĕritahu ⎫
kasitahu ⎭ inform, tell

apa sĕbab ⎫
sĕbab apa ⎭ why
sĕbab itu   for that reason
sudah itu   after that, then
ṇaik apa   how (of mode of transport)
bĕrapa lama   how long (of time)
apa macam   how are you; how was it; what sort of
orang di ⎫
sĕbĕlah rumah ⎭ next-door neighbours

LESSON NOTES

46. *balik*   This word is often used without a following noun because the place (**rumah, kampung,** etc.) is understood. The phrase **balik kerja** is most often used as 'return from work'. At other times **balik** is used to support another verb and then merits only the translation 'back' in English.

> **Bĕri fail ini balik kĕpada Ĕncik Mahmud.**
> Give this file back to Mr Mahmud.

47. *cukup*   Like **banyak** and other words indicating quantity, this word precedes the noun it describes, as in,

> **cukup bĕras**   sufficient rice

unless, of course, 'This rice is enough', (**Bĕras ini cukup**). It occupies the preceding position, unlike the English 'enough', when linked with adjectives.

> **tak cukup jauh**   not far enough

48. *dulu*   To see all the possible implications of **dulu** (written **dahulu**) you must accept a very broad interpretation of 'previous'. The English synonyms for the various possible contexts are numerous.

tunggu dulu   wait *awhile*
awak pĕrgi dulu   you go *first/ahead*
dulu dia kĕrja sini   he *used to* work here
bila awak jumpa dia dulu   when did you *last* see him
macam dulu   as *before*

49. *jumpa* As you may observe from the second from last example, **jumpa** translates 'see' when it means 'meet'. It is a useful reminder to translate ideas rather than words.

50. *pandai* Like the word 'nice', 'good' is used to excess in English. In Malay you should choose the word appropriate to the context and say, for example, 'She is clever at cooking' for 'She is a good cook'. Good food is, of course, 'tasty' or 'nourishing', and a good worker works 'industriously'.

In some parts of the Malay world **pandai** is used also for 'like to' where in English statements it would be omitted.

I don't (like to) smoke
He doesn't (like to) eat chicken.

51. *sĕbĕlah* This word comes from **bĕlah** (to split in two). It is used for a side or a half, when things are divided into two. The exercises in this lesson emphasise the difference between phrases using **sĕbĕlah mana** before and after nouns.

sĕbĕlah mana jalan   which side of the road
jalan sĕbĕlah mana   the road on which side (which of the alternative roads)

Sĕbĕlah is used not only for right and left sides but for rear, front, top and bottom sides also; and in time phrases **di sĕbĕlah** is sometimes used for 'during'.

di sĕbĕlah pagi/pĕtang/malam   during the morning/afternoon/night

52. *sudah, 'dah* This word and its abbreviated form are used as a tense indicator, showing that an action or phase has been completed, and so it is similar to 'have' when used with verbs, as in 'have gone' and 'has written'. It should not be confused with **ada** (have, possess), nor with **mĕsti** (must, have to).

In the absence of a verb **sudah** must sometimes be seen as 'is now' or 'has become'.

28

Kapal sudah jauh The ship is now far away.
Hari sudah malam. It is now night-time.
Anak dia sudah bĕsar. His child has grown up.

If you can see that the idea of 'already' is contained in **sudah,** you will soon appreciate that the negative of it is **bĕlum** (not yet). Do not use **tak sudah** for 'have not'. You may hear **sudah tak,** but this has a different meaning which we need not consider at this stage.

53. *Yes/no* In this lesson **mahu, tahu, sudah, belum** and **boleh** are used, like **ada** in the last lesson, for the short yes/no responses.

54. *Sentence balance* Notice how pairs of words are used at times to balance one part of a sentence against another in order to indicate meaning by contrast. In this lesson examples of words in balance are

sudah ... baru ... (in which **baru** means 'only then')
dulu ... sĕkarang ...

55. *Omission of words* You are reminded that **pĕrgi** is often omitted from colloquial speech, just as we can change to 'off'.

Dia kĕ bandar. He is off to the town.

Similarly, **di** and **kĕ** are often dropped from the full prepositional forms, producing phrases like **dalam kapal** for **di dalam kapal.**

EXERCISES

Read and translate:

A. 1. Bila ĕncik nak balik? Habis kĕrja, baru boleh balik.
2. Saya mahu bawa bĕras ini balik kĕ kĕdai. 3. Mĕreka bĕlajar Inggĕris di sĕkolah di bandar. 4. Apa dia cakap tadi? Dia mahu tahu jalan kĕ rumahsakit. 5. Tak ada cukup kĕrusi di pĕjabat ini. 6. Dulu bĕras murah di pasar, sĕkarang sudah mahal.
7. Bilakah ĕncik pĕrgi kĕ rumahsakit dulu? 8. Pĕrgilah awak dulu. Saya ada sĕdikit kĕrja di opis. 9. Ahmad sudah naik bas kĕ Mĕlaka nak jumpa pĕgawi polis di sana. 10. Kita pĕrgi naik kapal, balik naik apa? Naik kĕreta. 11. Pĕtang sĕmalam saya mĕsti pĕrgi kĕ rumahsakit. 12. Orang mĕsti bawa kĕreta di sĕbĕlah kiri jalan? Mĕsti. 13. Kĕrja di pĕjabat itu macam mana?

29

Bagus. 14. Apa sĕbab dia mahu balik dulu? Sĕbab anak dia sakit. 15. Dia naik kapal fĕri tadi, nak kĕ mana? Nak kĕ Batu Pahat. 16. Sĕkolah Mĕlayu itu ada di sĕbĕlah kanan sungai. 17. Ĕncik boleh tunggu bas di situ. 18. Istĕri saya bĕlum pandai cakap Inggĕris. 19. Bĕrapa lama ĕncik kĕrja di bandar itu. 20. Kĕrja 'dah habis, marilah kita naik teksi kĕ rumah Ĕncik Rahman.

B. 1. Tuan mahu jumpa saya? Mahu, ĕncik. 2. Apa kami boleh masuk sĕkarang? Bolehlah. 3. Awak tahu di mana dia duduk sĕkarang? Tahu. 4. Osman sudah hantar istĕri dia balik bĕlum? Bĕlum. 5. Anak ĕncik sudah bĕsarkah? Sudah. 6. Anak mĕreka suka bĕlajar Inggĕris di sĕkolah? Suka. 7. Rumah doktor itu jauh dari sini? Tak jauh. 8. Apa pakaian di kĕdai itu murah? Tidak, cukup mahal. 9. Sĕbab apa dia tak datang kĕrja hari ini? Sĕbab sakitlah. 10. Apa anak ĕncik mĕsti tinggal di rumahsakit? Ya, mĕsti.

C. 1. Istĕri dia bĕlum pandai bawa kĕreta. 2. Rumah Ĕncik Rahman di kampung baru itu bĕlum sudah. 3. Anak dia sudah boleh baca buku sĕkarang. 4. Kapal sudah jauh, baru mĕreka datang. 5. Bila anak kami sudah bĕsar, kami nak hantar dia bĕlajar di Kuala Lumpur. 6. Bila kami jumpa dia di rumahsakit, dia bĕlum boleh cakap. 7. Saya tak mahu, kĕreta 'ni tak cukup bĕsar. 8. Bagaimana ĕncik boleh tahu? Orang di sĕbĕlah rumah kasitahu kĕpada saya. 9. Orang kĕdai bĕritahu kĕpada saya bĕras di bandar sudah cukup. 10. Bĕlum banyak orang di kampung itu tahu cakap Inggĕris. 11. Di sĕbĕlah rumah awak ada kĕreta sakit, tahukah? 12. Di sĕbĕlah mana jalan ĕncik nak tunggu? 13. Buka pĕti itu sĕbĕlah atas. 14. Laci sĕbĕlah mana dia taruh fail itu tadi? Sĕbĕlah kanan. 15. Di kiri kanan sungai ada kampung Mĕlayu. 16. Bukit itu ada di sĕbĕlah sana bandar. 17. Apa sĕbab dia tak datang sĕkolah pagi 'ni? Sĕbab air sungai sudah naik. 18. Dulu dia boleh cakap Mĕlayu sikit, sĕkarang bagaimana? 19. Dulu awak tak pandai buat kĕrja itu, sĕkarang bagaimana? 20. Apa saya mĕsti pusing kanan sĕkarang? Jangan dulu. 21. Ĕncik Daud, apa macam? Bagus, tuan. 22. Cik Zuraidah suka pĕrgi pasar sĕbĕlah pĕtang.

Substitute in the following exercises:

D. *pattern:* Sĕbab kĕreta itu tak cukup bĕsar.
bilik, bĕsar; orang, pandai; air, dalam; pejabat, bĕrsih; kĕrja, baik; air minum, sĕjuk

E. *pattern:* Dia datang sini sĕbab apa?
mahu balik; mahu pĕrgi naik bukit; tak mahu pĕrgi sĕkolah;
sudah pusing kiri; bĕlum balik kĕrja; tak boleh naik kapal

F. *pattern:* Rumah sĕbĕlah mana dia masuk tadi? Sĕbĕlah
kanan.
laci, taruh surat itu, atas; jalan, masuk, kiri; bilik, keluar,
kanan; pintu, kĕluar, bĕlakang; kasut, cari, kiri; lampu, mĕsti
tutup, kanan

G. *pattern:* Bila awak jumpa Mat itu dulu?
jumpa doktor; jumpa pĕgawai itu; jumpa orang kampung itu;
balik kampung; naik kapal kĕ sana; naik kĕ atas bukit itu

H. *pattern:* di sĕbĕlah kanan jalan
kiri kapal; sana sungai; sini jalan; kanan rumah; bawah pĕti;
kiri pasar

I. *pattern:* Sĕbĕlah mana bandar dia tinggal?
bandar, kĕrja; bilik, dudak; pĕti, buka; benk, masuk; jalan,
taruh kĕreta; kĕdai, kĕluar tadi

J. *pattern:* Pĕrgilah awak dulu.
makan; balik; duduk; bikin; ambil; masuk

K. *pattern:* Anak sudah bĕsar.
hari, malam; kapal, jauh; makanan cukup; Omar, pandai;
pakaian, murah sikit; bĕras, mahal sikit

L. Read each sentence aloud and give the response appropriate
for 'Yes' each time.

   e.g. Tuan ada kĕreta? (Response) Ada.

1. Ĕncik mahu balik sĕkarang? 2. Tuan suka duduk di Malaysia?
3. Awak sudah kasitahu dia? 4. Ĕncik tahu cakap Inggĕris?
5. Apa saya boleh masuk? 6. Apa kami mĕsti tunggu?

M. Again, here are long sentences broken down into short
conversational patterns:

Pagi tadi Omar sudah naik teksi kĕ bandar sĕbab dia mahu jumpa
pĕgawai kastam.
Omar sudah pĕrgi kĕ mana? Sudah pĕrgi kĕ bandar.
Bila dia pĕrgi? Pagi tadi
Dia pĕrgi naik apa? Naik teksi.
Apa sĕbab dia mahu kĕ bandar? Mahu jumpa pĕgawai kastam.

Hassan tunggu di hadapan benk nak naik bas pĕrgi kĕ Mĕlaka.
Di mana Hassan?   Dia di hadapan benk.
Apa dia bikin di situ?   Dia tunggu nak naik bas.
Dia nak kĕ mana?   Kĕ Mĕlaka.

Roslan pĕrgi naik teksi kĕ pasar nak bĕli bĕras di sana sĕbab bĕras di kĕdai kampung sudah mahal.
Roslan pĕrgi pasar naik apa?   Naik teksi.
Apa dia nak bĕli di sana?   Mahu bĕli bĕras.
Sĕbab apa dia tak bĕli di   Sĕbab bĕras di situ sudah mahal.
   kĕdai kampung?

Lesson Six

Numerals and the numerical coefficient *orang*; *sě/satu* as the indefinite article, 'one' and 'each'; uses of the particle *nya*; *batu* illustrates changes of meaning according to word order; the use and non-use of numerical coefficients; problems of interpretation with *lagi, běli* and *cukup*.

Vocabulary

bapa   father
batu   stone, mile, milestone
běrapa   how much, how many
bětul   correct, exact, indeed
bulan   month, moon
cuti   holiday, leave
ela   yard (36 ins.)
ěmak   mother
gaji   wages, pay
gantang   unit of capacity (about 1¼ gallon)
gudang   warehouse, godown
harga   price, value
jam   clock, watch, hour
jual   sell
kaki   foot, leg, 12 ins.
kali   time, occasion

kati   1¼ lbs., 625 grms.
kěrani   clerk
kosong   empty, zero
lagi   additional, another, more, again
lebar   wide
minggu   week
panjang   long
ringgit   dollar
saja ⎫
sahaja ⎭   only, just
syarikat   a firm, company
tahun   year
tětapi ⎫
'tapi ⎭   but
těrbang   to fly
tinggi   high, tall
wang   money

Malayanised English words:

inci   inch
nombor   number

sen   cent
talipun   telephone

33

Phrases

ĕmakbapa parents
kaki lima pavement
kapaltĕrbang aeroplane
batu sĕjam (b.s.j.) miles per
  hour
minggu dulu last week

jalan kaki go on foot
naik harga rise in price
harga mahal high price
tak bĕrapa not very
baca jam tell the time

Cardinal Numbers

0	kosong	11	sĕbĕlas
1	satu, sĕ—, suatu	12	dua bĕlas
2	dua	13	tiga bĕlas
3	tiga	14	ĕmpat bĕlas
4	ĕmpat	15	lima bĕlas
5	lima	16	ĕnam bĕlas
6	ĕnam	17	tujuh bĕlas
7	tujuh	18	lapan bĕlas
8	lapan. dĕlapan	19	sĕmbilan bĕlas
9	sĕmbilan		

10	sĕpuluh	hundred **ratus**
20	dua puluh	thousand **ribu**
30	tiga puluh	million **juta**
40	ĕmpat puluh	one hundred **sĕratus**
50	lima puluh	one thousand **sĕribu**
60	ĕnam puluh	one million **sĕjuta**
70	tujuh puluh	246 **dua ratus ĕmpat puluh**
80	lapan puluh	**ĕnam**
90	sĕmbilan puluh	3,587 **tiga ribu lima ratus**
		lapan puluh tujuh

Lesson Notes

56. *Numbers* When 0 to 10 have been memorised, the Malay numbers are quite easy to learn. The numbers 11 to 19 add **bĕlas** as the equivalent of '-teen', the only other variation being the contraction of **satu** to **sĕ** in **sĕbĕlas**. This contraction is used also with nouns and is very much like the change from 'one' to 'a' in English. The equivalent of our '-ty' in the multiples of ten is **puluh**. There is no need to translate 'and' as it is used in 120 and 1,069.

57. *Numerical coefficients* After numbers and **bĕrapa,** when they are applied to nouns, you will find certain words which vary according to the class of noun described. These numerical coefficients have been compared with 'sticks' and 'head' as used in 'two sticks of dynamite' and 'fifty head of cattle'. If you use 'how many' instead of 'how much' before the English uncountable nouns such as rice/cement/water/cloth/wood, you will feel the need for words like bags/cupfuls/pieces, which resemble Malay numerical coefficients.

In this lesson **orang** is used as a numerical coefficient after **bĕrapa** and numbers when people are referred to. It is better to say,

> **dua orang kĕrani** *rather than* **dua kĕrani** (two clerks)
> *and* **bĕrapa orang anak** *rather than* **bĕrapa anak** (how many children)

Sometimes you will hear a different word order:—

> **kĕrani dua orang** *and* **anak bĕrapa orang**

—but, on the whole, the translation does not alter.

It is important to remember that numerical coefficients are not used in expressions of measurement (of time, distance, money, etc.).

> **satu hari** one day   **sĕbatu** a mile
> **sĕringgit** a dollar

58. *Sĕ* The use of **sĕ** or **satu** will now enable you to show that nouns are definitely singular, though, it should be remembered, context may make their use superfluous.

An extension of their use covers the meanings of 'per' and 'each', just as 'a' is used in this way in 'four times a day'. Again, the Malay word order is not as rigid as the English:

> **tiga kali sĕminggu** ⎫
> **sĕminggu tiga kali** ⎬ three times a week
> **dua ringgit sĕorang** two dollars per person
> **sepuluh ringgit satu** ten dollars each

59. *Nya* This particle has several different uses.
1. It can be attached to nouns to mean his/her/its/their.

> **Hassan kĕrja lama sĕhari 'tapi** *gajinya* **kĕcil.**
> Hassan has a long working day but *his wages* are poor.

35

2. It can be attached to verbs to mean him/her/it/them.

>   **Dia naik bas di batu ĕnam,** *turunnya* **di sini.**
>   She boarded the bus at the sixth milestone and *got off* it here.

3. It can change adjectives like high/wide/deep into their appropriate nouns: height/width/depth, and so forth. In such cases there is no need to translate the 'in' required by a certain English word order.

>   **Tingginya bukit itu lapan ratus kaki.**
>   The height of the hill is eight hundred feet.
>   **Bukit itu sĕmbilan ratus kaki tingginya.**
>   The hill is nine hundred feet in height.

60. *Batu* A number following this word invariably indicates a particular milestone, and preceding it shows the number of miles. A similar distinction is made with the use of **bĕrapa,** as can be seen from the examples below. To state a number of stones one would have to use the numerical coefficient introduced in the next lesson.

>   **lapan batu**   eight miles
>   **batu lima**   the fifth milestone
>   **bĕrapa batu**   how many miles
>   **batu bĕrapa**   which milestone

61. *sudah* (*bĕrapa*) *lama* This is the 'is now' use of **sudah** mentioned in the notes in Lesson Five.

>   **Sudah lama dia boleh baca jam**
> *is literally,*   It is now a long time he can read the clock
> *for,*   He has long been able to tell the time.

When, however, the verb after the **sudah lama** phrase is negative, the English translation may use 'since' and dispense with the negative.

>   **Sudah lama kita tak jumpa.**
>   It is a long time since we met.

62. *Bĕlum . . . lagi* In this construction **lagi** does the work of 'still' in English.

e.g. **Dia bĕlum makan lagi.**
>   He still hasn't eaten yet.

63. *Lagi* Notice how this word changes considerably in interpretation according to various contexts:

Mahu minum lagi? Want any more to drink?
tak lama lagi soon (not long more)
Datang lagi Come again
lagi dua hari (in) another two days
Dia sakit lagi She is still ill
tak sakit lagi no longer ill

64. *Běli = pay for* Use **běli** for 'pay for' as seen in exercise **D** of the Substitution drills.

65. *cukup = good* **Cukup** is often used like 'good' in such phrases as **cukup ěnam kaki** (a good six feet) and **cukup dua jam** (a good two hours).

66. *Harga mahal* Notice that prices are **mahal** and not **tinggi**.

EXERCISES

Read and translate:

A. 3; 6; 4; 5; 8; 1; 7; 2; 10; 14; 16; 23; 25; 27; 89; 64; 33; 54; 101; 146; 211; 346; 486; 914; 522; 1,069; 7,537; 8,712; 4,600; 1,020,128; 8,573,210.

B. 1. Gaji dia lima bělas ringgit sěhari. 2. Měreka ambil çuti tiga puluh hari sětahun. 3. Saya běri měreka lima pulun sen seorang. 4. Di sini orang městi bawa kěreta tiga puluh batu sějam. 5. Běras itu dua ringgit sěgantang. 6. Baju ini běrapa? Sembilan ringgit satu, ěncik. 7. Sěluar itu sudah naik harga dua puluh lapan ringgit satu. 8. Jam macam ini cukup dua ratus ringgit satu. 9. Dia pěrgi kě rumahsakit sěminggu dua kali. 10. Orang dalam sjarikat ini dapat gaji sěbulan sěkali. 11. Kapalterbang turun di sana sěhari tiga kali. 12. Běrapa orang kěrani kěrja di gudang ini? Ada sěorang saja. 13. Běrapa orang istěri dia ada? 14. Sungai itu tak běrapa lěbar. 15. Kampung saya tak běrapa batu dari sini. 16. Bukit di sěbelah sana sungai itu tak běrapa kaki tingginya. 17. Běrapa ringgit harganya kasut baru itu? 18. Běrapa kali dia dapat cuti sětahun? Dulu satu kali, sěkarang dua kali. 19. Sudah běrapa kali Ismail pergi cuti tahun ini? 20. Sudah bĕrapa lama mĕreka tunggi di sana? Cukup satu jam.

C. 1. Bapa saya jual kĕretanya dua bulan dulu. Belum beli lagi. 2. Minggu dulu dia masuk askar lagi. 3. Lagi ĕmpat bulan ĕmak bapa dia mahu datang ke Malaysia. 4. Wang ini tak cukuplah. Kasi saya lima ringgit lagi. 5. Lagi lima hari Ismail balik dari cuti di kampung. 6. Bilakah anak awak mĕsti masuk rumahsakit lagi? 7. Bĕrapa orang lagi boleh naik kapal? Lagi ĕnam orang cukuplah. 8. Bĕras itu tak bĕrapa cukup. Ĕncik mahu lagi? 9. Awak baru ambil sĕpuluh hari cuti, apa lagi awak mahu? 10. Kĕreta itu cukup murah. Apa lagi? Bĕlilah. 11. Orang pĕriman itu sudah kĕrja tiga minggu 'tapi bĕlum dapat gaji lagi. 12. Bĕrapa jauh lagi kita mĕsti jalan? Ĕmpat batu bĕtul. 13. Harga bĕras sudah naik lima puluh sen sĕgantang. 14. Ĕmak istĕri saya pĕrgi kĕ pasar tiga kali sĕminggu. 15. Bĕri mĕreka wang ini lima bĕlas ringgit sĕorang. 16. Bĕrapa batu sĕjam orang boleh bawa kĕreta di jalan ini? 17. Bĕrapa ringgit awak bĕli buku itu? Sĕringgit tujuh puluh satu. 18. Sĕbab istĕri dia sakit dia mĕsti duduk sĕmalam di kampung. 19. Dalamnya air itu bĕrapa kaki? Cukup ĕnam kaki sĕkarang. 20. Di batu bĕrapa rumah dia? Di batu tiga puluh satu Jalan Ipoh. 21. Bĕrapa lama awak nak balik rumah? Lagi ĕmpat puluh minit baru boleh balik. 22. Bĕrapa lama awak nak jalan pĕrgi kĕ pasar? 23. Cukuplah dua minggu lamanya saya duduk di rumahsakit ini. 24. Sungai itu cukup lebar 'tapi airnya bĕlum cukup dalam. 25. Dia kĕrja lama sĕhari 'tapi gajinya kĕcil saja. 26. Baju ini kĕcil saja tĕtapi harganya mahal.

Substitute in the following exercises:

D. *pattern:* Bĕrapa ringgit **awak** bĕli **kĕreta** itu?
dia, kasut; awak, jam; mĕreka, kapal; istĕri ĕncik, bĕras; bapa, sĕluar; ĕmak, almari; Kasim, lampu kĕreta; ĕmak bapa awak, kĕrusi meja

E. *pattern:* **Kĕreta** itu tak bĕrapa **bĕsar.**
gaji, mahal; kapaltĕrbang, lama; bukit, tinggi; sungai, lebar; jam, murah; cuti, lama; air sungai, dalam; rumah, panjang

F. *pattern:* Bila awak nak **pĕrgi sĕkolah** lagi?
datang sini; ambil gaji; balik kampung; naik kapaltĕrbang; pĕrgi cuti; jumpa Ismail; masuk rumahsakit; buka kĕdai

G. *pattern:* Běrapa batu lagi dia mahu pěrgi?
orang, hantar; minit, tunggu; jam, kěrja; hari cuti, ambil; jauh, jalan; tinggi, naik; banyak, ambil; lama, cari.

H. *pattern:* Ada sěorang polis dalam kěreta.
kěrani, opis; pěgawai kastam, gudang; Cina, kědai; Inggěris, kapal; doktor, rumah; askar, kědai kopi

I. *pattern:* Saya bělum jumpa dia lagi.
naik kapaltěrbang; dapat wang itu; boleh ambil cuti; pandai cakap Mělayu; tahu bawa kěreta; masuk rumahsakit.

J. *pattern:* Sudah lama dia tahu bawa kěreta.
pandai cakap Inggěris; kěrja di sini; nak pěrgi kě England; boleh baca jam; tunggu di kaki lima; kěrja polis

K. *pattern:* Sudah lama kita tak jumpa.
jumpa Ěncik Ismail; balik kampung; dapat surat; pěrgi cuti; pakai kěreta itu; naik bas kě sana; makan di kědai itu

L. *pattern:* Sudah běrapa lama ěncik tunggu di sini?
tunggu kapal; duduk di Batu Pahat ini; cari rumah dia; bělajar Inggěris; buat kěrja kěrani; cari kěrja

M. Translate: Cik Ali di kědai Cik Mat

Mat—Sělamat pagi, Cik Ali.
Ali —Sělamat pagi, Cik Mat.
Mat—Apa khabar?
Ali —Khabar baik, těrima kasih.
Mat—Hari ini Cik Ali tak kěrja?
Ali —Tidak, hari ini saya cuti.
Mat—Běrapa hari cuti sěminggu, Cik Ali?
Ali —Saya cuti sěhari sěminggu.
Mat—Nak běli apa hari ini, Cik Ali?
Ali —Saya hěndak tiga gantang běras dan sěkati kopi.
Mat—Apa sěbab sikit běli běras, Cik Ali?
Ali —Saya běli běras dua kali sěbulan. Tak banyak kopi di kědai awak, Cik Mat.
Mat—Kopi datang sěbulan sěkali, Cik Ali, minggu děpan baru datang.
Ali —Běrapa harga sěgantang běras, Cik Mat?
Mat—Murah, sěkarang dua ringgit sěpuluh sen sěgantang. Dulu dua ringgit ěmpat puluh sen.
Ali —Běrapa harga běras dan kopi itu, Cik Mat?

Mat—Tak banyak, lapan ringgit sěmbilan puluh sen, Cik Ali.
Ali —Ini wangnya, Cik Mat.
Mat—Těrima kasih, Cik Ali. Ini běras dan kopi.
Ali —Saya nak pěrgi kě pasar sěkarang.
Mat—Cik Ali tak bawa kěreta?
Ali —Tidak, pasar 'tu tak běrapa jauh, Cik Mat.
Mat—Sělamat jalan, Cik Ali.
Ali —Sělamat tinggal, Cik Mat.

Lesson Seven

The days of the week; telling the time; the numerical coefficient *biji*; the employment of *malam, pada, jam, pukul, padang* and *barang*: the fractions *sětěngah* and *suku*; quantity indicators like *cawan* and *sěbělah* preclude use of numerical coefficients; introductory examples of the prefix *běr*.

Vocabulary

antara   between, among
bangun   get up, wake up
bangunan   a building
barang   thing, goods
běrhěnti   to stop, cease
běrlabuh   to dock, anchor
běrlěpas   set off
běrpuasa   to fast
běrtugas   be on duty, work
cawan   a cup
cukur   to shave
děngan   with, by (transport)
gambar   picture, photograph
hutan   jungle, forest
kějutkan   wake someone, surprise, startle
kilang   factory, mill
kurang   less, lacking
lěbih   more
main   to play
mandi   bathe, wash
měsjid   mosque

mulai   begin
pada   at, on
padang   field
pasukan   team, army unit, force
pukul   to hit, o'clock
sampai   arrive, reach, until, as far as
sěmbahyang   pray
sětěngah   half
songkok   the rounded Malay cap
suku   a quarter
tangan   hand
tělur   egg
tengok   look at, see, watch
tiap-tiap   every, each
tidur   to sleep, go to bed
wayang   a show (theatrical)
děraiber   driver
talipun   telephone
bola   a ball

41

PHRASES

lĕbih kurang approximately, more or less

ambil gambar take photographs

bangun pagi get up in the morning

bĕrhĕnti kĕrja retire from work

buka puasa to break a fast

bulan puasa the fasting month

di antara—dĕngan/dan between—and—(time and place)

jam tangan wristwatch

pukul bĕrapa? what time?

pukul talipun to telephone, ring up

kĕrja kosong work vacancy

pasukan/padang bola football team/field

pasar malam evening market

pĕrgi tengok wayang gambar to go to see a film show

padang kapaltĕrbang airfield

pasukan polis hutan police field force

rumah batu brick or stone house

kakitangan staff, personnel

bĕrsĕmbahyang Jumaat to perform the Friday prayers

DAYS OF THE WEEK

Sunday **hari Ahad (hari minggu)**

Monday **hari Isnin (hari satu)**

Tuesday **hari Sĕlasa (hari dua)**

Wednesday **hari Rabu (hari tiga)**

Thursday **hari Khamis (hari ĕmpat)**

Friday **hari Jumaat (hari lima)**

Saturday **hari Sabtu (hari ĕnam)**

LESSON NOTES

67. *Days of the week* The names of the days derived from Arabic (**Ahad, Isnin,** etc.) are those used in all printed matter and they are given capital letters. In common speech the form given in brackets is usually used. The phrase **hari apa** ('what day of the week') has a fixed word order.

68. *Malam = eve of* There is a difference of 24 hours between **malam Rabu** (Tuesday night) and **malam hari Rabu** (Wednesday night). In other words, when the word **hari** is included, the form is that which is nearest to the English; and if **hari** is not included, **malam** should be thought of as the eve of the day mentioned, just as Christmas Eve precedes Christmas Day.

42

69. *Pada* This word is used more often of time than place, though you will hear phrases such as **pada kampung saya.** It is also useful because it can translate 'on' (not meaning 'on top of'), which sometimes appears as 'to', as in 'I have no money on me' and 'stuck to the wall'.

70. *Biji* This word has the meaning 'seed, pip', but in this lesson it is used as the numerical coefficient for small, round objects such as eggs, fruit, watches, cups, saucers and hats. Notice here the meaning established with the use of **biji** and a particular word order:

> **Běrapa batu?** How many miles?
> **Běrapa biji batu?** How many stones?
> **Di batu běrapa?** At which milestone?

71. *Pukul/jam* **Pukul běrapa** and **Jam běrapa** are both used for 'What time', but the latter tends to be used in areas where there has been Indonesian influence. Further changes of meaning with the use of a numerical coefficient and a particular word order are seen here:

> **Běrapa jam?** How many hours?
> **Běrapa biji jam?** How many clocks/watches?
> **Jam běrapa?** What time?

72. *Telling the time*

(1) *Divisions of the day:* The day is divided into 4 parts, the approximate times of which are:

> from 4.00 a.m. to 11.30 a.m. **pagi**
> from 11.30 a.m. to 2.00 p.m. **těngah hari** (midday period)
> from 2.00 p.m. to 7.00 p.m. **pětang**
> from 7.00 p.m. to 4.00 a.m. **malam**

(2) *The hour-hand:* Either **pukul** or **jam** can precede the number of the hour.

> **pukul satu** one o'clock
> **pukul ěmpat pětang** four o'clock in the afternoon
> **pukul dua bělas těngah malam** twelve o'clock midnight

(3) *The minute-hand:* In time 'to' the hour, **kurang** and **lagi** are interchangeable. In time 'past' the hour, the word **minit** is optional.

43

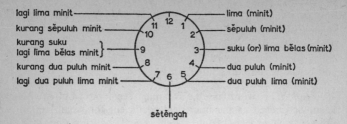

lagi lima minit — lima (minit)
kurang sĕpuluh minit — sĕpuluh (minit)
kurang suku / lagi lima bĕlas minit } — suku (or) lima bĕlas (minit)
kurang dua puluh minit — dua puluh (minit)
lagi dua puluh lima minit — dua puluh lima (minit)

sĕtĕngah

It can be seen that, as in English, 5.40 can be given as: **pukul lima ĕmpat puluh** *or* **lagi dua puluh minit pukul ĕnam**. Hence, at the 45 minute position there are 4 possible alternatives;

8.45—eight and three quarters (**pukul lapan tiga suku**)
—eight and forty-five minutes (**pukul lapan ĕmpat puluh lima**)
—a quarter to nine (**lagi suku pukul sĕmbilan**)
—fifteen minutes to nine (**kurang lima bĕlas minit pukul sĕmbilan**)

It only needs a little regular practice to master this system. Remember that when giving time *to* the hour you begin with **lagi** or **kurang**, and for time *after* the hour you begin with **pukul** or **jam**. Here are some more examples to illustrate these notes:

11.55   **lagi lima minit pukul dua bĕlas**
12.30   **pukul dua bĕlas sĕtĕngah**
10.20   **pukul sĕpuluh dua puluh**
6.50   **kurang sĕpuluh minit jam tujuh**
12.30 p.m.   **pukul dua bĕlas sĕtĕngah tĕngah hari**
8.15 p.m.   **jam lapan suku malam**

73. *Padang* This word is not used for cultivated fields. It suggests either waste land, as in ' desert ', or land reserved for a particular activity, as in 'football field', 'airfield' and 'firing range'.

74. *Sĕtĕngah/suku* Change the word order of English phrases like 'four and a half hours' and 'two and a quarter miles' so that the noun comes before the fraction, making 'four hours and a half' and 'two miles and a quarter', to see the word order of the Malay:

ĕmpat batu sĕtĕngah (and) **dua batu suku.**

44

75. *Barang* This word is usually reduplicated to become **barang-barang,** suggesting a variety of objects. The simple form **barang** has a few other functions. It can be used for the indeterminate 'ever' in 'whatever', 'whoever' and 'wherever'.

> **Barang apa dia mahu běrilah kěpada dia.**
> Give him whatever he wants.

It can also be used for 'approximately'.

> **Pěrgilah běli nasi barang lapan puluh sen.**
> Go and buy about eighty cents' worth of rice.

76. *Lěbih kurang* In the Borneo states and Indonesia the word order **kurang lebih** is usually employed.

77. *Cawan, bělah* When words like **cawan** and **gělas** are used as indicators of quantity, they make the use of a numerical coefficient unnecessary:

> **Sěgelas bir** (a glass of beer) *but* **sěbiji gělas** (a glass)
> **dua cawan kopi** (2 cups of coffee) *but* **dua biji cawan** (2 cups)

With limbs or parts of the body appearing in pairs, the word **bělah** is used in a similar way:

> **tangan sěbělah kiri**   the left hand
> **kaki sěbělah kanan**   the right leg
> **děngan dua bělah tangan**   with both hands

78. *běr.* This is a prefix which will be explained in a later lesson. It is attached to the stem words **labuh** (hanging down), **lěpas** (free), **puasa** (a fast) and **tugas** (duty, task) in this lesson. The **běr** of **běrhěnti** is rarely detached from its stem word.

EXERCISES

Read and translate:

A.   1. Hari ini hari apa? Hari ini hari Sabtu.   2. Besok hari apa? Besok hari Ahad.   3. Tuan nak běrlěpas kě Singapura hari apa? Hari Isnin pagi.   4. Minggu děpan kami dapat gaji hari Khamis. 5. Tiap-tiap hari Jumaat sěmua kakitangan tak běrtugas. 6. Hari apa awak tak kěrja? Tiap-tiap hari Jumaat dan Ahad. 7. Dia pěrgi tengok wayang gambar tiap-tiap hari Rabu.   8. Omar bërtugas di padang kapaltërbang hari Sëlasa ini. 9. Hari ëmpat minggu ini bapa saya nak bërhënti kërja di kilang. 10. Pasukan bola Jëpun sampai dëngan kapaltërbang malam hari satu. 11. Malam apa istëri ëncik mahu përg tengok wayang gambar? Malam hari minggu. 12. Sëkarang pukul bërapa? Kurang dua puluh minit pukul tujuh. 13. Ëncik bangun pagi pukul bërapa? Pukul lima tiga suku. 14. Jam bërapa Ëncik Zainal pukul talipun tadi? Jam sëpuluh bëtul. 15. Këjutkan saya pada pukul lima sëtëngah pagi esok. 16. Anak saya bangun pukul tujuh nak përgi sëkolah. 17. Kapal Jëpun itu nak bërlabuh lëbih kurang pukul lima pëtang. 18. Kami përgi bërsëmbahyang Jumaat pukul dua bëlas sëpuluh. 19. Pukul bërapa wayang mulai pëtang ini? Lëbih kurang pukul tujuh lima bëlas. 20. Kami boleh buka puasa lëbih kurang pukul ënam pëtang. 21. Ëncik Harun përgi kë mësjid pukul sëbëlas, bëlum balik lagi. 22. Dalam bulan puasa kami kërja di antara pukul lapan dëngan pukul dua bëlas dan dari pukul satu sampai pukul tiga sëtëngah pëtang. 23. Omar sudah jalan kaki dari batu ëmpat sëtëngah sampai batu sëmbilan suku. 24. Sëmua kakitangan makan tëngah hari di antara pukul dua bëlas dan pukul satu. 25. Bapa saya suka tidur pëtang antara jam dua dëngan jam tiga.

B. 1. Bërapa ringgit Mat bëli dua biji jam tangan itu? 2. Bawa batu itu këmari lagi sëpuluh biji. 3. Dia përgi kë pasar bëli tiga puluh biji tëlur. Tiap-tiap sëbiji dua puluh sen. 4. Sëmalam saya jumpa sëbiji songkok baru dalam pëti itu. 5. Di batu bërapa ëmak bapa Omar tinggal? Di batu lima sëtëngah. Dari sini kë rumahnya itu bërapa jauh? Lëbih kurang sëtëngah batu. 6. Bërapa batu dari sini kë bangunan Western Assurance? Lëbih kurang ënam batu tiga suku. 7. Bërapa jam awak kërja sëhari? Lëbih kurang tujuh jam. 8. Jam bërapa ëncik cukur sëbëlah pagi? Jam tujuh tiap-tiap hari kërja. 9. Dia pakai dua biji jam, sëbiji tangan kiri, sëbiji tangan kanan. 10. Bapa dia bërhënti kërja satu tahun sëtëngah dulu. 11. Mëreka tunggu nak naik bas 'tapi bas tak bërhënti. 12. Sudah tiga kali saya pukul talipun kë Muar, bëlum dapat cakap lagi dëngan Ëncik Kadim di sana. 13. Saya 'dah baca dalam suratkhabar syarikat itu mahu dëraiber ënam orang lagi. 14. Kasitahu Ëncik Hashim dia bolih ambil cuti di antara hari Sëlasa dëngan hari Jumaat. 15. Ada banyak rumah di kiri kanan jalan dari batu lima sampai batu tujuh. 16. Mana Zainal? Dia përgi bëli suratkhabar nak cari kërja kosong. 17. Bangunan itu tak sampai dua ratus ela dari pĕjabat saya. 18. Bĕras dalam pĕti itu tak sampai tiga gantang sĕtĕngah. 19. Harganya lima biji apul itu sĕringgit dua puluh. Tuan mahu bĕli? 20. Sĕmua kĕreta mĕsti bĕrhĕnti di jalan bĕsar itu. 21. Dia orang mulai main bola pukul ĕnam, habis pukul tujuh sĕtĕngah. 22. Pada hari satu Ĕncik Karim mulai kĕrja dĕngan pasukan polis di Muar. 23. Bĕrapa batu lagi mĕsjid itu dari sini? Dari sini kĕ mĕsjid itu bĕrapa batu lagi? Mĕsjid itu dari sini bĕrapa batu lagi?

Substitute in the following exercises:

C. *pattern:* **dua ringgit** sĕtĕngah
ĕmpat hari; ĕnam jam; dua minggu; tujuh bulan; lima tahun; sĕpuluh ringgit; tiga batu; lapan ela

D. *pattern:* lĕbih kurang **tiga tahun** lagi
lapan jam; tujuh ringgit; ĕmpat minggu; dua kali; ĕnam orang; tiga biji; lima bulan; sĕmbilan batu

E. *pattern:* di antara **pukul satu** dĕngan **pukul dua**
pukul sĕpuluh, pukul dua bĕlas; jam ĕmpat, jam lapan; pukul lima, pukul tujuh; hari Isnin, hari Khamis; hari tiga, hari ĕnam; hari Sĕlasa, hari Jumaat; batu dua, batu lima; batu tiga, batu ĕnam

F. *pattern:* dari **pukul tujuh pagi** sampai **pukul tiga pĕtang**
jam lapan pagi, jam sĕpuluh pagi; pukul sĕmbilan pagi, pukul dua bĕlas tĕngah hari; jam satu tĕngah hari, jam dua bĕlas tĕngah malam; pukul ĕmpat pĕtang, pukul sĕpuluh malam; hari minggu, hari dua; hari satu, hari tiga; batu ĕmpat, batu ĕnam sĕtĕngah; batu lima, batu tujuh suku

G. *pattern:* tak sampai **lima ela**
tiga jam; lima batu; dua kati; ĕnam ratus ringgit; dua puluh kaki; sĕtĕngah jam lamanya; ĕmpat batu jauhnya; sĕratus lima puluh kaki tingginya

H. *pattern:* Bĕrapa nombor **teksi** ĕncik?
talipun; kĕreta; teket; rumah; tĕrak; kapaltĕrbang; buku; fail; askar

I. *pattern:* Pukul bĕrapa awak **makan pagi?**
makan malam; bangun pagi; cukur; mulai kĕrja; mandi; habis kĕrja; pukul talipun; tidur

47

J. *pattern:* Hari apa ĕncik nak **balik kampung?**
main bola; main golf; bĕrlĕpas kĕ Sabah; ambil cuti; dapat gaji;
pĕrgi ke kilang; pĕrgi tengok wayang gambar; kĕrja di gudang;
masuk hutan

Lesson Eight

More numerical coefficients and quantity
indicators; *punya* for possession; *sangat* and
problems of degree.

VOCABULARY

ayam chicken
bĕbĕrapa several, some
bĕtina female (of animals)
binatang animal
bungkus wrap, parcel up,
  packet (cigarettes)
curi steal
daging meat
dĕkat near, nearly
gĕtah rubber
hilang lost. missing
hisap suck
ikan fish
itik duck
jantan male (of animals)
kĕbun garden, plantation
kĕlapa coconut
kotak carton, box
ladang estate, field (not
  irrigated)
lĕmbu ox
mati die, dead

mĕninggal die, pass away
nama name
nampak see, notice, catch
  sight of
parang short chopping
  sword
pasang fix, assemble, install,
  to light, pair
pisau knife
pokok tree
punya (see note)
putih white
rokok cigarette
sangat very, too, extremely
sĕnapang rifle
tanam to plant, bury, invest
tangkap catch, arrest
injin engine
lesen licence
paun pound (£ and lb.)
pistol pistol
rĕstoran restaurant

PHRASES

anak lembu calf
ayam itik poultry

ada lagi still alive
daging lembu beef

49

jalan mati	cul-de-sac	siapa punya?	whose?
harga mati	fixed price	siapa nama?	what is the name of (person)?
pisau cukur	razor-blade		
ladang getah	rubber estate	apa nama?	what is the name of (thing)?
baju mandi	bathing suit		
sĕluar mandi	bathing trunks	air pasang	high tide
hisap rokok; merokok	to smoke	tuan punya	the owner
		tak nampak lagi	out of sight

MORE NUMERICAL COEFFICIENTS

kĕping	(piece, fragment)—for thin flat things not folded easily, like photographs; becomes 'piece' for glass and wood, 'slice' for bread and meat.
hĕlai	(fold)—for things easily folded such as clothes, paper, blankets.
batang	(stick, stem)—for stick-like objects such as cigarettes, trees, pencils and oars.
buah	(fruit)—for large objects, natural features like hills and rivers, and for books.
bilah	(cutting edge)—for cutting instruments such as knives, swords and razor-blades.
ekor	(tail)—for non-human living creatures.
laras	(barrel of gun)—for firearms.
pucuk	(sprout, shoot)—for letters and firearms.
pintu	(door, gate)—for houses or shops in a row.

LESSON NOTES

The words given in brackets after the numerical coefficients indicate their basic meanings. It can be seen that sometimes objects will fit into more than one category so that, for example, **batang** or **buah** can be used for rivers and roads. There are several other numerical coefficients but their use is so restricted that they fall outside the scope of this book. You have seen that some words like 'cup' and 'glass' can become quantity indicators, and are used like the numerical coefficients; other such words are the collective nouns like 'herd' and 'group'. In this lesson **pasang** is used as 'pair' but not with 'trousers', for which **hĕlai** should be used.

Another new word in this lesson is **bĕbĕrapa**, which (like **bĕrapa** and numbers) requires the use of numerical coefficients except in expressions of measurement.

79. *Punya* This is the stem of the verb 'to possess'; it is used to make possessive forms equivalent to 'mine', 'yours' and 'ours', *i.e.* the possessive pronouns and nouns with the apostrophe 's'.

Buku ini siapa punya Whose book is this?
Rumah itu Ěncik Mat punya. That house is Ěncik Mat's.
Kěreta ini saya punya. This car is mine.

In what is called 'bazaar Malay', **punya** is greatly over-used, causing ambiguity. The tendency is to say **saya punya kampung** instead of **kampung saya.**

80. *mati/měninggal/ada lagi* When referring to the death of relatives and close friends, the more euphemistic **měninggal** is preferred to **mati**. It is derived from **tinggal** and the full phrase used is **měninggal dunia** (leave the world). The phrase **ada lagi** in particular contexts regarding people is used to mean 'still alive'.

Ěmakbapa ada lagi? Are (your) parents still alive?

81. *Hilang* It is better to change the form of such sentences as 'I have lost my pen' to 'My pen is lost'; otherwise it sounds like a deliberate action in Malay. This word is not used in the expression 'losing the way'. Those readers familiar with English grammar will note that the passive form 'is lost' is not reflected in the Malay.

82. *Daging* It sounds better in Malay to say 'eat chicken meat' rather than just 'eat chicken'.

83. *Sangat* If you read through the progression fairly/rather/ quite/very/extremely—too/ you will notice that a borderline has been crossed when 'too' is reached; and we are now in the area of the unwanted—too slow, too many, etc. In Malay there is no clear dividing line between 'very' and 'too'. The word **sangat** can suggest either according to the context. It is a problem that will be met again with other words of degree. Observe the use of the word carefully at first and you will see that the context makes plain which English word is appropriate for the translation. **Sangat** can be used either before or after the word it describes.

84. *Pasang* There is considerable variation in the use of this word. It covers two different meanings of 'fix', both 'fit, put in

51

position' and 'repair, put into working order'. In addition, its old use of applying a flame to light something has been extended to cover the switching on of electrical devices. (See also the preceding notes on the numerical coefficients.)

EXERCISES

Read and translate:

A. 1. Běrapa pasang kasut sudah hilang dari gudang? Lěbih kurang lima puluh pasang. 2. Běrapa batang rokok awak hisap sěhari? Sěkarang sěpuluh batang saja. 3. Ada dua buah sěkolah di sana, sěbuah sěkolah Mělayu, sebuah Inggěris. 4. Pětang saya mahu pěrgi kě kampung běli dua ekor ayam bětina. 5. Taruh baju tiga hělai itu dalam almari. Baju ini saya nak pakai. 6. Sěkarang bapa dia ada ayam itik běrapa ekor? Sěmuanya ěnam puluh ekor. Minggu dulu dia běli lagi lima ekor. 7. Dalam sěkotak pisau cukur ada běrapa bilah? Dalam kotak kěcil ini lima bilah. 8. Dia orang nampak běběrapa ekor binatang děkat sungai. Tidak sěekor dapat tangkap. 9. Binatang itu sangat běsar dan ekornya panjang. 10. Apa kěrja Hashim di kěbunnya tadi? Dia tanam tiga batang kělapa. (Why is 'pokok' unnecessary here?) 11. Dia pěrgi běli buah di pasar pagi tadi, sěkarang mahu běli kělapa dua biji lagi. 12. Tadi saya běli dua kěping teket, sěkarang sudah hilang. 13. Ěmpat buah kapal itu sudah jauh, tak nampak lagi. 14. Děkat sungai ada běběrapa buah kampung. Adakah orang putih suka duduk děkat sungai? 15. Surat itu sudah hilang. Hantarlah sěpucuk lagi. 16. Surat mana ěncik cari tadi? Dua pucuk di dalam fail itu. 17. Taruhlah dua hělai sěluar mandi itu dalam beg. 18. Makanan saya pagi ini dua kěping roti saja. Marilah kita pěrgi makan di kědai Cik Long. 19. Dia běli dua buah rumah murah, jualnya mahal. 20. Běrapa ringgit harganya sěhělai baju putih? 21. Sěpaun daging lěmbu harganya běrapa ringgit? 22. Daging itu tak cukup. Ambillah lagi sěkěping. 23. Sěmua askar bawa sěnapang satu laras dan sěbilah parang bila dia pěrgi masuk hutan. 24. Ahmad dapat tangkap ěnam ekor ikan di sungai malam tadi.

B. 1. Siapa punya kěreta di luar bangunan běsar itu? Itu saya punya. 2. Ayam itik di kěbun itu siapa punya? Sěmuanya Hashim punya. 3. Siapa nama tuan punya kědai dua pintu itu. Namanya Long. 4. Ada běběrapa buah kěreta di sana. Kěreta mana Ěncik Karim punya? Kěreta putih itu dia punya.

5. Apa nama kapal ĕncik turun tadi? Namanya 'ss. Bahagia'.
6. Apa nama restoran Cina sĕbĕlah kanan jalan ini? 7. Dua orang perempuan orang putih itu siapa nama? Saya bĕlum tahu namanya. Suaminya kĕrja di dua buah ladang gĕtah dĕkat Kota Tinggi. 8. Bapa Omar mĕninggal tahun dulu 'tapi ĕmaknya ada lagi. 9. Sudah dĕkat pukul tujuh baru dia mahu pasang lampu di rumah. 10. Saya bĕlum boleh balik. Mĕsti pasang injin kĕreta dulu. 11. Saya sangat suka mandi bila air pasang. 12. Apa ĕncik nak bĕli rumah batu di bandar? Tak bolehlah sĕbab mahal sangat. 13. Rokok ini tak cukup. Tolonglah bĕri lagi sĕbungkus. 14. Apa sĕbab orang polis sudah masuk gudang pĕtang tadi? Orang sudah curi barang. 15. Sĕmua barang itu harganya mati. 16. Jangan masuk jalan lagi satu itu. Jalan mati. 17. Saya lĕtak kĕreta tuan di jalan mati di sĕbĕlah kiri jalan ini. Di sana sĕlamat bĕtul. 18. Parang ini sangat panjang. Tolong kasi saya sĕbilah pisau. 19. Pĕrgi kasitahu Ĕncik Harun ada sĕekor lĕmbu dalam kĕbunnya. 20. Cik Ali sudah jual kapalnya. Apa dia nak bĕli kapal baru? Tidak, mahu tanam wangnya.

Substitute in the following exercises:

C. *pattern:* Dia sangat suka **kĕrja di kĕbun.**
kĕrja di ladang gĕtah; makan daging ayam; makan tĕlur itik; mandi di sungai; pĕrgi tengok wayang gambar; naik kapal; tangkap ikan; hisap rokok

D. *pattern:* Saya tak bĕrapa suka **kĕrja di kĕbun.**
Use the phrases in C again.

E. *pattern:* Tak bolehlah sĕbab **bukit** itu **tinggi** sangat.
air, panas; ladang, jauh; sungai, lebar; daging, mahal; parang panjang; bĕras, sikit; pokok, tinggi; ikan, kĕcil

F. (You are required to use the correct numerical coefficient in the next 4 exercises.)
pattern: tiga **buah lori** saja
rokok; pisau; bukit; binatang; topi; kasut; kĕlapa; ladang; ikan; sĕluar; roti; polis

G. *pattern:* Bĕrapa **ekor itik** ada?
songkok; sĕnapang; sungai; rumah; baju; kĕrani; surat; pokok; lĕmbu bĕtina; ringgit; apul; gambar

H. *pattern:* **baju** dua **hĕlai** itu
binatang; pisau; pĕrempuan; surat; ayam; kĕlapa; pokok; kapal; buku; parang; pistol; kĕreta

I. *pattern:* **Buku** ini tak cukup. Běri lagi sě**buah.**

kělapa; pisau; cawan; rokok; ikan; pěti; baju; gambar; roti; kěrusi

J. Change the pattern of the sentences so that, for example, **Ini kěreta Hashim** becomes **Kěreta ini Hashim punya.**

Itu rumah Tuan Smith; ini wang Cik Ali; itu kědai bapa saya; ini buku Cik Fatimah; itu kapal orang Cina; ini baju orang putih itu.

K. *pattern:* **Sěmua** orang di kampung ini kěrja di ladang Cik Harun. (becomes) Orang di kampung ini sě**muanya** kěrja di ladang Cik Harun.

Sěmua kěrani di sjarikat ini orang Mělayu.
Sěmua orang di sěbělah rumah saya sudah pěrgi cuti.
Tiap-tiap tahun sěmua kědai kopi tutup dalam bulan puasa.
Sěmua orang di kampung tidak kěrja pada hari Jumaat.
Sěmua kědai di sini tutup pada pukul sěmbilan malam.

L. Find the matching half-sentences.

1. Rumah saya tak běrapa běsar,
2. Sěkolah itu tak běrapa juah,
3. Pisau cukur ini tak běrapa mahal,
4. Ladang itu tak běrapa běsar,
5. Kotak itu tak běrapa panjang,
6. Pokok kělapa itu tak běrapa tinggi,

1. lěbih kurang sěkaki saja.
2. ada sěratus batang pokok saja.
3. ada tiga buah bilik saja.
4. lěbih kurang 30 sen saja sěbilah.
5. lěbih kurang sěbatu saja dari sini.
6. lěbih kurang 20 kaki saja.

Lesson Nine

The causative and prepositional functions of the suffix *kan*; dates; uses of *tĕmpat* and *jadi*; *bĕrapa* in questions of quantity.

VOCABULARY

abang elder brother
adik younger brother or sister
amah female servant
bayar to pay
bĕlayar to sail
besoknya the following day
borang form
duit money, cash
elaun allowance
isi(nya) contents
jadi become, be born, outcome, so, as
kahwin marry
kakak elder sister
kĕtua head, chief
kursus a course
lahir to be born
lalu go past, and then, last (year, month, etc.)
lambat late, slow

lantai floor
latihan training, practice
lĕkas quick(ly), soon, early
lĕlaki ⎫
laki-laki ⎬ male (of people)
lĕpas past, free (not caught)
pindah move, transfer
sĕbĕlum before
sĕlama for (time)
sĕlĕpas after
sĕmalamnya the previous day
suruh order, tell (to do)
tarikh date
tĕmpat place
tong bin, barrel
tunjuk show, point out
umur age
botol bottle
gostan go astern, reverse
mekanik mechanic

PHRASES

adik bĕradik brothers and sisters
isikan borang fill in a form

elaun kahwin marriage allowance
hari jadi birthday

tarikh lahir	date of birth	
kĕrani bĕsar	chief clerk	
kĕtua kampung	village chief	
boleh jadi	it could happen (that)	
dapat tahu	find out	
pindah rumah	move house	
banyak sikit	quite a few	
bĕrapa umur?	how old?	
tarikh bĕrapa?	what date?	

tahun lĕpas ⎫
tahun dulu ⎪
tahun lalu ⎬ last year
tahun sudah ⎭

bĕrapa tahun? how many years?
tahun bĕrapa? which year?
bĕrapa bulan? how many months?
bulan bĕrapa? which month?

LESSON NOTES

85. *Kan* This suffix is attached to verbs for two main reasons:
(1) Its causative use gives the idea of 'causing to' or 'causing to be' the meaning of whatever stem word is used. This is easily seen in examples:

> bĕrsihkan to clean (cause to be clean)
> naikkan raise, hoist (cause to go up)
> barukan to renew
> masukkan to insert

It should be remembered that the English synonyms for such **kan** verbs will vary considerably according to context. This is why, due to limited space, it is difficult to include all of the possible meanings in glossaries and dictionaries.
Other verbs created in this way are:

baikkan repair
bĕsarkan enlarge
balikkan reverse *i.e.* put upside down, inside out, or back to front
bolehkan enable
bangunkan erect, build, develop
bungkuskan wrap, parcel up
bĕrhĕntikan stop
lĕpaskan release
tugaskan detail, assign
dudukkan sit someone down

gambarkan illustrate, imagine
habiskan use up, exhaust
hilangkan lose, get rid of
jalankan carry out, set going
kĕcilkan reduce in size
kotorkan to dirty
kurangkan reduce in amount
mandikan bathe someone
kĕluarkan expel, produce
panaskan to heat
sĕbabkan cause
sampaikan to present, deliver

56

tinggalkan leave, abandon	**sĕlamatkan** rescue, save
turunkan to lower	**poskan** to post
tidurkan put to bed	

Notice that the suffix **kan** denotes deliberate action. Care must be taken, therefore, in translating English sentences like 'I dropped my bag' and 'I lost my money'; if the action is unintentional, the form 'My bag fell' and 'My money was lost' should be used.

(2) The suffix is also used for the word **akan,** which can cover the various meanings 'to, towards, for, at, about'. There is no one-word equivalent in English for **akan,** the work being done by prepositions attached to certain verbs for particular reasons. The difference between 'laugh' and 'laugh *at*', and between 'listen' and 'listen *to*', illustrates this function of **kan.** In the following phrases the implications of the suffix are shown in brackets:

> **bĕlikan saya rokok** buy (for) me cigarettes
> **ambilkan saya buku itu** fetch (to/for) me the book
> **bawakan kĕreta saya** drives my car (for me)
> **bacakan saya surat itu** read (to) me the letter.

In bazaar Malay **kan** is rarely used. In its causative use the suffix is replaced with **kasi,** and the prepositional function is performed often by **sama.**

86. *Dates* Days of the month:

> 1st **satu haribulan**   8th **lapan haribulan**
> 12th **dua bĕlas haribulan**   24th **dua puluh ĕmpat haribulan**

For months of the year either the Malayanised spelling of the English month names (shown in exercise A.) is used, or the number of the month follows **bulan.**

> **bulan satu** (or) **bulan Januari** January
> **bulan tiga** (or) **bulan Mac** March
> **bulan enam** (or) **bulan Jun** June

When the day is combined with the month, the word **bulan** will occur twice, and so the second one is optional. If it is retained there is a slight pause between the two. In letters **hb.** is used for **haribulan.**

57

10th August   sĕpuluh haribulan bulan lapan
             (or) sĕpuluh haribulan lapan

For years there are three possible variations, but you must always begin with the word **tahun**.

1960   **tahun sĕribu sĕmbilan ratus ĕnam puluh**
       tahun sĕmbilan bĕlas ĕnam puluh
       tahun ĕnam puluh

The last, abbreviated form is used for years in this century only. An example of a complete date could, therefore, be

tiga haribulan bulan ĕnam tahun sĕribu sĕmbilan ratus tiga puluh dua   (3rd June, 1932)

87.   *Brothers and sisters*   The term **adik bĕradik** is also used if there are sisters only or brothers only. The word **abang** (abbreviation **bang**) is used as a form of address by wives to their husbands. Sometimes you may hear these words applied affectionately to people unrelated to the speaker.

You may be confused by the fact that, when asked how many **adik beradik** he has, a Malay will include himself in the number.

88.   *Tĕmpat*   This word is commonly used where English nouns have particular names, as in **tĕmpat talipun** (telephone box) and **tĕmpat bas** (bus stop). In some sentences **tĕmpat** should be seen as 'place where', or simply 'where'.

Saya tak tahu tĕmpat dia duduk   I don't know where he lives.

89.   *Bĕrapa*   This continues to be the questioning word when a number is expected in the reply. Some students are confused by the variety of possible English forms.

Bĕrapa jauh?   How far is it?
             What is the distance?

90.   *Jadi*   The English synonyms for this word are numerous. The extension of the idea of 'become' to 'come about' and 'happen' is easily followed. (It is probably the most suitable word for 'to be' in Hamlet's soliloquy.) The other idiomatic uses of the word are not so easily traced. Its conjunctive function as 'so/therefore/hence' is quite easily recognised:

Musa sudah sakit jadi tak   Musa is ill so he isn't coming
    datang kĕrja   to work.

At other times it says 'suitable/will do' (**Kĕrja itu tak jadi**) and here it is probably related to the subjunctive 'let be' as in 'Let there be light'. It should not be too difficult to see that **jadikan** is used for 'create/make/bring about'.

EXERCISES

Read these dates:

A.

1. 21 Mac   2. 10 November   3. 14 Febrari   4. 22 Jun   5. 17 Oktober   6. 30 April   7. 15 Julai   8. 11 Mei   9. 3 September 10. 9 Ogos   11. 6 Disember   12. 1 Januari   13. tahun 1933 14. tahun 1959   15. tahun 1965   16. tahun 1976   17. 10/11/69 18. 14/5/44   19. 12/9/49   20. 10/3/73

Read and translate:

B.   1. Lesen ini mati dua puluh satu haribulan ini.   2. Kakak saya nak kahwin ĕnam bĕlas haribulan bulan dĕpan.   3. Kursus itu habis sĕpuluh haribulan Oktober.   4. Abang saya masuk askar pada dua puluh dua haribulan sĕmbilan tahun sudah. 5. Ĕncik Salim jadi kĕtua pĕjabat satu haribulan satu tahun ini.

6. Awak lahir tahun bĕrapa? Tahun lima puluh tiga.   7. Tarikh bĕrapa dia sudah pindah rumah? Lapan bĕlas haribulan bulan lalu.   8. Adik lĕlaki saya nak pindah sĕkolah pada tujuh haribulan September.   9. Bulan bĕrapa kapal itu bĕlayar balik kĕ sini? Saya bĕlum dapat tahu. Boleh jadi bulan lapan.   10. Bĕrapa bulan awak nak ambil kursus latihan itu? Sĕlama sĕbulan saja.   11. Tahun bĕrapa ĕncik mulai kĕrja sini? Tahun ĕnam puluh.   12. Bĕrapa tahun lagi tuan boleh bĕrhĕnti kĕrja? Lagi tiga tahun.   13. Tarikh bĕrapa awak kahwin dĕngan istĕri? Pada dua puluh lapan haribulan tujuh tahun ĕnam puluh lima. 14. Tarikh hari jadi? Sĕbĕlas haribulan Julai tahun lima puluh tiga.   15. Bĕrapa umur adik pĕrĕmpuan ĕncik? Umurnya baru sĕmbilan tahun saja.   16. Bulan bĕrapa sjarikat itu nak pindah kĕ Kuala Lumpur? Boleh jadi bulan ini.   17. Apa sĕbab Dollah minta cuti sĕhari? Dia mahu pindah rumah sĕpuluh haribulan ini.   18. Bĕrapa haribulan dia mulai dapat elaun kahwin itu? Dari lapan haribulan.   19. Sudah bĕrapa tahun ĕncik kĕrja jadi kĕrani? Sudah dua puluh tahun sĕtĕngah.

20. Amah itu cakap dia mahu balik kampung pada dua haribulan dĕpan.

C. 1. Zainal mahu panjangkan cuti lagi dua hari. 2. Sĕmua dĕraiber mĕsti bĕrhĕntikan kĕreta di jalan bĕsar. 3. Suruh orang pĕrgi bĕrsihkan lantai gudang itu. 4. Sĕbĕlum balik rumah awak mĕsti habiskan kĕrja itu dulu. 5. Tunjukkan dia orang bagaimana nak isikan borang itu. 6. Sudah masuk rumahsakit baru dia lahirkan anak. 7. Di mana awak tinggalkan wang sebĕlum hilang? 8. Saya tinggalkan lori di batu ĕnam Jalan Muar. 9. Bila saya suruh lĕkaslah naikkan tong itu. 10. Tugaskan dua orang pĕrgi tolong mekanik hari ini. 11. Bunguskan barang-barang kĕcil itu, isikan kĕ dalam tong. 12. Orang di kĕdai cakap dia boleh bĕsarkan gambar itu sĕlĕpas hari tiga. 13. Jam itu lambat sikit. Tolong lĕkaskan lima minit. 14. Sĕlĕpas bapanya mĕninggal dia habiskan sĕmua wangnya. 15. Amah sudah mandikan dan tidurkan anak. 16. Sĕbĕlum boleh pukul talipun awak mĕsti masukkan duit dulu. 17. Dalam sĕminggu cuti ini Ahmad mahu barukan rumahnya di kampung. 18. Tolonglah ambilkan suratkhabar saya dari opis. 19. Pĕrgilah kĕ kĕdai bĕlikan saya rokok dua bungkus. 20. Suruh dia buatkan kopi kita sĕkarang. 21. Apa ĕncik boleh tunjukkan saya jalan mana pĕrgi kĕ Kampung Danau? 22. Hashim boleh ambilkan gaji saya minggu ini. 23. Sudah makan malam saya bacakan buku kĕpada anak kĕcil saya. 24. Sĕmua pĕjabat tutup pukul lima jadi saya mĕsti lĕkas balik kĕ bandar. 25. Saya naik bas sampai Johor Bahru lalu jalan kaki dari sana. 26. Kĕreta tak boleh pusing di sini, tuan. Mĕsti gostan sikit dulu. 27. Pĕrgi lalu sĕbĕlah pasar, di situlah rumah Ĕncik Ali dĕkat tĕmpat talipun. 28. Surat ini tak jadi. Suruh dia tulis sĕkali lagi. 29. Bĕrapa orang adik bĕradik ĕncik ada? Sĕmuanya ĕnam orang, dua orang abang, sĕorang kakak, dan dua orang adik—pĕrempuan dan laki-laki. 30. Adik bĕradik bapa ĕncik ada lagi? Abangnya 'dah mĕninggal, tinggal dua orang kakak dan sĕorang adik laki-laki saja.

Substitute in the following exercises:

D. *pattern:* Bĕrapa tahun awak **kĕrja jadi mekanik?**
pĕrgi sĕkolah; duduk di bandar; kĕrja di ladang gĕtah; bĕlajar Inggĕris; tinggal di kampung istĕri; duduk di Kuala Lipis; kĕrja dalam sjarikat itu; kĕrja baikkan kĕreta

E. *pattern:* Tahun bĕrapa dia **jadi kĕtua kampung?**
lahir; buat latihan itu; kahwin dĕngan istĕri; pindah rumah baru;
ambil kursus Inggĕris; bĕrhĕnti kĕrja; jadi kĕrani bĕsar; mulai
kĕrja di sini

F. *pattern:* Bulan bĕrapa awak nak **pĕrgi kĕ Kuantan** lagi?
jumpa dia; pĕrgi cuti; ambil kursus; hantar wang; naik kapal
kĕ sana; kahwin; pĕrgi jumpa doktor; naikkan gaji dia

G. *pattern:* Bĕrapa umur **awak? Dua puluh tiga** tahun lĕbih.
istĕri awak, 29; abang awak, 40; kakak awak, 35; adik pĕrĕmpuan, 18; adik lĕlaki, 17; kĕtua kampung, 47

H. Translate:

Osman—Apa khabar, Cik Aziz?

Aziz —Khabar baik.

Osman—Sudah lama bĕtul saya tak jumpa awak. Kĕ mana
ĕncik pĕrgi?

Aziz —Saya 'ni 'dah pindah ke Kampung Sĕntosa dan sĕlĕpas
pindah saja lalu balik cuti. Sĕbab itulah awak tak
nampak saya di opis.

Osman—Apa macam tinggal di rumah baru sĕkarang, Cik Aziz?

Aziz —Rumah baru saya 'tu macam rumah lama di Jalan
Padang Bola, 'tapi biliknya bĕsarlah sikit. Ada ĕmpat
buah bilik sĕmuanya.

Osman—Baguslah, Cik Aziz. Saya dapat tahu dari orang
kampung ĕncik nak kahwinkan anak pĕrĕmpuan. Apa
bĕtulkah khabar ini, Cik Aziz?

Aziz —Ya, bĕtul. Sĕbab itulah kami lĕkas pindah. Rumah
baru itu bolehlah isikan banyak sikit orang bila sampai
tarikhnya.

Osman—Bila ĕncik nak buat kĕrja kahwin itu?

Aziz —Tarikhnya saya bĕlum tahu lagi, 'Man. Sĕbĕlah lĕlaki
mahu tunggu sampai dia habis latihan. Sĕlĕpas itu dia
nak ambil kursus di Johor. Dia kĕrja polis.

Osman—Kĕrja polis itu bagus, Cik Aziz. Gajinya bĕsar, dapat
elaun kahwin dan rumah.

Aziz —'Tapi, 'Man, rumah polis tak boleh dapat lĕkas.

Osman—Apa sĕbabnya?

Aziz —Ada banyak polis bĕlum dapat rumah lagi. Sĕorang
polis baru kahwin mĕstilah isikan borang dulu dan
tunggu sampai ada rumah kosong.

Osman—Baiklah, Cik Aziz, saya 'dah lambat. Hari ini hari jadi
        anak lělaki saya. Umurnya cukup tujuh tahun.
Aziz —Baiklah, sělamat jalan.

(Notice in the conversation how 'Osman' is abbreviated to
''Man', following the Malay practice of retaining the last few
letters of a name when shortening it.)

Lesson Ten

Uses of the emphatic negative *bukan*; *bĕgini*
and *bĕgitu* in phrases of degree or extent; *yang*
in restrictive relative clauses and phrases; ordinal
numbers; *baik* and *eloklah* used as the advisory
'should'; more on *nya* and *lah*; reminders of *kan*.

Vocabulary

atau or
badan body
bĕgini ⎫
bĕgitu ⎭ so, such
bĕrat heavy, weight
bĕrdiri to stand
bukan no, not
elok lovely, fine
gĕmuk fat, stout
hal matter, affair, case, fact
ikat tie, fasten
ikut follow, obey,
  accompany, via
ingat remember, think
jambatan bridge
jika ⎫
kalau ⎭ if
kĕrajaan government
kuat strong, powerful
kuih cake
kurus thin (of living and
  growing things)

masa time, period
mĕnyĕbĕrang to cross
pĕlajaran lesson, education
pendek short
pĕngurus manager
potong to cut
ringan light (weight, injuries)
sĕbĕrang across
sĕdap tasty, pleasant (to the
  senses)
sĕmpit narrow, tight
sĕnang easy, at ease,
  comfortable
susah difficult, uneasy,
  worried
tali rope, string, cord
tĕgap sturdy, well-built
yang which, who
yang pĕnghabisan the final,
  the last
yang pĕrtama the first

63

PHRASES

bĕrat badan body weight

barang-barang makanan foodstuff

barang-barang rumah household effects

badanya tĕgap he is well-built

bukankah bĕgitu? isn't that so?

kalau bĕgitu if that's the case

janganlah susah don't worry

air kĕlapa coconut milk

sĕpotong kuih a piece of cake

potong jalan }
ikut jalan dĕkat } take a short-cut

potong gaji cut wages

matikin injin switch off engine

Some of these new words can take the suffix **kan**:

ingatkan remind, think about

ikatkan to tie

kuatkan strengthen

pendekkan shorten

potongkan cut

ringankan lighten, alleviate

sĕnangkan make easier, make comfortable

susahkan to trouble, make difficult

LESSON NOTES

91. *Bukan* This negative is used to contradict an impression that is, or may be, in someone's mind.

1. This can be seen most easily in simple denials.

> Omar comes from Selangor   *No*, he comes from Perak.
>   (*or*)He does *not* come from Sĕlangor.

2. It can be used for the negative question tags which are so common at the end of English conversational sentences, such as 'don't you', 'won't they', 'can't she' and 'shouldn't he'.

> **Dia kĕrani bĕsar, bukan?** He is the chief clerk, isn't he?

3. Placed in front of a pronoun (saya, awak, etc.) or a name, and often with **yang** following, it suggests 'not the one who'.

> **Bukan saya yang bĕritahu dia** It wasn't I who told him.

4. With **kah** it will, of course, be used in direct questions.

Bukankah dia pĕngurus? Isn't he the manager?
Bukankah awak tahu? Didn't you know?

5. Occasionally one comes across it used like 'non'.

orang bukan Mĕlayu non-Malays

6. The use of **bukan tak** is similar to 'not un— —'.

Dia bukan tak suka; tak boleh He is not unwilling; he can't.

7. **Bukannya** as used in Exercise K suggests 'To my mind . . .
not'.

92. *Bĕgini/bĕgitu* These words, saying literally 'like this' and
'like that', are formed from **bagai** (like) and **ini** and **itu**. There
are many ways of conveying in English the meaning of the words,
but 'so' and 'such' will be found most useful. They cannot,
however, be used for the exclamatory use of 'such a'. (Such a
nice man!)

bukanlah bĕgitu it wasn't like that
orang yang bĕgitu banyak so many people
kĕreta yang bĕgitu kĕcil such a small vehicle
bĕgini lambat as late as this

93. *Yang* The difficulties of this word for students are not as
great as some grammar books have suggested. A feeling for the
proper use of the word can be developed without complicated
explanation. It means 'who/which' relating to a previously-
mentioned person or thing; and so it is not a questioning word
like **siapa**. At times it does not need to be translated, and com-
monsense is the best guide in this case. Notice the word positions
in the following development:

yang itu that one
yang pendek ini this small one
yang di dalam laci itu the one in the drawer

Do not try to use prepositions before **yang** in the way of English
phrases like 'from whom' and 'by which'. To ask the question
'Which one?' use **Yang mana satu?** or its short form **Yang mana?**

94. *kĕ—/yang ke—* The affix **kĕ** is not very common; it has
been used so far only in **kĕtua**. Ordinal numbers are formed
with **kĕ,** and **yang** is the word linking the ordinal with its noun;

and so this, the 10th lesson, is **pĕlajaran yang kĕsĕpuluh.** You only need to learn the exception **yang pĕrtama** (the first), and the rest are quite regular:

yang kĕdua the 2nd; **yang kĕtiga bĕlas** the 13th;
yang kĕdua puluh satu the 21st.

Remember to use the system already studied for the dates and not this equivalent of the English ordinals.

The affix **kĕ** is also used to give stress when indicating all-embracing numbers and quantities—

sĕmuanya (all of them) *but* **kĕsĕmuanya** (every one of them)
and other uses you will see in a later lesson.

95. *Apa hal* This phrase resembles the 'what matter' in 'What matter brings you here?' (**Apa hal awak datang ke mari?**). It should be contrasted with **Bagaimana hal dĕngan dia?** (How are things with him?).

96. *Baik, eloklah* In addition to their basic meanings these two words are used idiomatically to mean 'had better'. Usage indicates that the **elok** should carry **lah** and that **kita** is used after them more than the other pronouns.

Baik kita tunggu dulu We'd better wait awhile
Eloklah kita pĕrgi sĕkarang We had better go now.

97. *Ingat* The clear distinction between 'think' and 'remember' in English is not paralleled in Malay by the colloquial use of this word. Though given in dictionaries as the verb 'to remember' it is also used for 'think, be of the opinion'. The word **ingatkan** can be used to demonstrate this and also the two functions of **kan** described in the last lesson.

Saya ingatkan dia bĕbĕrapa kali I reminded him several times.
Apa yang awak ingatkan? What are you thinking about?

98. *Sĕbĕrang, menyĕbĕrang* When 'across' means 'on the other side' use **sĕbĕrang**: but when 'across' is used with an action 'to the other side', the appropriate word is **mĕnyĕbĕrang**:

66

Di sěběrang sungai ada rumah Across the river there is a house

Dia pěrgi měnyěběrang sungai He went across the river.

99. *Nya* In this lesson we see two instances of what appears to be a noun form in Malay becoming verbal in English:

Orang yang kětiga itu namanya Ali The 3rd man is called Ali

Bangunan itu lětaknya di Jalan Mahkamah The building is situated in Mahkamah Road.

100. *Lah* The implications of this particle go far beyond the simple explanation given in Lesson 4. Notice how, at the beginning of a sentence or a half-sentence, it seems to take on the function of the indeterminate English 'it', particularly in the absence of other pronouns.

Susahlah nak měnyěběrang sungai It will be difficult to cross the river.

At other times **kalau** at the beginning of a sentence is balanced by **lah** on the first word of the main clause:

Kalau wang di dalam benk sudah cukup, bolehlah kita běli. If we now have enough money in the bank, we can buy it.

EXERCISES

Read and translate:

A. 1. Saya boleh ingat hari yang pěrtama dia datang kěrja di sini. 2. Apa hal ěncik datang nak jumpa pěngurus pagi ini? 3. Dia bukan orang Mělayu, orang Cina. 4. Siapa nama tuan punya kědai yang kědua itu? 5. Kalau barang itu běgitu běrat, macam mana dia boleh bawa sěmuanya? 6. Orang yang kurus itu baru kěluar dari rumahsakit. 7. Omar bukan orang yang gěmuk macam itu. 8. Kalau makanan itu tak sědap janganlah běli. 9. Tuan Nasir duduk di rumah yang elok. Lětaknya dua batu jauh dari sini. 10. Bila pěngurus suruh, lěkaslah sěmua orang kěrani ikut. Běgitulah halnya dalam sjarikat itu. 11. Ingatkan Ěncik Salim saya mahu jumpa dia sěbělum dia pěrgi kě pějabat pělajaran. 12. Pělajaran yang kěmpat itu sěnang, tak susah macam pělajaran yang kěěnam. 13. Awak boleh sampai kě rumahnya ikut jalan yang sěmpit ini. 14. Ikat kuat binatang itu dĕngan tali ini. 15. Saya mahu awak potong tali yang kuat itu pendek macam ini. 16. Taruh barang yang bĕrat itu di bawah dan barang yang ringan di atas. 17. Dulu badannya tidak bĕgitu bĕrat macam sĕkarang ini. 18. Bĕrapa bĕrat badan kĕreta ĕncik? Tiga tan lĕbih. Kalua bĕgitu, tak boleh ikut jambatan sĕmpit yang di hadapan itu. 19. Janganlah awak susah! Saya boleh cakapkan hal itu kĕpada tuan pĕngurus. 20. Saya tak tahu hal itu sĕbab sĕmalam saya sakit di rumah. 21. Bila orang bĕsar sampai di padang sĕmua orang bĕrdiri. 22. Di kampung itu orang pĕrĕmpuan buat kĕrja yang sĕnang saja. 23. Bĕrapa bĕrat badan ĕncik? Sĕratus lima puluh paun saja. 24. Barang ini tak boleh saya bawa masuk. Kalau bĕgitu, boleh saya taruh di sini saja?

B. 1. Sĕkarang bapa saya duduk sĕnang di kampung, tak susah macam dulu di bandar. 2. Orang yang tĕgap badannya itu namanya Wahid, bukan? 3. Apa yang awak susahkan? Hal itu bukanlah bĕsar. Sĕnang saja awak boleh buat. 4. Jam tangan dia sudah hilang dalam air sungai. Susahlah nak cari barang yang bĕgitu kĕcil. 5. Saya ingat barang-barang itu sĕribu ringgit harganya. Bukanlah begitu mahal. 6. Kami bukan hĕndak mĕnyĕbĕrang sungai. Mahu tangkap ikan. 7. Bila saya sĕnang bĕgini saya suka duduk di rumah dĕngan anak istĕri. 8. Siapa yang bĕrdiri di pintu opis tadi? Saya tak tahu namanya, ĕncik. Saya ingat dia cari kĕrja. 9. Yang mana daging awak suka makan, daging lĕmbu atau daging ayam? 10. Pada masa ini banyaklah orang yang cari kĕrja di bandar sĕbab di sana gaji mahal. 11. Banyaklah kĕreta yang di hadapan itu; lambat kita sampai di pĕjabat pagi ini. Kalau bĕgitu, baik kita potong jalan di sini. 12. Ĕncik boleh ikut makan di rumah saya pĕtang ini, macam mana? Eloklah bĕgitu, tĕrima kasih banyak. 13. Air kĕlapa ini sĕdap bĕtul. Bukankah bĕgitu, Cik Kadir? 14. Ĕncik Harun nak balik tak lama lagi. Eloklah kita tunggu dia di sini saja. 15. Pĕti yang dia bawa itu bukan bĕrat, ringan saja. 16. Hari sudah pĕtang. Eloklah kita bĕrlĕpas lĕkas. 17. Saya ingat kali yang pĕrtama dia datang kĕ rumah saya tiga tahun dulu. 18. Bungkuskan sĕmua barang kĕcil ini, lalu ikat dĕngan tali. 19. Kalau ĕncik mahu duduk di rumah kĕrajaan isikanlah borang sĕkĕping ini. 20. Makanannya tĕngah hari sĕpotong kuih saja. Eloklah dia pĕrgi jumpa doktor pĕtang.

Substitute in these exercises:

C. *pattern:* Itu **buku** yang **baik.**
makanan, sĕdap; hal, kĕcil; kĕrja, bĕrat; jambatan, sĕmpit; kĕreta, elok; jam, lambat; hal, susah; masa, panjang.

D. *pattern:* Dialah yang **kasitahu** saya.
tunjukkan; ingatkan; bĕlikan; carikan; susahkan; hantarkan; buatkan

E. *pattern:* Yang **tulis surat** itu siapa?
bĕrdiri di pintu; tĕgap badannya; ikat tali; ikut di bĕlakang; potong pokok; nak mĕnyĕbĕrang jalan; potong jalan

F. *pattern:* Yang mana satu, yang **ini** atau yang **itu**?
bĕsar, kĕcil; bĕrat, ringan; pendek, panjang; kurus, gĕmuk; mahal, murah; bĕrdiri, duduk; di hadapan, di bĕlakang

G. *pattern:* Bukan **saya** yang **bĕritahu dia.**
awak, dia cari; dia, hilang wang; dia, mĕninggal; pokok gĕtah, saya tanam; saya, dia suruh; anak dia, polis tangkap

H. *pattern:* Dia **bawa kĕreta lama,** bukan?
ambil kursus pendek; ambil cuti panjang; pindah rumah baru; ikut jalan dĕkat; duduk di sĕbĕrang sungai; jual barang-barang rumah; mĕsti matikan injin

I. *pattern:* Orang yang **gĕmuk** badannya itu namanya **Ali.**
kurus, Omar; kuat, Kadir; tĕgap, Hassan; tinggi, Hashim; sakit, Wahid

J. *pattern:* Susahlah nak **naik bukit** yang bĕgitu **tinggi.**
jalan kĕ tĕmpat, jauh; bawa pĕti, bĕrat; mĕnyĕbĕrang sungai, lebar; ikut jalan, sĕmpit; jalankan tugas, susah; bawa kĕreta, lama

K. *pattern:* Bukannya **bĕsar rumah** yang dia **bĕli** itu.
murah kĕreta, bĕli; bĕrat barang, bawa; susah kĕrja, buat; susah hal, cakapkan; mahal barang-barang makanan, jual; kuat tali, pakai

L. *pattern:* Apa yang awak **tengokkan**?
tunggukan; carikan; susahkan; ingatkan; bĕlikan dia; tinggalkan di sana

Lesson Eleven

Functions of the *bĕr* prefix; the distinctions
between *tukang*, *juru* and *pakar*.

ahli   member, expert
atur   arrange
bahasa   language, manners
bangsa   race, type
bĕrani   brave, dare
bĕrĕnang   swim
bĕrjabat   grasp, hold
biru   blue
budak   lad, girl
buruh   labourer, labour
gaduh   to quarrel
gunting   clip, cut, scissors
hijau   green
hitam   black
hubung   communicate, get
   in touch
jabatan   department
juru   skilled worker
kelabu   grey
kolam   pool, pond
kumpul   collect, gather,
   congregate
kuning   yellow
langgar   collide, invade,
   break (law)
merah   red, brown
minta   ask for, request

muda   young, light (of
   colour), unripe (of fruit)
padi   unhusked rice, rice
   plant
pangkat   rank, status
rambut   hair (of the head)
rehat   rest, break
rosak   damaged, broken
   down
saudagar   merchant, trader
sĕmbunyi   to hide
sĕnjata   weapon
susun   stack, arrange
tĕrus   straight on, straight
   away, continue
tua   old (of people), dark
   (colour)
tukang   craftsman
tukar   change, exchange
warna   colour
coklat   dark brown, chocolate
kĕlab   club
mesin   machine
paip   pipe, tap
tangki   tank, cistern
tayar   tyre
wayar   wire

70

PHRASES

Apa bolen buat? What can one do? What's to be done?

Mana boleh? How's it possible?

lampu těrapik traffic-lights

běrjabat tangan to shake hands

pěgawai kěrajaan government official

rumahsakit běranak maternity hospital

kolam mandi swimming-pool

sěpasang gunting a pair of scissors

cuti tak běrgaji unpaid leave

air paip tap-water

Jabatan Pělajaran Education Department

Jabatan Imigěresen Immigration Department

Jabatan Buruh Labour Department

Some of these words will accept the affixes **an** and **kan**. When the derived word has an obvious meaning, as in **sekumpulan** (a group, gang), no special explanation need be given; but the not-so-obvious, such as **těrusan** (canal), will be pointed out when used. Use **mainkan** for 'play' with musical instruments and rôles; and note the deliberate intention indicated by **kan** as in **langgarkan** (ram).

LESSON NOTES

101. *Ber* This prefix is shortened to **bě** on **kěrja** and stem words beginning with **r**. With this prefix words that have been used as both nouns and verbs, like **kěrja** and **jalan,** can now be given a purely verbal form. Some words (**běrhěnti, bělayar, běrlěpas, běrpuasa, bělajar, běrdiri, běrtugas**) that you have already used carry the prefix. The serious student will soon find that some stem words never appear in isolation except in dictionaries. **Jabat,** for example, the stem of **berjabat, pějabat** and **jabatan,** never occurs by itself. You will also meet occasionally words like **běrani** which appear to carry this prefix, but do not in fact do so. A few words, like **běrhěntikan** and **běrsěnjatakan** (armed with), can carry **běr** and **kan** simultaneously; but it is generally true to say that the two affixes are opposites in function. The action of **běr** verbs is not carried out on someone or something else; the performer remains the only one affected by it. In other words, such verbs tend to be intransitive and reflexive; whereas **kan** verbs have direct objects and are, therefore, transitive. Those

71

not familiar with these grammatical terms should see the distinction easily in these examples:

Dia běrsembunyi   He hid (himself)
Dia sěmbunyikan wangnya   He hid his money
Dia běrmandi   She bathed (herself)
Dia mandikan anak   She bathed the children.

Whereas some běr verbs, such as běrmalam (to spend the night) and běrtaruh (to bet, wager), are difficult to fit into any particular category, Malay teachers usually classify the functions of běr as follows:

1. Intransitive and reflexive

běrjalan (travel), běrmain (play), běkěrja (work), běrcukur (shave), běrkumpul (congregate), běrlatih (do training), běrpindah rumah (move house)

2. Using, wearing, having, attending

běrnama (to be called), běristěri/běrsuami (to be married), běrsěkolah (attend school), běrtopi (wear a hat), běrumur (have the age of), běrwarna (to be coloured), běrpakaian (to be dressed), běrsěnjata (armed), polis běrkěreta (mobile police), běrkaki ayam (in bare feet), běrisi (contain).

3. Reciprocal actions

In these actions, which involve different parties equally, the běr combines with děngan:

běrjumpa děngan (meet), běrhubung děngan (communicate with), běrkahwin děngan (marry), běrbaik děngan (be on good terms with), běrlanggar děngan (collide with), běrgaduh děngan (quarrel with)

4. Having offspring

běranak (to bear children), běrbuah (bear fruit), běrtělur (lay eggs)

5. Earning a livelihood (only rarely used)

Bapa saya běrjual kěreta   My father is a car-salesman
Dia běrtanam padi   He is a rice-planter.

102. *Tak běr*   The English 'without' before a noun, or 'less' on the noun, is often rendered by **tak běr**:

tak bĕrharga   valueless
tak bĕrtopi   without a hat

103. *Tukang/juru* These words are used to indicate trades and profession. The difference between them is similar to the distinction between blue and white-collar workers. Further up the professional scale the word **pakar** (expert, specialist) is often used.

tukang paip	plumber	jurubahasa	interpreter
tukang batu	mason	jurutaip	typist
tukang kasut	cobbler	jurucakap kĕrajaan	
tukang letrik	electrician		government spokesman
tukang roti	baker	juruteknik	technician
tukang gambar	photographer	juru odit	auditor
tukang wang	cashier	juru x-ray	radiographer

104. *Bahasa* In the same way that 'well-spoken' is linked with good manners, so **berbahasa baik** can mean 'of good manners'.

105. *Budak/anak* **Anak** is used when the kinship of 'child' is known (*e.g.* **anak saya**) but when it is not known, or not necessary to state it, the word **budak** is appropriate.

Ada budak bermain di jalan There are some children playing on the road

EXERCISES

Read and translate:

A. 1. Apa warna baju yang dia bĕli itu? Baju bĕrwarna putih. 2. Sĕmalam dia pakai sĕluar yang bĕrwarna kĕlabu. 3. Apa bangsa kĕreta yang Cik Omar bĕli itu? Bangsa Toyota. 4. Orang buruh dalam jabatan kĕrajaan itu bĕrbangsa Cina. 5. Apa sĕbab orang tua itu bĕrjalan tak bĕrkasut. 6. Kasut yang bĕrwarna hitam itu sangat mahal. 7. Istĕrinya masuk rumah-sakit bĕranak pukul dua suku pagi ini. 8. Kĕretanya rosak sĕlĕpas bĕrlanggar dĕngan sĕbuah lori. 9. Banyaklah budak yang suka pakai sĕluar panjang yang bĕrwarna coklat. 10. Pĕgawai buruh itu bĕrnama Ĕncik Karim. 11. Apa dia nak? Dia nak bĕrhubung dĕngan kĕrani bĕsar di jabatan buruh. 12. Bĕrapa umur jurutaip di opis dĕpan itu, tahukah? Saya ingat dia bĕrumur lĕbih kurang sĕmbilan bĕlas tahun. 13. Dia

73

běrjalan dari pějabat těrus kě kolam mandi. 14. Sampai di kolam mandi dia těrus paki sěluar mandi lalu masuk air. 15. Bila polis datang cari dia, dia těrus běrsěmbunyi. 16. Suruh sěmua kakitangan běrkumpul di opis saya. 17. Aturkan sěmua kěrusi meja macam dulu. Sělěpas itu suruh orang buruh běratur nak dapat gaji. 18. Orang muda itu běrbahasa baik 'tapi dia bělum běristěri lagi. 19. Tukang wang mahu jumpa pěngurus pagi ini nak minta cuti tak běrgaji. 20. Bila kěretanya rosak dia těrus běrjalan kaki kě kampung minta tolong di sana. 21. Lampu těrapik sudah tukar hijau baru ěncik boleh jalan těrus. 22. Běrapa lama awak duduk di sěkolah latihan itu? Saya běrlatih di sana sělama ěnam bulan.

B. 1. Dalam masa rehat Ishak balik rumah nak tukar baju sěbab baju yang dia pakai itu sudah kotor. 2. Ěncik nak tukar tayar, saya boleh tolong. 3. Sěbělum orang muda itu bolih masuk Singapura dia městi běrgunting rambut dulu. 4. Apa boleh buat? Kěreta sudah rosak, tak dapatlah kita pěrgi sěkarang. 5. Mana bolen dia datang kěrja hari ini kalau dia sakit kuat sěmalam? 6. Kalau badan awak tak cukup tinggi, mana bolen masuk polis? 7. Lěmbu Ěncik Ahmad sudah lěpas dan měnyěběrang jalan. Itulah sěbabnya dua buah kěreta itu běrlanggar. 8. Polis yang běrtugas di pintu benk městilah běrsěnjata. 9. Abang saya běrtanam padi di Kedah dan adik laki-laki saya běrsěkolah di sana. 10. Dia ambil sěminggu cuti bulan dulu, tak běrani minta cuti lagi. 11. Kalau dia pěrgi ke kělab malam malam tadi, saya běrani běrtaruh dia lambat sampai kěrja pagi ini. 12. Kalau tong itu tak běrisi lagi, susunlah di luar gudang. 13. Apa boleh buat? Saya nak běli rokok, kedai sudah tutup. 14. Dulu měreka banyak běrgaduh, sěkarang sudah běrbaik. 15. Budak macam itu tak cukup běrani nak běrmalam di hutan. 16. Barang yang hilang itu tak běrharga. Janganlah awak susah. 17. Sampai di kaki bukit měreka těrus naik kě atas. 18. Awak jangan běrhenti. Běkěrja těrus sampai habis sěmuanya. Sělěpas itu boleh běrehat sěsuku jam. 19. Anak saudagar Cina itu mahu těruskan pělajarannya di England. 20. Bila dia datang hari itu, kětua jabatan běrjabat tangan sěmua orang kami. 21. Dulu Hashim kěrja jadi tukang gunting, sěkarang dia běrjual kěreta di bandar. 22. Dia běrjumpa děngan banyak saudagar Jěpun sělěpas dia jadi ahli kělab golf.

Substitute in the following exercises:

C. *pattern:* Apa warna **kĕreta** yang dia pakai?
baju; kasut; songkok; sĕluar; kotak; baju pasukan; tali; pensil

D. *pattern:* **Cuti 'dah habis,** apa bolen buat?
mesin, rosak; wang, hilang; kapal, bĕlayar; benk, tutup;
makanan, habis; lĕmbu, mati

E. *pattern:* **Budak** itu tak **bĕrduit.**
pokok, buah; botol, isi; barang, harga; orang tua, kasut; polis,
kĕreta; askar, topi

F. *pattern:* Dia bĕrjalan dari **rumah** tĕrus kĕ **rumahsakit.**
sĕkolah, padang bola; kapal, bandar; gudang, jabatan buruh;
kolam mandi, tĕmpat kĕrja; rumah, benk

G. *pattern:* Sampai di **rumah** kami tĕrus **tidur.**
pintu, masuk; sĕkolah, bĕlajar; jalan bĕsar, bĕrhĕnti; hutan,
bĕrjalan kaki; sungai, bĕrmandi; kolam, bĕrĕnang

Lesson Twelve

Active and passive uses of *kĕna*; *nanti* as
indicator of future time and as alternative
conjunction; *tĕntu* in balance with *kalau* and
nanti, and *sudah tĕntu* in the conditional past;
dĕngan in adverbial phrases of manner; introduction of *juga*.

VOCABULARY

adu   complain, charge
api   fire, flame, light
basah   wet
buang   throw away, discard
bunuh   kill, murder
cukai   tax, duty
darah   blood
dĕnda   a fine
gigi   teeth
gigit   to bite
guru   teacher
hukum   punish, sentence
jaga   look after, guard, be
   awake, be alert
jatuh   fall, trip, occur
juga   also, nevertheless, still,
   quite
kĕna   suffer, get, hit
kĕpala   head (of body or
   group)
luka   wound, hurt
marah   angry
masak   to cook, boil (water),
   make (tea, etc.), ripe
minyak   oil, grease, petrol

nakal   naughty
nanti   wait
nyamuk   mosquito
panggil   call, invite
parah   severe (of injuries)
pĕrut   stomach
rĕndah   low, short (of people)
rompak   rob, burgle
rotan   rattan, cane
salah   guilty, wrong(ly)
sĕkĕjap   awhile, a second
sĕrang   to attack
simpan   keep, save, put away
tembak   to shoot
tĕntu   sure, certain(ly)
tipu   deceive, cheat
undang-   laws
   undang
basikal   bicycle
gerej   garage
kad   card
komunis   communist
lotĕri   lottery
pam   pump

76

PHRASES

nanti dulu ⎫ wait a bit
nanti sěkějap ⎭

kěna buang kěrja   get sacked
naik marah   get angry
naik pangkat   get promotion
tukang masak   a cook
tukang kěbun   gardener
kěpala kumpulan   head of
   group/gang
simpan wang   save money
wang simpanan   savings
panggil talipun   to telephone
panggilan kahwin   wedding
   invitation
jatuh sakit   fall ill
orang luar   stranger, outsider

jaga baik   take care, watch
   out
těmpat pam minyak
   petrol station
orang yang kěna adu   the
   accused
pějabat běsar   head office
Amerika Sjarikat   the U.S.A.
ambil běrat   take seriously,
   take pains over
kerětapi   a train
jatuhkan hukuman   pass
   sentence
pegawai běrpangkat   junior
   rěndah   officials

By adding affixes to some of the words in this vocabulary we can create these meanings: běradu (compete), běrdarah (bleed), kěnakan (levy, impose), marahkan (scold), salahkan (blame), and těntukan (make sure, fix, determine).

LESSON NOTES

106. *Kěna*   The nearest English word to kěna is 'get' when used as 'hit' (He fired and got it), and as 'suffer', 'have to' and 'affected by'. Examples to illustrate these uses are:

Dia tembak, tak kěna.   He fired and missed.
Dia kěna běkěrja hari ěnam.   He has got to work on
   Saturday.
Baju dia kotor kěna minyak.   His shirt got stained with oil.
Dia kěna gigit.   He got bitten.

You will notice that kěna has a passive use, that is, when the subject is suffering, not performing, the action. When it is necessary in this case to state the performer of the action, the agent, there is no need to translate 'by'. The agent follows the verb.

Dia kěna tipu orang kědai   She was cheated by the shop-
   assistant.
Dia orang kěna tangkap polis   They got caught by the police.

77

Except sometimes in its use as 'hit', **kĕna** is only appropriate for misfortunes and tedious chores. That is why this lesson is depressingly concerned with accidents and calamities, and why many of the sentences are of the type commonly found in newspapers.

107. *Nanti* Although its basic meaning is 'wait', this word often indicates an unaccentuated future tense in the way that 'will' is contracted to ''ll' in English. In other contexts it can mean 'soon', 'time', 'coming', and 'or else'; so, until you are familiar with the word, it is best (where 'wait' is not appropriate) to think of it as 'by-and-by' and then choose the best English word to fit the context.

> **Simpanlah wang itu,** Put that money away or else it will
>   **nanti kena curi**   be stolen
> **Nanti saya datang** I'll be along soon
> **tiga hari nanti** in three days' time
> **minggu nanti** the coming week
> **satu hari nanti** someday, sometime

Regarding the position of **nanti,** notice how it tends to appear at either the beginning or end of its sentence or phrase. In its sense of 'or else' it usually introduces the second half of the sentence, the first half being introduced by a command.

108. *Tentu* This is a common and useful word. Like **nanti** it often begins the second half of a sentence (very often balancing the introductory word **kalau**); but when it indicates future time, the future is definite, the certain result of some preceding statement. In the following example **tĕntu** and **nanti** have been included in the second clause, **tĕntu** to indicate a definite result, and **nanti** a vague future:

> **Kalau awak ikut jalan saya ini, tĕntu awak tak kĕna buang nanti.** If you do it my way, you won't get fired.

Students will find that **tĕntu** can be translated at times by 'of course', 'bound to', 'obviously' and other such words; but you are advised not to use it much in conversation until you are fully acquainted with the types of sentence in which it is normally used. Further practice is given in the next lesson. In Exercise G of this lesson notice how **sudah tĕntu** shows a definite result in the

78

past, requiring the English 'would have' or 'would certainly
have'.

109. *Juga* As can be seen from the vocabulary list, this word
has several uses, which are best studied separately. In this lesson
it functions as 'nevertheless, all the same, anyway'.

Mahu tak mahu kita kĕna pĕrgi juga.
Whether we want to or not, we have to go nevertheless.

110. *Dĕngan* Adverbs of manner, words describing how an
action is carried out, have been used before or after the verb.

lambat bĕrjalan (or) **bĕrjalan lambat** walking slowly

Putting **dĕngan** before the adverb does not alter the meaning;
it stresses the adverbial nature of the word in the sentence, like
'ly' in English. The normal position for the adverb is then after
the verb, though it may be brought forward in the sentence for
emphasis (cf. Lesson 3, Notes).

Dia bĕrjalan dĕngan lambat He is walking slowly.

111. *Minyak* This is a general word for greasy substances.
More often than not the type of substance is obvious in context.
If not, more words are added; hence,

minyak injin engine-oil   **minyak kĕlapa** coconut-oil
minyak rambut hair-oil   **minyak sapi** lard

112. *Cikgu* This is a form of address and a title for teachers.
It is derived from **ĕncik guru.**

113. *Undang* This is the stem of the verb 'to invite'. Only
when it is reduplicated does it refer to 'laws, ordinances'. **Hukum**
too can be used for 'law, regulations'.

EXERCISES

Read and translate:

A. 1. Kĕreta dia kĕna curi malam tadi. Dia pĕrgi tadi nak
adukan hal itu kĕpada polis. 2. Tangan Cik Harun kĕna potong
pisau, tĕrus bĕrdarah. Bajunya kotor kĕna darah. 3. Malam
tadi anak saya kĕna gigit nyamuk. 4. Kasut awak kotor kĕna

minyak. 5. Pějabat pos di Jalan Swettenham kěna rompak minggu lěpas. 6. Ěncik Dollah kěna adu polis sěbab dia lětak kěreta di sěbělah sini jalan. 7. Inilah těmpat dua orang polis kěna bunuh komunis. 8. Hamzah kěna suruh pěrgi běrjumpa pěngurus. 9. Istěri saya kěna masak pukul tiga pagi dalam bulan puasa. 10. Dia kěna panggil tuan pěngurus sěbab dia tak datang kěrja hari satu. 11. Měreka kěna děnda dua ratus ringgit sěorang. 12. Dia kěna simpan wang di rumah sěbab rumahnya jauh dari benk. 13. Malam tadi saya kěna jaga anak di rumah sěbab istěri saya jatuh sakit. 14. Saudagar itu kěna bayar cukai dua ribu ringgit. 15. Kědai makan itu kěna rompak dua orang běrsěnjata. 16. Bila dia kěna tipu pěrěmpuan itu lěkaslah dia naik marah. 17. Tahun dulu banyak orang buruh kěna buang kěrja. 18. Bapa dia kěna pindah kě Kuala Lipis bulan sudah. 19. Sěbab tak ada jambatan měreka kěna běrěnang menyěběrang sungai itu. 20. Kalau dia nak naik pangkat lagi, dia kěna bělajar bahasa Inggěris. 21. Orang yang curi barang-barang makanan itu sudah kěna tangkap polis. 22. Orang polis itu tembak tětapi tak kěna. 23. Dia tembak binatang itu dan kěna di pěrutnya. 24. Saya kena bekěrja tiap-tiap hari ěnam bulan ini.

B. 1. Janganlah simpan wang di rumah; simpanlah di benk. Kalau di rumah těntu kěna curi nanti. 2. Dia tak bayar wang cukai. Těntu kěna děnda nanti. 3. Bětulkanlah susunan kotak itu, nanti jatuh. 4. Těntukan sěmua tong itu běrisi minyak. 5. Banyak orang yang tinggal di luar bandar London datang kěrja děngan kěretapi tiap-tiap hari. 6. Husin, awak 'ni suka buat nakal. Siapa buat nakal těntu kena rotan. Bagaimana boleh pandai nanti kalau tak bělajar děngan bětul? 7. Bila dia sampai nanti, tolonglah ambilkan wang itu, běrikan dia surat ini. 8. Polis bělum dapat tangkap lagi kěpala kumpulan yang bunuh tuan punya kědai itu. 9. Pěgawai yang běrpangkat rěndah itu kěna marah kětua jabatan. 10. Orang luar itu minta tolongkah? Minta api rokok saja. 11. Suruhlah budak itu jangan main api, nanti kěna bajunya. 12. Kalau běgitu halnya, kita městi adukan kěpada polis. 13. Sěorang budak sěkolah mati di rumahsakit sělěpas kěna sěrang sěekor binatang děkat kampungnya. 14. Janganlah awak susah. Sěkějap lagi sampailah kěrani běsar. Boleh jadi dia dapat tolong. 15. Tukang kěbun itu kěna hukum ěnam bulan kěrja běrat. 16. Ini bukan kali yang yang pěrtama dia langgar undang-undang. 17. Orang yang rompak kĕdai radio itu tidak bĕrani kĕluar dari tĕmpat mĕreka bĕrsĕmbunyi. Mĕreka tahu kalau mĕreka kĕluar, polis tĕntu sahaja dapat tangkap mĕreka. 18. Dah pukul lima sĕkarang, ĕncik. Marilah kita balik. Nanti sĕkĕjap, saya mahu habiskan kĕrja 'ni dulu. 19. Yusuf sudah kĕna lotĕri. Itulah sĕbabnya dia mahu bĕrhĕnti kĕrja sĕkarang. 20. Jaga baik bila mĕnyĕbĕrang jalan di sana. Kalau tidak, tĕntu kĕna langgar. 21. Apa hal yang hĕndak awak bĕritahu itu, Yusuf? Cakapkanlah sĕkarang! Nanti, kalau bas sudah datang, awak tidak dapat bĕrcakap dĕngan saya lagi. 22. Minyak di dalam tangki itu bukannya banyak. Eloklah awak bĕrhĕnti di tĕmpat pam minyak yang dĕkat. 23. Guru bĕsar sĕkolah itu kĕna luka ringan bila kĕretanya langgar pokok. 24. Kalau awak ambil bĕrat sikit, tĕntulah pĕlajaran ini tidak bĕgitu susah.

Substitute in the following exercises:

C. *pattern:* **Kĕreta** dia **rosak,** kĕna apa? Kĕna **langgar bas.**
baju, kotor, minyak injin; wang, hilang, curi orang; kaki, sakit, batu bĕsar; kĕpala, bĕrdarah, pukul orang; sĕluar, basah, minyak petrol; badan, luka, tembak komunis

D. *pattern:* Sĕbab itulah dia orang kĕna **adu.**
buang; hukum; dĕnda; marah istĕri; bayar

E. *pattern:* Bukan **awak** yang bĕrsalah, **saya**lah.
saya, dia; kami, mĕreka; anak saya, budak nakal; kĕrani, tukang wang; tukang letrik, tùkang paip; orang kita, orang luar

F. *pattern:* Nanti **sĕtĕngah jam** lagi dia nak **bĕrlĕpas.**
dua minggu, bĕrpindah rumah; dua jam, balik; tujuh jam, kahwin; ĕmpat bulan, ambil kursus itu; tiga minggu, balik kĕ Amerika Sjarikat

G. *pattern:* Kalau saya tahu **kĕreta** itu bĕgitu **murah,** sudah tĕntu saya **bĕli.**
makanan, sĕdap, bĕli; rumah, jauh, tak ikut; kĕrja, susah, tak buat; peti, bĕrat, tinggalkan; tali, kuat, pakai; badannya, sakit, panggil doktor

H. *pattern:* Mahu tak mahu dia kĕna **masuk rumahsakit** juga.
tolong kĕrani; bayar balik; bĕlajar Inggĕris; pindah rumah; bĕrmalam di sana; bĕrhĕnti sĕkolah

Lesson Thirteen

Particular expressions employing *nya*; the *yang . . . nya* combination; *děkat nak*; colloquial use of *kuat* and *banyak*.

Vocabulary

barangkali perhaps, maybe
bodoh foolish
cantik beautiful
cuba try, test
gadis teenage girl
hidup alive, to live
hujan rain
kawasan area
kěmas tidy, neat
kěrbau water-buffalo
kěrtas paper
lari run, flee
lěbat thick (foliage, hair), heavy (with fruit, rain)
luas wide (of area), spacious
malas lazy
mělawat to visit
měrbahaya dangerous
memang of course, naturally, indeed

něgara state, national
něgeri state, country
pělan-pelan slowly, quietly (pěrlahan-lahan)
pěnat tired
pěriksa examine, inspect
pěta map
pinjam borrow
rupa appearance, shape
saudara relative, cousin
sěsat astray, lost
tanda a sign, mark
tangga ladder, steps, stairs
ular snake
betěri battery
ekar acre
cek cheque
kělas class

Phrases

hari hujan it's raining
bukan main extraordinarily (ain't 'arf!)
kěrusi malas easy-chair

tandatangan signature
tanda jalan road-sign
wang kěrtas bank-notes
bapa saudara uncle

ĕmak saudara aunt
dalam bahaya in danger
sĕsat jalan lose the way, be lost
cek tipu false cheque
minta lalu excuse me (to get past)

buat apa? why? what for?
tangga gaji salary scale
mesin taip typewriter
saya kurang pĕriksa I don't know, I haven't looked into
saya malas nak I can't be bothered to

Affixes that you have studied can be used to form these words: **larikan** (abscond with, abduct), **lawatan** (a visit), **hidupkan** (start, switch on), **cantikkan** (decorate, make pretty), **luaskan** (widen), and **pinjamkan** (lend). An alternative for **mĕrbahaya** is **bĕrbahaya.**

LESSON NOTES

114. *Gadis* This is used for a girl of marriageable age (taking note of the fact that girls may often marry at an earlier age than their Western counterparts).

115. *luasnya* Luas means 'wide' in the sense of 'long radius'. **Luasnya** means 'area' (length times breadth); and a 'wide area', referring to land etc., would be **kawasan luas.**

116. *Nampaknya, rupanya* In these two expressions **nya** is doing the work of an indeterminate 'it', saying literally 'the look of it' and 'the form of it'. Both can be translated by 'it seems' or 'seemingly' but there is a difference between the two. **Nampaknya** is based on an impression which may be false, whereas **rupanya** is nearer to fact. To get used to the difference, think of **nampaknya** as 'it seems', and **rupanya** as '(but) it turns out that', unless as in Exercise **C** **rupanya** obviously refers to physical appearance and means 'looks'.

117. *Dĕkat nak* Think of this combination as 'about to'.

118. *Kuat, banyak* These words are often used adverbially in colloquial speech. **Dia kuat makan** means 'He is a good eater', whereas **Dia banyak makan** is 'He is eating a lot' (the idea being limited to one occasion).

83

119. *Yang . . . nya* This combination usually becomes 'whose' in English.

saudara yang rumahnya a relative whose house

120. *Nĕgĕri, nĕgara* The word **nĕgĕri** can refer to 'state' (equivalent to the British county) and 'country', as physical and geographical entities. **Nĕgara** is 'state' as a corporate unit of society, with an administrative system, *etc.* Used after another noun it sometimes becomes 'national' as in **Stadium Nĕgara** (National Stadium) and **Mĕsjid Nĕgara** (National Mosque).

EXERCISES

Read and translate:

A. 1. Tĕntukan sĕmua bilik kĕlas itu kĕmas. Nanti guru bĕsar datang nak pĕriksanya. 2. Kalau dia orang tak bawa pĕta, tĕntulah sĕsat di kawasan itu nanti. 3. Dalam lawatannya kĕ Kuala Lumpur dia pĕrgi bĕrsĕmbahyang Jumaat di Mĕsjid Nĕgara. 4. Dulu saya ingat gadis itu sudah mĕninggal, rupanya dia hidup lagi. 5. Kalau hujan lĕbat nanti, tĕntulah susah nak cari jalan. 6. Barangkali satu hari nanti kita boleh pĕrgi mĕlawat kĕ Muzium Nĕgara. 7. Mĕreka kĕna bĕrjalan pĕlan-pĕlan saja sĕbab hujan kuat turun. 8. Luasnya padang ini dua ekar sĕtĕngah. Saudara saya yang punya. 9. Kita mĕsti luaskan kawasan ini sĕbĕlum boleh buat padang bola. 10. Sĕbĕlum balik rumah kĕmaskan opis ini dulu. 11. Kalau dia tak tahu baca pĕta, bagaimana boleh cari jalan yang bĕtul? 12. Bawalah pĕlan-pĕlan sikit. Saya mahu baca tanda jalan itu. 13. Buat apa dia tak boleh masuk kawasan itu? Rupanya askar nak bĕrlatih di sana. 14. Tĕmpat itu sangat mĕrbahaya. Banyaklah kĕreta yang sudah langgar di situ. 15. Cuba susun barang-barang ini dĕngan kĕmas. 16. Cuba tengok buku ini. Cantik bĕtul gambar di dalamnya. 17. Buat apa dia simpan fail ini dalam laci, awak tahu? Saya kurang pĕriksa, tuan. Nanti saya boleh bĕritahu tuan. 18. Bukan main bodoh budak itu. Hujan lĕbat bĕgini dia manu bĕrĕnang di sungai itu juga. 19. Jaga baik! Ular yang warnanya macam itu mĕrbahaya. 20. Jangan-lah hantar surat itu sĕbĕlum pĕngurus turunkan tandatangannya. 21. Saudara saya manu pĕrgi bĕlajar di luar nĕgĕri. 22. Dia kĕluar nĕgĕri tahun dulu, balik tahun dĕpan. 23. Saya lahir di Nĕgĕri Sĕmbilan dalam tahun sĕribu sĕmbilan ratus lima puluh

tujuh. 24. Dia kěna buang kěrja sěbab apa? Sěbab malas.
25. Askar memang tahu pakai kěmas.

B. 1. Dia rupanya macam orang India tětapi ěmak bapanya
běrbangsa Siam. 2. Bawalah fail itu kě opis saya. Saya mahu
pěriksa sěmua surat itu. 3. Omar kěrja di ladang? Bukan, tadi
dia pěrgi cari kěrbau, nanti dia balik. 4. Saya tak těntu di
mana dia sěkarang. Barangkali dia pěrgi kě rumah bapa saudaranya. 5. Těntu badannya pěnat. Sampai sěminggu dia kěna
běkěrja malam. 6. Bila turun bukit běrjalanlah pělan-pělan
nanti jatuh. 7. Hidupkan injin bila saya suruh. Lěpas itu
jalankan kěreta pělan-pělan. 8. Nampaknya tong itu bukan
bětul těmpatnya. Kami městi pindahkan. 9. Buat apa dia
bělum balik dari cuti? Nampaknya dia těrus sakit sělěpas jatuh
sěmalam. 10. Minta lalu, ěncik. Banyaklah orang di sini, susah
nak jalan. 11. Dia datang minta tolong, bukan? Běgitulah
nampaknya. 12. Ahmad pěrgi talipun; rupanya istěri dia děkat
nak běranak. 13. Gambar yang běgitu cantik těntu dia mahu
běli. 14. Saya ini malas, tak mahu kěmaskan meja itu sěkarang.
15. Saya malas nak tulis surat sěkarang. Besok sajalah. 16.
Pěrěmpuan muda itu bukan gadis lagi. Sudah kahwin. 17.
Budak yang duduk děkat jalan běsar itu těntu hidup dalam
bahaya. 18. Budak itu bukan main kuat lari. Sěkějap saja dia
sampai di sana. 19. Běrhěnti běli minyak di situ. Minyak
děkat nak habis. 20. Bila děkat nak habis kěrja nanti, suruh
budak itu kěmaskan barang-barang ini. 21. Betěri děkat nak
habis; těntulah susah nak hidupkan injin besok. 22. Měreka
buat děkat nak habis, 'tapi kita baru sikit saja. 23. Gaji bělum
lagi těrima, wang sudah děkat nak habis. 24. Hari děkat nak
malam; běrhěnti saja di sini makan malam. 25. Hujan lěbat
děkat nak turun, dia pěrgi juga cari rotan di hutan.

Substitute in the following exercises:

C. *pattern:* **Dia** rupanya macam **orang Jěpun.**
kěreta itu, kěreta saya; anak itu, bapanya; binatang itu, kěrbau

D. *pattern:* Dia **pěrgi kampung,** rupanya nak **mělawat
saudara.**
potong pokok, luaskan kawasan itu; minta tali tadi, ikat barang;
balik lěkas, kěmaskan rumah dulu; jumpa pěgawai polis, adukan
hal; jual kěrbau, kahwinkan anak; pěrgi rumah saudara, pinjam
duit

85

E. *pattern:* Nampaknya **orang sakit** itu banyak **makan** hari ini.
budak, tidur; anak saya, bĕrmain; kĕrbau, kĕrja; saudara saya,
bĕrcakap; budak yang kĕna rotan, bĕlajar; gadis, minum

F. *pattern:* Dia orang barangkali **nak balik kĕ mari.**
bĕrmalam di bandar; sĕsat jalan; nak bayar dĕngan cek; kĕna
buang; kĕna langgar kĕreta; nak minta pinjam wang

G. *pattern:* Sudah tĕntu dia **sĕsat jalan.**
mĕlawat kĕ kampung saudara; pĕnat sangat; tak ikut jalan ini;
nak datang lagi; nak bĕrgaduh; tak 'ndak jumpa saya; tak 'ndak
balik hari ini.

H. *pattern:* Tĕntukan **air betĕri cukup.**
kawasan itu cukup luas; sĕmua fail ada; tangki bĕrisi minyak;
tak ada orang dalam gudang; dia orang habiskan kĕrja itu

I. *pattern:* Pĕriksalah kalau **air betĕri cukup.**
minyak injin cukup; sĕmuanya bĕrjalan dĕngan bĕtul; ada
barang yang jatuh; surat yang hilang; sĕmua orang ada

J. *pattern:* **Barang-barang** yang bĕgini **cantik** tĕntulah **mahal.**
minyak petrol, banyak, mĕrbahaya; orang, malas, tak dapat
naik pangkat; orang, bodoh, susah nak bĕlajar; hujan, lĕbat,
kĕreta mesti bĕrjalan pĕlan-pĕlan

K. *pattern:* **Pĕrĕmpuan muda** itu bukan main **gĕmuk.**
gadis, cantik; kĕrbau, bĕsar; tĕmpat, mĕrbahaya; dia, pĕnat;
ular, panjang; orang polis, tinggi

L. *pattern:* **Tanda** itu bukan bĕtul tĕmpatnya.
tanda jalan; almari fail; lori minyak; pĕti; tong

Lesson Fourteen

Standard forms of comparison of adjectives and adverbs; additional information on *kurang,* *lĕbih* and *lagi*; *sĕkali* as 'extremely'.

VOCABULARY

anjing   dog
bĕruang   a bear
bĕsi   metal, iron
buaya   crocodile
cadar   bed-sheet
cĕpat   quickly, fast, early
cĕrmin   mirror, window
durian   large, thick-skinned
   thorny fruit
ganas   fierce, wild
ilmu   study of
jahat   wicked, bad
kain   cloth, clothing
kaya   rich
kayu   wood, wooden
kĕras   hard, harsh, obstinate
kira   calculate, reckon
lapang   open (of ground), free
   (of time)
lapar   hungry
lĕmah   weak, feeble
lĕmbut   soft, pliable

limau   citrus fruit
manis   sweet
masam   sour
monyet   monkey
mutu   quality, grade
nanas   pineapple
nipis   thin (of objects)
paling   extremely, the most
pisang   banana
rajin   industrious
rambutan   red, hairy fruit
sama   same, together
sarung   skirt, sheath,
   envelope
sĕlimut   blanket
sihat   fit, healthy
susu   milk
tanah   land, ground
tĕbal   thick
tingkap   window
tuala   towel

PHRASES

lapangan tĕrbang   airport
antarabangsa   international

binatang hutan   wild animal
   (not tame)

87

binatang ganas wild (dangerous) animal

sama macam the same as, the same sort

tak kira bĕrapa— no matter how—

kira-kira approximately, accounts

kira-kira benk bank account

ilmu kira-kira arithmetic

ilmu politik political science

pĕti bĕsi a safe

tanda harga price-tag

limau manis orange

limau masam lemon

tukang kayu carpenter

kain tingkap curtain

Two affixed words have been included in this vocabulary. They are **durian** (**duri**—thorn) and **rambutan** (**rambut**—hair).

LESSON NOTES

121. *Comparison* Some forms of comparison with adjectives and adverbs have already been used, because comparison was implicit in the context. It was apparent to all participants in the conversation and no additional words were needed to convey precision. According to context, **Yang ini bĕsar** could mean 'This is a big one', 'This is the bigger', or 'This is the biggest'. In order to be more precise on other occasions, the standard forms of comparison are practised in this lesson. (Other variations are given later in the book.)

1. Equal comparison: **Macam** and **dĕngan** are interchangeable here. The basic pattern is,

    sama + adjective + **macam/dĕngan** (as + adjective + as)

2. Unequal comparison: Three forms are given; the first two are common.

    tak sama + adjective + **macam/dĕngan** (not as + adjective + as)

    lĕbih + adjective + **dari** (more + adjective + than)

    kurang + adjective + **dari** (less + adjective + than)

3. Superlative degree: Of several forms, these are probably the most common:

    yang + adjective + **sĕkali**
    yang + **paling** + adjective } (the most + adjective)

122. *Kurang* The word **kurang** contains the idea 'lacking' and it is often used as 'not' or 'not very' when it is being suggested that a desired quality is lacking.

Dia kurang cantik She isn't pretty
Tali ini kurang panjang This string isn't long enough.

In bazaar Malay, the word **lagi** tends to be used for all the work of **lĕbih**. In standard Malay **lĕbih** is used for 'more' when there is a direct comparison between two different things, or when one thing is compared in two different states; and it is used with adjectives and adverbs. **Lagi**, as 'more', is used with nouns. The two can combine in phrases to produce 'even more'.

Bĕrjalanlah lagi sĕpuluh ela Go another ten yards
Ipoh lĕbih jauh dari Lumut Ipoh is further than Lumut
Pĕrgilah lĕbih jauh lagi Go even further

The meaning of **lĕbih** with nouns comes into a later lesson.

123. *Sĕkali* As you have seen, this word can be used to produce the superlative degree. Used with adjectives without **yang**, it means 'extremely'. Again, there are other functions of the word in later lessons.

124. *Cĕrmin* Though the dictionary meaning of this word is 'mirror', be prepared to hear it used for sheets of ordinary glass, as in **cĕrmin kĕreta** (car window) as opposed to **cĕrmin nampak bĕlakang** (rear-view mirror). **Meja cĕrmin** is often used for 'dressing-table'.

125. *Kira* This word can be used for two senses of 'reckon', that is, 'calculate' and 'believe'.

126. *Ilmu* This word introduces the names of academic subjects and branches of knowledge. It may be dropped if the meaning is obvious without it.

Hari ini kami kĕna buat kira-kira We had to do arithmetic today.

Here there is no confusion with the other meaning of **kira-kira**.

127. *Kain, sarung* The meaning of 'clothes, clothing' for **kain** is seen in such phrases as **pakai kain** (get dressed) and **kedai kain**

baju (clothing shop). **Kain tingkap** is the commonest expression for 'curtains' in speech, but **langsir, tabir, tirai** and **bidai** are various words used for curtains, partitions and screens. **Sarung** as an article of clothing is commonly known in the West, but it is not often realised that it is used for various sheath-like cases, hence **sarung pisau** (knife-sheath), **sarung tangan** (gloves) and **sarung benet** (bayonet frog).

EXERCISES

Read and translate:

A. 1. Jam awak itu sama macam jam saya. Bĕrapa ringgit awak bĕli? 2. Sĕlimut itu kurang baik. Bĕrilah yang lĕbih tĕbal. 3. Buah di hutan lĕbih masam dari buah di kĕbun. 4. Bukit itu tinggi sĕkali dan naik kĕatasnya paling susah. 5. Siapa orang yang paling tinggi dalam sjarikat? Saya tak tahu, 'tapi saya kira yang paling tinggi Omar. 6. Lapangan tĕrbang mana yang bĕsar sĕkali di Singapura? Saya kira lapangan tĕrbang di Sĕletar yang paling bĕsar. 7. Kapaltĕrbang itu sampai lagi dua puluh minit. 8. Dĕraiber itu ikut jalan sĕmpit sĕbab apa? Sĕbab jalan itu lĕbih dĕkat pĕrgi kĕ lapangan tĕrbang. 9. Kĕdai kain baju yang baru itu lĕbih bĕsar dari yang lama. 10. Yang mana lĕbih manis, nanas atau durian? Sudah tĕntu nanas lĕbih manis. 11. Janganlah ambil buah itu sĕkarang. Kalau buah itu cukup masak tĕntulah lĕbih manis lagi. 12. Kayu ini kĕras sĕkali, susah nak potong. 13. Harga cadar ini lĕbih mahal di Kuala Lumpur. Lĕbih baik bĕli di sini. 14. Dia tak bĕrapa pandai sĕkarang, tĕtapi di bĕrlatih banyak, tĕntu dia lĕbih pandai nanti. 15. Umur dia sama macam umur anak saya. Sĕbab apa dia tak boleh bĕrhĕnti sĕkolah? 16. Saya tak sama kaya macam Tuan Mahmud, jadi tak dapat bĕli kĕreta yang begitu mahal. 17. Dia orang kĕna bĕrjalan lĕbih cĕpat kalau nak lĕkas sampai di sana. 18. Ini cĕrmin yang baik tĕtapi cĕrmin itu lĕbih baik lagi. 19. Monyet itu ganas sĕkali; janganlah dĕkat. 20. Kalau orang sakit itu tak makan dua hari tĕntulah dia paling lapar sĕkarang. 21. Daripada sĕmua kĕrani dalam sjarikat ini Zainallah yang rajin sĕkali. Sĕbab itu dia cĕpat naik pangkat. 22. Minggu dulu saya sakit sangat; sĕkarang badan saya lĕmah lagi. 23. Kĕreta susah bĕrjalan di tanah lĕmbut ini. Cari tĕmpat yang lĕbih kĕras. 24. Di mana tĕmpatnya tanah yang paling luas? Yang paling luas saya kira di antara bukit dĕngan sungai. 25. Bĕtul dia sihat sĕkarang, 'tapi kalau dia pĕrgi cuti dua hari nanti dia lĕbih sihat lagi.　26. Cantik bĕtul sarung awak hari ini, Kadir. Sarung barukah?　27. Minuman apa ĕncik suka minum? Yang saya suka sĕkali susulah.　28. Hari ini saya nak bĕli kain tingkap yang baru lagi cantik.　29. Tingkap di sini lĕbih bĕsar dari tingkap di bilik sĕbĕlah. Tĕntukan kainnya lĕbin panjang.　30. Lĕtakkan surat itu balik dalam sarungnya.　31. Siapa lĕbih lĕmah, Jalil atau Mahmud? Saya kira Mahmud lĕbih lĕmah daripada Jalil. 32. Mana lĕbih ganas, bĕruang atau monyet? Saya kira bĕruang lĕbih ganas dari monyet.　33. Yang mana lĕbih kĕras, tanah di sini atau di sana? Saya kira yang di sini lĕbih kĕras.　34. Daripada sĕmua orang itu siapa yang pandai sĕkali? Yang pandai sĕkali Ĕncik Yusuf.　35. Saya ingat buku awak itu lĕbih baik dari buku saya. Marilah kita bĕrtukar.　36. Kain ini bĕrmutu tinggi. Bĕlilah sĕkarang dĕngan harga murah!

Substitute in the following exercises:

B. *pattern:*　**Jam** ini sama macam **jam** itu.
kayu, kain, rokok, pokok, pĕta, buku, cĕrmin

C. *pattern:*　**Buah ini** tak sama **manis** macam **nanas.**
anjing ini, ganas, monyet itu; Ali, jahat, Hussin; betĕri ini, lĕmah, betĕri itu; orang kampung, kaya, orang bandar; bĕsi ini, lĕmbut, bĕsi itu; dia, sihat, dulu; buah ini, masam, buah muda itu

D. *pattern:*　**Rumah** itu kurang **tinggi.**
kain, cantik; minuman, manis; buah, masak; orang, sihat; tuala, tĕbal; kĕrani, rajin; kayu, kĕras; budak, pandai

E. *pattern:*　Yang mana lebin **sĕdap, makanan Mĕlayu** atau **makanan Cina?**
manis, durian, rambutan; ganas, monyet, bĕruang; kĕras, kayu ini, bĕsi; mahal, cadar, sĕlimut; lĕmbut, roti lama, roti baru; nipis, kain ini, kain itu

F. *pattern:*　**Nanas** itu kurang baik, ambillah yang lĕbih **manis.**
sĕlimut, tĕbal; pisang, masak; susu, baru; tuala, bĕrsih; ayam, gĕmuk; daging, lĕmbut; roti, lĕmbut; kayu, kĕras

G. *pattern:*　Dia orang mĕsti **bĕrjalan** lĕbih **jauh** lagi.
tunggu, lama; bĕkĕrja, rajin; naik, tinggi; buat, kĕmas; bĕrjalan, cĕpat

H. *pattern:* Dari sĕmua **orang** itu siapa yang paling **tua?**
(*You must substitute* **mana** *for* **siapa** *when things and animals are discussed*)

budak, malas; binatang, ganas; buah, sĕdap; jurutaip, pandai; sjarikat, bĕsar; orang buruh, rajin; jalan, lebar

Lesson Fifteen

The standard passive (without agent); more uses of *juga*; *sĕkali* as 'completely'; problems of *biasa, guna, sĕmula* and *pulang*.

VOCABULARY

alat   equipment, device
bakar   burn, bake, toast
bĕrniaga   to trade
biasa   usual, used to, accustomed to
butang   button
cuci   wash, rinse, develop (film)
daftar   register
dingin   cold, chilly
goreng   to fry, fried
gulung   roll up, a roll
guna   use
hawa   atmosphere, climate
jĕmu   bored, fed up
jĕmur   to dry in the sun
kata   say, words
kawat   wire, telegram
kĕring   dry, dried
kirim   send (things)
larang   prohibit, forbid
laut   sea
lurus   straight (not crooked)

miskin   poor, needy
pantai   shore, coast
payung   umbrella
pĕnuh   full
pĕrkakas   kit, equipment, tools
pulang   return
rumput   grass
sampah   rubbish
sĕlalu   often, always
sĕmula   again, re-
sĕntuh   to touch
siap   ready, prepared
siram   to spray
tĕkan   to press
tĕpi   edge
ubat   medicine, remedy
untuk   for, for the purpose of, in order to
waktu   time (of day), time when
filĕm   film

PHRASES

alat hawa dingin   air-conditioner

bas bĕrhawa dingin   air-conditioned bus

93

nasi goreng fried rice	**sĕbĕrang laut** overseas
goreng pisang fried banana	**tĕpi pantai** beach
(notice the word order)	**tong sampah** rubbish-bin
surat kawat telegram	**tĕkan minyak** press the
ubat nyamuk mosquito spray	accelerator, accelerate
(or coil)	**macam biasa** as usual
roti bakar toast	**sĕgulung kĕrtas** a roll of
pĕnuh dĕngan full of	paper
dilarang masuk entry	**mel bĕrdaftar** registered mail
forbidden	

Affixed words: **berguna** (useful), **bĕrjĕmur** (sunbathe), **bĕrsiap** (get ready), **siapkan** (prepare something), **bĕrsiram** (take a shower), **ubatkan** (treat medically), **biasanya** (usually).

LESSON NOTES

128. *Passive voice* One form of the passive voice has already been used with **kĕna,** and you have seen that some active verbs in Malay, such as **sĕsat, hilang** and **rosak,** are often rendered passively in English. In this lesson the standard passive form, in which the verb is prefixed with **di,** is introduced. Thus we have **tangkap** (to catch) and **ditangkap** (to be caught), **suruh** (to order) and **disuruh** (to be ordered). This means that the prefix **ber** is dropped to make way for the **di** on all verbs that you know except **bĕrhĕntikan.** The suffix **kan,** however, is retained wherever it is necessary. The passive is not as common in Malay conversation as it is in English. At times, however, it must be used because it is not known, or not considered necessary to state, who performed an action. In this lesson no agent is given. (Students who are in doubt about these English terms are advised to re-read the notes on **kĕna** in Lesson 12.)

129. *Nak/mahu + passive* This combination parallels the conversational English form 'wants/needs + verb(ing)' as in,

> **Tuala ini mahu dijemur** This towel needs drying (needs to be dried)

130. *Juga* Three more uses of **juga** are illustrated in this lesson:

1. 'Also': considerable ambiguity can arise if **juga** is used as haphazardly in Malay as 'also' is sometimes used in English.

94

In Malay the word should follow the word it is meant to qualify,
For example, in the sentence 'I also worked in Ipoh'.
does the 'also' imply 'I in addition to someone else', 'worked
as well as lived', or 'Ipoh in addition to another place'? In
English the correct meaning is often indicated by stress, which
belies the actual word position of 'also', but in Malay the
position of **juga** must be correct.

2. 'Quite/fairly': again **juga** follows the word it describes.
Students should avoid confusion with 'quite' that means
'completely', as in 'You are quite wrong'.

   bĕsar juga (quite big)   **sĕlalu juga** (fairly often)

3. 'Very/very same': this use of **juga** appears mostly in time
phrases.

   sĕkarang ini juga   this very minute, right now
   hari itu juga   that very same day

131. *Biasa*   We have seen that 'used to', meaning 'previously',
can be translated with **dulu**. It should not be confused with 'to be
used to' where **biasa** can be employed. Notice in these examples
how **dĕngan** is used before a noun but not before a verb:

   Saya tak biasa dĕngan kĕrja ini   I am not used to this work
   Saya tak biasa bĕkĕrja waktu malam   I am not used to working at nights.

Used adjectivally, **biasa** means 'common, ordinary'.

132. *Guna*   The phrase **apa gunanya** can have two different
translations: 'what's the use of' and 'what is — used for'.

   Apa gunanya pĕrkakas lama itu? Buang saja.
   What's the use of that old kit? Just throw it out.
   Apa gunanya butang di mesin ini?
   What is the function of the button on this machine?

133. *Sĕkali*   The function of **sĕkali** in the last lesson is taken
one stage further so that it becomes 'completely' in this lesson;
and so,

   bakar sĕkali   burn completely, burn the lot
   sĕmua sĕkali   every single one

95

134. *Sĕmula* This sense of 'again' is 'as at first' and not simply 'once more, in addition', for which **lagi** has been used so far. The English prefix 're' often suggests this return to a previous condition, as in 'rearrest' and 'replace, put back'. There is much common ground in the use of both **sĕmula** and **balik** in this case (**bayar balik**—repay; **ambil balik**—recover, get back) and students must find out by experience where each is preferred in common usage. You will find from extended study that **kĕmbali,** another verb 'to return', is used in a very similar way to **balik.**

135. *Pulang* This verb covers the commonest sense of 'return' ('going back to a starting place') but it does not have the subsidiary uses of **balik** shown in the previous note. Once again, the place to which one is returning (usually 'home') is usually known in the context, and not stated.

EXERCISES

Read and translate:

A. 1. Kami mĕsti sĕlalu tolong orang yang susah, tak kira orang itu miskin atau kaya. 2. Anak saya yang tua itu sudah jĕmu bĕlajar. Tak mahu pĕrgi sĕkolah lagi. 3. Goreng pisang awak itu tinggal bĕrapa lagi? Tinggal lagi lapan kĕping saja, ĕncik. Bungkuslah sĕmua sĕkali. 4. Marilah kita pulang sĕkarang. Hari sudah pĕtang. Nanti, bila hari malam, tĕntu susah hĕndak cari jalan pulang kĕ rumah. 5. Dulu saya malas bĕlajar. Barulah saya tahu pĕlajaran sĕkolah itu sangat bĕrguna. 6. Tiap-tiap pagi dan tiap-tiap pĕtang kami siram sĕmua pokok di sini dĕngan air. Kalau ada rumput di bawah pokok itu, sĕmuanya kami buang. Dĕngan itu pokok kami sĕlalu sihat. 7. Tĕntukan tong itu pĕnuh dĕngan air bĕrsih. 8. Gunakan tuala ini, yang itu basah sĕkali. 9. Dia sĕlalu pĕrgi kĕ tĕpi laut waktu air pasang. 10. Janganlah buang sampah di sana sini. Taruh dalam tong sampah itu. 11. Jangan buang tali itu, barangkali ada gunanya. 12. Nasi sudah siap, marilah kita makan, nanti sĕjuk makanan itu. 13. Kalau tangan awak basah jangan sĕntuh tĕmpat lĕtrik. 14. Sudah sampai waktunya awak mĕsti makan ubat lagi. 15. Tolong pasangkan kawat antara pokok di kĕbun untuk jĕmur kain. 16. Orang yang sakit itu mahu diubatkan dĕngan lĕkas. 17. Kayu basah ini susah nak dibakar. Carilah kalau ada yang kĕring. 18. Orang dilarang bunuh binatang dalam kawasan hutan itu. 19. Butang sudah hilang dari baju ini. 20. Waktu dia cuci lantai di rumah saya cuci kĕreta di tĕpi jalan. 21. Baik kita bawa payung; nampaknya nak hujan lagi. 22. Payung kuning sĕlalu disimpan untuk sultan dan raja.

B. 1. Ambil kawat dua gulung itu dari lori. Dia nak dipasang di sini. 2. Sĕmua baju ini basah; nampaknya nak dijĕmur. 3. Apa macam anak istĕri di kampung? Baik juga. 4. Lama juga mĕreka kĕna tunggu kapaltĕrbang itu. 5. Dia kĕluar ikut pintu bĕlakang nak cari Zainal, 'tapi waktu itu juga Zainal masuk dari pintu hadapan. 6. Ĕncik Omar pĕrgi cuti hari tiga, 'tapi dia diminta pulang dĕngan lĕkas hari itu juga. 7. Dulu saya duduk di kawasan ini, 'tapi sĕkarang saya sudah tak biasa dĕngan jalan ini lagi. 8. Biasanya dia bĕrjĕmur di tĕpi pantai waktu pĕtang, hari ini tidak. 9. Saya ingat dia askar biasa, 'tapi rupanya dia sĕorang pĕgawai. 10. Alat ini ada banyak gunanya. Dia jangan dipindahkan. 11. Bila anak saya pulang dari sĕkolah sĕlalu dia siapkan kĕrja untuk hari esok. 12. Talipun tak ada, dia boleh dihubungkan sĕmula dengan surat kawat. 13. Siapa tahuh, satu masa nanti barang-barang lama itu sĕmuanya bolih digunakan sĕmula. 14. Barang ini bĕrharga mahal; kotaknya jangan ditĕkan. 15. Hawa di dalam bilik itu panas sangat sĕbab alat hawa dingin mahu dibĕtulkan. 16. Pĕrut saya tak lapar, sĕkĕping roti bakar cukuplah. 17. Jalan di antara bukit itu tidak bĕgitu lurus. 18. Sĕkarang orang boleh berjalan dĕngan bas bĕrhawa dingin ke nĕgĕri Siam. 19. Saya bĕrjumpa dĕngan Ĕncik Lim tadi. Katanya dia mahu bĕrniaga kĕlapa kĕring. 20. Injin tidak bĕrjalan dĕngan bĕtul dan saya tak ada pĕrkakas untuk bĕtulkannya. 21. Apa guna kĕretanya itu kalau belum didaftarkan lagi? 22. Pĕrgi katakan kĕpada Ĕncik Ahmad ada orang hĕndak bĕrjumpa dia.

Substitute in the following exercises:

C. *pattern:* **Rumput** itu mahu di**potong**.
hal, pĕriksa; tong, isikan; tuala, jĕmur; jam, bĕtulkan; sampah, buang; kawat, luruskan; lantai, cuci

D. *pattern:* **Kĕrtas** ini jangan di**buang**.
butang, tĕkan; tong, pindahkan; kawat, potong; filĕm, cuci; barang, ambil; alat, sĕntuh.

E. *pattern:* Sĕmua orang dilarang **mĕrokok** di sini.
berenang; buang sampah; bĕrdiri; bĕrmain; bakar kĕrtas; bĕrjalan

97

F. *pattern:* Biasanya dia **pĕrgi cuti kĕ Singapura**, 'tapi kali ini tidak.

bĕrhubung dĕngan talipun; bĕkĕrja dĕngan rajin; cuci sampai bĕrsih; ikut jalan bĕsar itu; isikan air dĕngan pĕnuh; sampai waktu pĕtang

G. *pattern:* **Ubat** itu tak ada gunanya lagi; bolehlah **dibuang.**

kĕrtas, bakar; kĕreta, jual; butang, simpan; tali, potong; kawat, gulung sĕkarang; barang, pulangkan kĕ gudang

H. *pattern:* Apa gunanya **fail** itu lagi, **bakarlah.**

kĕrtas, bakarlah; kayu, bakar sĕkali; surat, bakar sĕkali; ubat, buang sĕkali; pĕrkakas, buang saja; payung, buang saja

I. *pattern:* **Ubat** itu sangatlah bĕrguna nanti.

ubat nyamuk; tali; alat radio; payung; kawat; tong
(*Repeat, using:* **Kawat** itu sudah bĕrguna sangat)

J. *pattern:* Sudah sampai waktunya **bĕrlĕpas.**

buka puasa; bĕrsiap; bĕrehat; pasang lampu; bĕrtugas; bĕrjalan lagi

K. *pattern:* Dia tak biasa dĕngan **kerja** ini.

wang kĕrtas; waktu kĕrja; pĕrkakas; jalan di bandar; mesin

L. *pattern:* Saya tak biasa **bĕrmalam di hutan.**

duduk di nĕgĕri panas; bawa kĕreta bĕgitu bĕsar; bĕrjalan naik kapaltĕrbang; bĕkĕrja waktu malam; gunakan pĕrkakas ini; makan nasi goreng

M. *pattern:* Saya sĕlalu **siapkan makanan** waktu **itu.**

cuci kĕreta, pĕtang; pĕrgi kĕ tĕpi pantai, malam; bĕrmandi di tĕpi laut, pagi; pakai baju ini, kĕrja; bawa payung, hujan; sampai, yang sama

Lesson Sixteen

The passive voice with agent; first lesson on reduplication.

VOCABULARY

angin wind
arah direction
bĕrbual-bual chat, converse
bĕrhati-hati to be careful,
  pay attention
busuk rotten, stale
dĕngar hear, listen
gĕlap dark, the dark, secret
ganti substitute, replace,
  exchange
ibu mother
istana palace
kadang-kadang sometimes
kĕnapa why
kipas fan, propeller
kota fort, town, city
kunci key, lock
lalang a species of very tall
  grass

lalai negligent, careless,
  listless
malu shy, embarrassed,
  ashamed
masih still, yet
oleh by, on account of
pagar fence, hedge
parit drain, ditch
pĕkan small town
pĕrahu boat
putus snapped, severed
rasa taste, feel
rĕbus to boil in water
sayur vegetable
siang daylight, daytime
takut to fear, be afraid
tanah paya swamp
tiba to arrive
tiba-tiba suddenly
tiup to blow

PHRASES

gĕlapkan wang embezzle
  money
tĕlur rĕbus boiled egg
jaga baik-baik watch out, be
  alert, take good care of

kipas angin electric fan
makan angin have a stroll or
  short holiday
pasar gĕlap black market
tali kipas fan-belt

waktu siang daytime
arah kě in the direction of
jangan malu-malu don't be
  so shy
ibukota a State capital
tak apa never mind; it

doesn't matter
Istana Něgara State Palace
Jabatan Laut Marine
  Department
běrhati-hati take care, be
  alert

Affixed words:

arahkan to direct
arahan direction
di bawah arahan under the
  direction of
gantikan change, replace,
  substitute
kuncikan to lock
kipaskan to fan

lalaikan ignore, forget
malukan to shame
pagarkan to fence off
putuskan to decide, break off
běrasa feel, taste
takutkan frighten, be afraid
  of

LESSON NOTES

136. **Ibu, anak** Both of these words can have very general meanings, **ibu** as a source or main component, and **anak** as that which issues from, or is contained in, another. In most contexts **kunci** will mean 'key' but, when there can be ambiguity between 'key' and 'lock', **anak kunci** should be used for the former.

anak anjing puppy
anak kapal crew member
anak ayam chick
anak něgěri subject of a
  state
anak sungai tributary

anak tangga stair/step, rung of
  ladder
ibu kaki big toe
ibu tangan thumb
ibu pějabat head office

137. *Kota* This word is the equivalent of 'castle' in English place names.

138. *Passive voice (contd.)* The passive form given in the last lesson is now expanded by giving the agent—the person performing the action. The pattern is similar to that of **kěna**, with the agent coming immediately after the passive verb.

  Dia kěna pukul orang ⎫
  Dia dipukul orang   ⎬ He was struck by someone
                  ⎭

Sometimes the word **oleh**, much more common in written than in spoken Malay, precedes the agent and does the work of 'by'.

Ikan itu ditangkap oleh Ahmad The fish was caught by Ahmad

When **nya** is attached to a passive verb it too becomes an agent and must be thought of as 'by him/her/it/them'. However, the **di**+verb+**nya** form is usually given in English translation in the active voice.

buku yang dicarinya the book she was looking for (the book which was sought by her)
Apa yang ditakutkannya? What is it he's afraid of? (What is it that is feared by him?)

When the subject also follows the verb, the agent precedes the subject, as shown in the next example where the agent **nya** comes before the subject **tali**.

lalu diikatkannya tali itu and then she fastened the string (and then was fastened by her the string)

Despite the ugliness of the English literal translation, this is a neat and compact Malay construction whose value lies in its brevity and the relief it affords from continual use of the active voice.

139. **Sĕorang** It is quite normal for students to be plagued by doubts about correct constructions and true meanings. Most doubts can be dispelled by careful observation and regular contact with written and spoken Malay. A typical problem lies in the differing translations of these phrases

ditinggalkan sĕorang di rumah left alone at home
ditinggalkan orang di rumah left at home by someone

When it means 'alone', **sĕorang** will often be reinforced with **saja**.

sĕorang saja all alone

140. *Reduplication* Reduplication is the process of extending a word by repetition of all or part of the word, or by combining two rhyming words, one of which may have been coined especially for the purpose. You have already seen this process in **lĕlaki** and

laki-laki (which would have been printed previously as **laki2**). Many people get the erroneous idea that reduplication is used only to show plurality. Though this function is common in officialese and newspaper Malay, it is not the commonest function in general usage of the language. Nor is it necessary to reduplicate when a plural has already been indicated as, for example, in a number; it would be wrong to say **dua ekor lĕmbu-lĕmbu** for **dua ekor lĕmbu**.

Most of the work of this and the next lesson is to explain and illustrate reduplication. Some examples of reduplication and repetition in English can be used to illustrate, although poorly, the qualities of reinforcement, continuity, vagueness and variety in Malay reduplication.

1. Reinforcement of an idea or quality: *very, very good*; or (from children) *a big, big aeroplane*

2. Continuity of an activity or state: *Work, work, work, all day long; the drip, drip, drip of a tap; pitter-patter*

3. Vagueness and approximate resemblance: *hocus-pocus, airy-fairy, chitchat, claptrap*

4. Variety and diversity: *hotchpotch, raggle-taggle*

Students may decide for themselves the categories in which they would place others like *helter-skelter, dilly-dally, higgledy-piggledy* and *willy-nilly*. The fact that they may fit into more than one category brings out the point that you should not expect each Malay expression to fit into one category only. In different sentences they may express different ideas, and that is why one or two expressions are repeated in the following groups:

1. *Reinforcement:* **malam-malam**, late at night; **pĕtang-pĕtang**, late in the evening; **lama-lama**, eventually (or) a very long time; **sĕlalu-sĕlalu**, very often, as often as possible; **sĕkali-kali**, absolutely (see **sĕkali-sĕkali** in 3); **lĕkas-lĕkas**, very quickly, very early (see 3); **mula-mula**, at first, first of all; **pagi-pagi**, very early in the morning (see 2); **bĕtul-bĕtul**, properly, carefully, truly; **mahal-mahal**, very expensive; **sakit-sakit**, very ill (see 2).

2. *Continuity:* **hujan-hujan**, raining and raining; **sakit-sakit**, always ailing; **potong pendek-pendek**, cut into short pieces; **hari-hari**, day after day, daily; **pagi-pagi**, each morning.

(Most of the reduplicated verbs in the next lesson fit into this group.)

3. *Vagueness:* (As in the first example, **sikit** may indicate this category.) **lĕkas-lĕkas sikit,** a little quickish; **hitam-hitam,** blackish; **orang tua-tua,** elderly people; **muda-muda,** youngish; **siang-siang,** at first light (also a general 'early'); **di tĕngah-tĕngah,** about the middle of; **di tĕpi-tĕpi,** near the edge of; **besok-besok,** sometime in the future; **bila-bila,** whenever, anytime; **kalau-kalau,** if by chance; **kira-kira,** approximately (also 'accounts' and 'arithmetic'); **lama-lama,** oldish; **sĕkali-sĕkali,** once or twice, now and again.

4. *Variety:* (Plurality is automatically associated with this category; and the meaning 'all' is often implicit, as in **budak-budak yang jahat-jahat bĕgini**—'all youngsters who are very bad like this'.) **Tinggi-tinggi,** of varying height; **bĕrmacam-macam,** all kinds of; **suratkhabar-suratkhabar,** newspapers.

With a few nouns the suffix **an** will stress the variety of type. **Sayur-sayur,** vegetables, (but **sayur-sayuran,** various kinds of vegetables); **buah-buahan,** fruits of various kinds; **kayu-kayuan,** all kinds of wood; **bunga-bungaan,** all kinds of flowers; **tanam-tanaman,** all kinds of crops.

Some of the reduplicated words in this lesson require special mention:

(*a*) Notice the difference between these affirmative and negative wishes:

jangan-jangan it is to be hoped that . . . not . . .
harap-harap it is to be hoped that . . .

(*b*) In sentence B30 of the translation Exercises, **satu-satu** is linked with **itu** to mean 'a certain, a particular' and it can be found in Malay literature as **sĕsuatu.** At other times **satu-satu** can be used as 'one by one' and also 'spaced out'.

(*c*) Reduplication reinforces the effect of 'still not' in **bĕlum . . . lagi. Dia tidur bĕlum bangun lagi** may not invite comment, but **Dia tidur bĕlum bangun-bangun lagi** invites the question 'Why on earth isn't he up yet?'

EXERCISES

Read and translate:

A. 1. Taruhlah lurus-lurus. 2. Pĕrgilah lĕkas-lĕkas. 3. Bĕr-jalanlah bĕtul-bĕtul. 4. Jaga kĕreta itu baik-baik. 5. Simpanlah surat itu baik-baik. 6. Simpanlah buah itu baik-baik, nanti busuk. 7. Kira wang itu bĕtul-bĕtul. 8. Janganlah bĕli mahal-mahal. 9. Jangan cakap panjang-panjang. 10. Datang dĕkat-dĕkat sikit. 11. Baik pĕrgi lambat-lambat sikit. 12. Baik ikatkan tali pĕrahu itu kuat-kuat sikit. 13. Potong tali itu pendek-pendek. 14. Dia pĕrgi kĕrja pagi-pagi, balik pĕtang-pĕtang. 15. Kalau nak menyĕbĕrang tanah paya, kita mĕsti berlĕpas siang-siang. 16. Wayang gambar itu baik sĕkali. Teketnya siang-siang sudah habis dijual. 17. Besok-besok janganlah sĕkali-kali buat macam itu lagi. 18. Biasanya dia tak makan tĕlur rĕbus tĕtapi sĕkali-sĕkali dia makan juga. 19. Jangan masuk hutan sĕorang saja. Kalau-kalau sĕsat, siapa nak tahu? 20. Tiba-tiba tali itu putus sĕbab angin bĕrtiup kuat-kuat. 21. Tengoklah anak kunci ini. Kadang-kadang boleh buka, kadang-kadang tak boleh. Baiklah digantikan saja. 22. Bila-bila sĕnang dia suka sĕkali bĕrjalan di kawasan istana. 23. Tĕntukan kain yang nipis ini tidak diambil orang. 24. Daging itu sudah dimakan anjing. 25. Lalang itu sudah dipotong tukang kebun. 26. Tali kipas yang putus itu nak digantikan orang kĕdai. 27. Tĕntukan tugas itu tidak dilalaikan askar. 28. Tĕntukan kĕrja itu tidak dijalankan oleh kĕrani biasa. 29. Tĕntukan fail itu tidak diambil orang. 30. Kadang-kadang saya tidur pakai kipas angin. 31. Kadang-kadang mĕreka pĕrgi kĕ pĕkan naik pĕrahu. 32. Jaga baik-baik di dalam air yang dalam-dalam itu. 33. Bĕrhati-hatilah dalam hutan yang tĕbal-tĕbal itu. 34. Radio di rumah sĕbĕlah itu boleh didĕngar dari jauh. 35. Kĕnapa Omar tak kĕluar kĕ bandar? Dia baca buku. Buku apa yang dibacanya? Buku yang dibĕlinya sĕmalam.

B. 1. Tĕlur yang dirĕbus tadi bĕlum kĕras lagi. 2. Dibĕtul-kannya pagar yang rosak itu sĕmalam. 3. Sĕlĕpas ditiup angin dia tĕrus jatuh kĕ dalam parit. 4. Apa lagi yang ditunggu? Bukankah hari sudah malam? 5. Anak pokok itu kalau dijaga bĕtul-bĕtul tĕntulah tidak mati bĕgini. 6. Sayur yang dibĕlinya sĕmalam sudah habis dimakan lĕmbu. 7. Kalau awak sĕlalu datang bĕgini lambat tĕntulah nanti awak dibuang kĕrja. 8. Bapanya yang digigit anjing tiga minggu dulu masih bĕlum kĕluar

104

dari rumahsakit. 9. Pintu itu kalau dikunci sěbělum ditinggalkan dulu, těntulah orang tak dapat masuk. 10. Jěmurlah pakaian yang basah-basah itu di luar bilik. 11. Pasanglah lampu itu cěpat-cěpat sikit. Hari sudah nak gělap. 12. Sělalu-sělalu datang kě rumah saya bila-bila awak sěnang. 13. Tak apalah, dia běrmain di těpi-těpi jalan saja. 14. Sama-samalah kita tunggu sampai měreka datang. 15. Janganlah malu-malu. Kalau tak makan, pěrut awak lapar. 16. Anjing-anjing di rumah sěbělah it ganas-ganas rupanya. 17. Sudah sampai waktunya kita potong lalang yang těbal-těbal itu. 18. Sějuk-sějuk běgini, pakailah baju-baju yang těbal-těbal sikit. 19. Kalau dia bangun pagi-pagi těntulah dia boleh tolong ěmaknya. 20. Bila měreka baru-baru sampai dulu měreka sělalu sěsat jalan di ibukota. 21. Macam mana dia boleh běrehat lama-lama kalau banyak orang datang mělawatnya hari-hari. 22. Kěnapa orang Cina itu ditangkap polis tiba-tiba saja? 23. Apa lagi yang dicarinya malam-malam běgini? Besok sajalah! 24. Kadang-kadang budak itu dipukul ěmaknya sampai luka-luka. 25. Bila-bila dia sěnang, dibawa anak-anaknya makan angin di těpi pantai. 26. Saya tak nampak bila dia datang; tiba-tiba dia sudah ada di dalam opisnya. 27. Ali tidak tunggu lama-lama lagi; diikatnya tali pada pěti itu kuat-kuat. 28. Potonglah roti itu nipis-nipis, sělěpas itu barulah dibakar. 29. Tanah yang lapang-lapang běginilah yang dicarinya untuk buat rumah. 30. Kalau satu-satu kěrja itu dibuat bětul-bětul, barang yang susah boleh jadi sěnang. 31. Banyak-banyak buah, pisanglah yang saya suka sěkali. Awak suka jugakah? 32. Hujan-hujan běgini kěnapa tak běrtopi? 33. Buah yang busuk-busuk běgini kěnapa tidak dibuang? 34. Kalau takut-takut běgini kěnapa tinggal sěorang saja? 35. Kěnapa Hassan tak mahu pěrgi kě sungai? Dia takut. Apa yang ditakutkannya? Buaya yang dijumpa orang di sana.

Substitute in the following exercises:

C. *pattern:* Dia běrjalan arah kě **měsjid**.
sungai; pěkan; Kota Tinggi; pantai; bukit; Jabatan Laut

D. *pattern:* Dia **tidur** bělum **bangun-bangun** lagi.
kěrja, habis-habis; makan, sudah-sudah; cari, jumpa-jumpa; minta, dapat-dapat; jalan, sampai-sampai; tembak, kěna-kěna; potong, putus-putus; běrgaduh, baik-baik

E. *pattern:* Janganlah **pěrgi ke pěkan malam-malam** běgini, nanti **sěsat jalannya.**

pasang lampu siang-siang hari, habis minyaknya; cuci pakaian kuat-kuat, hilang warnanya; rěbus tělur lama-lama, kěras isinya; tutup pintu kuat-kuat, rosak kuncinya; potong sayur kěcil-kěcil, tak sědap rasanya; běrhěntikan lori tiba-tiba, jatuh barang-barangnya

F. In the following sentences, choose **jangan-jangan** or **harap-harap**, whichever is appropriate, to fill the blank spaces:

1. Sěkarang dia bělum sampai lagi, — — — dia sakit.
2. Siang-siang dia sudah běrlěpas, — — — dia sampai dulu.
3. Dia yang pěnghabisan kěluar, — — — pintu dikuncinya.
4. Hari ini dia běrjalan kaki, — — — kěretanya rosak.
5. Ini istěri saya datang, — — — dia bawa rokok.
6. Hari sudah gelap, — — — hujan nak turun.
7. Dia tak masak sayur itu, — — — sudah busuk.
8. Kipas angin itu sudah lama dibělinya, — — — boleh dipakai lagi.

Lesson Seventeen

Second lesson on reduplication; introduction of *pun*; peculiarities of *kata* and *pĕrnah*; distinguishing between *lain* and *lagi*.

VOCABULARY

angkat raise, lift
atap roof, thatch
belok turn, curve
bĕlukar secondary jungle
beza differ
bezanya difference
bujang single, unmarried
cap brand; to stamp, print
diam silent, motionless, to reside, live
garam salt
gosok rub, polish, iron
gula sugar
halus delicate, refined
hujung end
iaitu that, that is to say
ialah is, are (balance word)
jĕnis type, species
kaca glass
kawan friend, flock/herd
kulit skin, hide, bark, shell

lain different, other
lumba a race
manusia human, mankind
mata eyes
murid pupil
pĕnghulu headman
pĕrnah ever, used to, once
pondok hut, shed
pun too, even, at all
raya public, large
rugi lose, loss (opp. of 'profit')
sĕmpat have time/ opportunity
sĕmut ant
simpang junction, branch off
subur fertile, thriving
tambang fare (on transport)
tumbuh grow, sprout
untung profit, gain, lucky

PHRASES

tidak sĕorang pun not a single person
gantirugi compensation

(untuk) suka-suka saja just for pleasure

buat suka-suka saja do just as one pleases

kĕrjasama co-operate, co-operation

bagaimana bezanya (x) dĕngan (y) what is the difference between (x) and (y)

Hari Raya holiday at the end of Bulan Puasa

jalanraya (abbreviated **jaraya**) public road, highway

lain orang somebody else

(antara) satu sama lain with each other, among one another

sĕkawan binatang a herd of animals

sĕkawan ikan a shoal of fish

lumba lari running race

simpang ĕmpat cross-road

simpang tiga junction of three roads

hujung minggu end of week

ubat tidur sleeping-pills

dan lain-lain (dll.) etcetera (etc.)

pĕnghulu kampung village headman

Affixed words:

angkatan a force, generation

Angkatan Laut Navy

bezakan differentiate, discriminate

diamkan to silence, ignore

rayakan celebrate

rugikan cause loss to, damage

berbeza to be different

bĕrlainan to be different

sĕlain (dari itu) apart (from that)

gosokan ironing, ironed clothes

Lesson Notes

141. *Reduplication (contd.)* Students are reminded that reduplicated words can vary in translation according to the context. In the first of the following sentences **habis-habis** means 'till finally'; in the second the reduplication reinforces the 'still not yet' of **belum . . . lagi**:

> **Dia tak dapat gaji hari ini, habis-habis dia bergaduh dĕngan kĕrani bĕsar di opis.**
>
> **Sampai pukul ĕnam ini dia kĕrja bĕlum habis-habis lagi.**

The vagueness of the indeterminate English expressions involving 'some', 'any' and 'ever' is often conveyed in Malay by reduplication:

apa-apa, anything, any, whatever; siapa-siapa, anyone, whoever; bila-bila, whenever, any time; mana-mana tempat,
everywhere, wherever, all over.

The emphasis given by the English 'at all' in such expressions is
given by pun in Malay, though, particularly with bila-bila, the
word saja will often perform the same function.

Some English phrases, especially those involving numbers, have
clear parallels in Malay:

satu-satu, one by one, each one; dua-dua, in two's; kĕdua-
dua(nya), both (of them); kĕĕmpat-ĕmpat(nya), all four (of
them); bĕribu-ribu, thousands of; bĕratus-ratus, hundreds of;
bĕrpuluh-puluh, dozens of; bĕrjam-jam, for hours and hours;
bĕrbulan-bulan, for months on end.

Some expressions could be classed as metaphors because they
exhibit a vague resemblance to a thing or action:

anak-anak, doll (or anak-anak patung where it needs to be
distinguished from 'children', patung being 'statue, puppet');
mata-mata, police (recalling 'private eye'); gula-gula, sweets;
sakit sĕmut-sĕmut, the tingling of 'pins and needles'; ikan
lumba-lumba, porpoise, dolphin; buat-buat, pretend; main-
main, play around, in fun, 'kidding'.

Repetition of an action or state should now present few problems:

bĕrgaduh-gaduh, continually quarrelling, making a fuss;
bĕrganti-ganti, taking turns, in relay; pusing-pusing, go round
in circles, revolve, spin; tak bĕrhĕnti-hĕnti, unceasingly;
bĕrdiam-diam, remain silent; diam-diam, silently, secretly;
bĕrtumbuh-tumbuh, thrive, flourish; tumbuh-tumbuhan, vege-
tation, flora.

Occasionally two words of the same meaning have combined
without producing an additional meaning. In fact the kalau used
so far is a shortened form of jikalau, which is a combination of
two words, jika and lau, both meaning 'if'. Similarly, mĕrbahaya
is a combination of two words, mara and bahaya, meaning
'danger'. Apabila is another form of bila.

142. *Habis, sĕkali* Both of these words can be used for 'completely' but habis is generally used in this way to accompany only
verbal forms:

habis rosak, completely destroyed, damaged beyond repair; **tangannya habis bĕrdarah,** his hand was covered in blood; **habis dimakan,** eaten all up

143. *Kata* This stem word is really a noun; the verb 'to say' is **berkata,** although the form **katanya** (the words of him/her/them) is commonly used for 'he/she/they said'. The use of 'words' here is the same as in the English 'I wish to say a few words', that is, related words in meaningful speech. For isolated 'words' the Malay uses **pĕrkataan-pĕrkataan.**

144. *Pun* This is one of the most difficult Malay words for students to master. Yet, since it is used mainly to give emphasis, its absence rarely alters meaning. Try to develop the feel of it by learning complete phrases in which it appears.

145. *Pĕrnah* Since we use 'ever' and 'never' only in simple sentences that are interrogative and negative, students can be perplexed by the use of **pĕrnah** in *affirmative* Malay sentences, as though to say, for example, 'I have ever been to Japan'. In such cases, see the **pernah** as 'once', 'used to', or simply as an accentuated 'have/has'.

146. *Ini* This word can indicate nearness in time as well as space; hence the **sĕkarang ini** that you have already met, which is often shortened to just **ini** in ordinary conversation, and which is sometimes used for 'nowadays'.

147. *Lain, lagi* Whereas **lagi** relates to something 'additional', **lain** refers to 'difference'. In English 'another' is often used for both. In 'Give me another book', you would have to ascertain whether 'another' meant 'one additional to the one(s) I have' (**lagi satu**) or 'of a different kind' (**lain**).

EXERCISES

Read and translate:

A. 1. Kakak saya sudah lama bĕrkahwin tĕtapi abang saya masih bujang lagi. 2. Kĕlapa ialah sĕjĕnis tumbuhan yang sangat bĕrguna kĕpada manusia. 3. Pokok teh tumbuh dĕngan subur di bukit-bukit dalam nĕgĕri yang bĕrhawa panas. 4.

Angkat pěti itu baik-baik. Isinya ialah barang kaca yang halus, lěkas pěcah. 5. Memang bětul kata-kata awak itu dulu iaitu sěmua orang tua suka běrbual-bual. 6. Ali tidak jual mahal kěpada orang kampung; dia ambil untung sadikit saja. 7. Apabila cikgu běrtanya siapa tahu rumah murid yang sakit itu, Salim pun angkat tangan děngan cěpat. 8. Bila habis kěrja yang lain itu simpanlah gosokan ini di dalam almari. 9. Wang saya itu jika tak hilang kě mana pěrginya? Marilah tolong saya carinya. Untung-untung jumpa sěmula wang saya itu. 10. Wang yang hilang itu běrapa? Tak banyak. Lima puluh sen saja. Tětapi lima puluh sen pun wang juga. 11. Orang yang curi pun manusia juga. 12. Awak tunggu dulu di sini. Tětapi awak jangan pěrgi kě mana-mana, tahu? 13. Di těpi pantai běgini saya tak rasa pěnat, tak rasa apa-apa pun—tidak macam di rumah. Kalau di rumah, pěrut saya sělalu saja lapar. Saya pun rasa macam awak juga, Salmah. Kalau di rumah, saya sělalu saja rasa malas dan pěnat. 14. Kalau tuan nak pulang kě kota, městi balik kě simpang ěmpat lalu belok kiri. 15. Orang Mělayu kata, 'Ada gula ada sěmut', iaitu di mana-mana ada pěrěmpuan cantik di situ orang lělaki pun ada. 16. Tak ada sěorang pun dari kawan-kawan saya yang kěna běkěrja pada Hari Raya ini. 17. Bětul juga kata-kata dia itu, 'tapi kali ini bezanya sikit iaitu gula-gula cap ini sama mahal macam cap itu. 18. Kěreta ini sangatlah běrbeza dari kěreta yang pěrnah saya pakai dulu. 19. Kalau boleh, saya nak běrganti těmpat děngan Mahmud sěbab saya bělum sěmpat mělawat kě kota itu. 20. Saya tak pěrnah tengok sěmut-sěmut yang běgitu banyak di satu těmpat. 21. Dia tangkap ikan suka-suka saja, tak kira untungnya. 22. Sěmua orang kěna bayar wang tambang, tak kira běrapa harganya.

B. 1. Baik kita pusing di hujung jalan ini. Kita ikut jalan kěcil di sěbělah kiri itu saja. 2. Nampaknya ada běrmacam-macam binatang pěrnah duduk di bělukar itu. 3. Disuruh buat apa-apa dia buat suka-suka saja. Běgitulah budak-budak sěkarang ini, sělalu nak děngar radio dan tengok talivisyun saja. 4. Kalau lampu itu sudah merah, jangan sěkali-kali těkan butang ini. 5. Saya tak děngar sěorang pun di bilik kělas itu. Bětul-bětul murid itu běrdiam-diam di sana. 6. Saya disuruh hantarkan dia kěmana-mana dia suka, 'tapi rupanya dia tak 'ndak kěmana-mana pun. 7. Ada sampah di mana-mana těmpat. Běrsihkanlah. 8. Jika orang-orang kampung běkěrjasama děngan pěgawai kěrajaan, sěnanglah kěrja itu boleh dibuat nanti. 9. Duduk di

111

satu těmpat lama-lama běgini, kaki sěbělah kiri saya kěna sakit sěmut-sěmut. 10. Siapa-siapa yang mahu masuk lumba běrěnang běrganti-ganti itu, bolehlah. 11. Mata-mata itu suka main-main saja; sělalu buat-buat nak tangkap kawan-kawannya. 12. Tutup beg gula itu kuat-kuat, nanti sěmut dapat masuk. 13. Ubat yang awak makan dulu ubat tidur; yang ini ubat lain. 14. Janganlah pakai kěreta yang sudah rosak itu. Pakailah yang lain. 15. Sěmua murid di sěkolah ini městi belajar bahasa Mělayu, bahasa Inggěris, Ilmu Kira-kira, dan lain-lain lagi. 16. Saya tak sěmpat nak cakapkan hal itu sěkarang, lain kali sajalah. 17. Dia buat salah iaitu dia diam-diam masuk rumah orang lain dan bila dipěriksa polis dia běrdiam-diam saja. 18. Kalau awak nak kěmana, běritahu saya dulu. 19. Kasi saya buku macam ini lagi satu. Kalau tak ada, apa-apa buku yang lain boleh juga. 20. Těntukan tak ada siapa-siapa pun yang měrokok děkat těmpat minyak ini. 21. Bukan saja kěretanya habis rosak tětapi kawan-kawannya habis mati juga. 22. Apa ěncik pěrnah běrjumpa sěkawan binatang di těngah-těngah hutan? 23. Dalam pěti itu ada gula, gula-gula, garam, susu dan lain-lain-nya. 24. Měreka běkěrja běrsama-sama di satu bilik. 25. Pěnghulu-pěnghulu kampung sělalu běkěrjasama děngan kěrajaan. 26. Dia lari tak běrhěnti-hěnti sampai hujung jalan.

C. (The following groups of sentences demonstrate how emphasis is given by means of reduplication, **pun** and **saja**.)

1. Ada orang di dalam opis, běritahu saya. 2. Ada siapa-siapa dalam pondok, suruh dia kěluar. 3. Ada siapa-siapa pun dalam gudang, panggil dia kě mari.

4. Ada barang dalam kotak, ambillah. 5. Ada apa-apa dalam pěti sějuk, kěluarkanlah. 6. Ada apa-apa pun dalam tong, buanglah.

7. Di mana ada gula di situ ada semut. 8. Di mana-mana ada simpang městilah ada tanda jalan. 9. Di mana-mana pun ada kunci, carilah. 10. Di mana-mana těmpat ada sampah! Bersih-kanlah.

11. Bila ada sport, sělalu dia datang. 12. Bila-bila ada wayang gambar, sělalu dia tengok. 13. Kita boleh běrlěpas bila-bila saja.

Substitute in the following exercises:

D. *pattern:* Měreka tak **běrcakap apa-apa, běrdiam-diam** saja. bělajar bětul-bětul, mahu main-main; kěmana-mana, běrjalan-

112

jalan; ikut suruhan saya, buat suka-suka; bětul-bětul sakit, buat-buat; 'ndak kahwin, běrkawan-kawan.

E. *pattern:* Dia pěrnah **sakit** sampai **běrbulan-bulan lamanya.**
sěsat di hutan, běrhari-hari lamanya; tidur, běrjam-jam lamanya; simpan wang, běribu-ribu ringgit banyaknya; běli kěreta, běribu-ribu ringgit harganya; tanam pokok rambutan, běrpuluh-puluh batang banyaknya; naik bukit, běratus-ratus kaki tingginya; bawa běras, běrgantang-gantang běratnya.

F. *pattern:* Dia itu bukan saja **bodoh** tětapi **malas** juga.
lapar, sakit pěrut; tak měrokok, tak minum bir; kuat makan, kuat běrjalan; sělalu pakai kěmas, rajin běkěrja; pandai cakap Inggěris, pandai buat kira-kira; tahu pasang radio, tahu baikkan kěreta; pěrnah pěrgi kě Jakarta, pěrnah kě Hong Kong.

G. *pattern:* Bagaimana bezanya 'kěrjasama' děngan 'kěrja běrsama-sama'?
gula, gula-gula; mata, mata-mata; anak, anak-anak, buat, buat-buat; kata-kata, pěrkataan-pěrkataan; sayur-sayur, sayur-sayuran.

H. *pattern:* Dia tak sěmpat nak **běli garam** sěbělum **kědai tutup.**
belok, kěreta kěna langgar; pulang kě kampung, Hari Raya; jumpa saudaranya, kapal běrlěpas; buat apa-apa, dia jatuh; lari, dia ditangkap; balik rumah, hujan turun.

Lesson Eighteen

Uses of *sě* and *sěkali pun*; emphatic and reflexive pronouns; *lat* and *jaraknya*; *cuba* and
minta and the implicit 'please'; *agaknya,
rasanya, rupanya* and *nampaknya.*

VOCABULARY

agak to guess, rather
bakau mangrove
baring to lie down
ganggu disturb, interrupt,
  bother, annoy
hala direction
měnghala facing, pointing
jarak interval, space,
  distance between
kěsatuan union, unity
lat interval, cvcry (4th, 5th,
  etc.)
lompat to jump
maaf pardon, forgiveness
měsyuarat meeting,
  conference

pasal about, concerning
pěrsatuan association
pilih choose
pulau island
samar dim, obscure, vague
sawah padi wet rice-field
sěbagai as, like, resembling
sěndiri/diri self
sěngaja deliberately
sěmasa while
silap mistake, error
tahan endure, last out; stop,
  detain; defend
tanya ask, enquire
tarik to pull
tolak push, reject
wanita lady, woman

PHRASES

sěpanjang malam all night
  long
sěisi rumah/kampung the
  whole household/village
sěbagai ganti in place of,
  instead of, as a substitute

sěorang diri alone, by
  oneself
sěumur hidup all one's life
běkěrja sěndiri to be self-
  employed
apa pasal (pasal apa) why

114

jalan sěhala one-way street
sěkarang ini pun even now
waktu samar dusk, half-light
kayu bakau mangrove tree
hutan bakau mangrove swamp
jarak děkat/jauh short/long range
pilihan raya general election

kěsatuan sěkěrja trade union
kěsatuan buruh labour union
Pěrsatuan Wanita Women's Institute
wang pinjaman money loan

minta maaf ⎱
maafkan saya ⎰ forgive me; I beg your pardon

LESSON NOTES

148. *Sě* The particle **sě** may carry the inference of **satu, sama** or **semua**. Context, once again, will decide the particular implication; but division of the following terms into categories of **sama** and **sěmua** usage may serve as a guideline for students:

sama: **sějauh 20 batu**, for (as far as) 20 miles; **sělama 3 jam**, for (as long as) 3 hours; **sěumur**, of the same age; **sěbangsa**, of the same race; **sětěmpat**, in the same place; **sěwaktu**, at the same time, while; **sětibanya**, on his arrival;

sěmua: **sěpanjang sungai**, (all) along the river; **sěumur hidup**, all one's life; **sěisi rumah**, the whole family.

Into this category come also the expressions which indicate 'maximum extent':

sěboleh-bolehnya   to the best of one's ability
sělewat-lewatnya   at the latest, as late as possible
sěkuat-kuatnya   as tightly/strongly as possible
sětidak-tidaknya   at least, at any rate
sěkurang-kurangnya   at least (+ number)

Such expressions may or may not show reduplication, depending upon the amount of emphasis required. The two alternative forms that are fairly common in speech use **sěběrapa** and **sěhabis-habis**. The former, used affirmatively, is often not followed by the kind of word that we would expect to hear in English, as shown here in brackets:

Pergilah seberapa dekat (awak boleh)   Go as near as you can

Used negatively as **tak sěběrapa**, it will become 'not all that', so bringing it close to **tak běrapa**, as used in earlier lessons, and, though not so closely, to **bukan bĕgitu,** which is used when a comparison is being made with a previous statement. The form **sĕhabis-habis**—also means 'to the utmost extent', but it is also often used to impose a limit:

Dia boleh tidur sĕhabis-habis lama lapan jam
He can sleep for eight hours at the most

In other expressions, students may decide for themselves what use is being made of **sĕ:**

sĕbĕnarnya, actually, in actual fact; **sĕbaliknya,** on the contrary, on the other hand; **dan sĕbagainya,** and the like, and so forth; **sĕmĕstinya,** necessarily, by rights.

149. *Sĕkali pun* The notes on **sĕ** should throw light on the different uses of **sĕkali** as (1) once; (2) together, at the same time; (3) very, extremely. The following rather contrived sentence should show that 'together' and 'same' require thought as to whether they refer to time, place or activity, before being translated:

Mĕreka bĕrlĕpas sĕkali nak bĕlajar bĕrsama-sama di satu sĕkolah
They set off at the same time to study together in the same school.

The phrase **sĕkali pun** can mean 'just once' and, not so obviously, 'even though'. See if you can spot in Exercise **H** where the use of one meaning gives way to the other.

150. *Sĕndiri, diri* The English sentence 'He cooked himself' can have two meanings, one of them ridiculous. In the intended meaning 'himself' emphasises 'he' and its use is 'emphatic'; whereas in the other meaning 'he' appears to have performed the action on 'himself', and the action is said to be 'reflexive'. In Malay, **sĕndiri** is the emphatic and **diri** the reflexive form of the 'self' terms. (The reflexive use of **bĕr** was introduced in Lesson 11.) In the following examples of verbs that can take **diri,** the abbreviation 'o.s.' is used for 'one's self':

bunuh diri commit suicide	**hilangkan diri** absent o.s.,
matikan diri pretend to be	disappear
dead	**larikan diri** run off, abscond

116

besarkan diri show off, boast
samarkan diri disguise o.s.,
  camouflage o.s.
susahkan diri make trouble
  for o.s., disturb o.s.

diamkan diri keep quiet
lĕpaskan diri set o.s. free
senangkan diri relax,
  compose o.s.
bĕrtahan diri defend o.s.

When **sĕndiri** is used after **diri** in such expressions, it is only for added emphasis, the pronouns (**awak, kita,** *etc.*) being used in a similar way, so that most stress comes with the use of all three, as in **diri sĕndiri awak.**

Depending upon its position in a sentence, **sĕndiri** can mean 'own'.

> **Dia bawa kĕreta sĕndiri** He drove his own car
> **Dia sĕndiri bawa kereta** He himself drove the vehicle

151. *Lat, jaraknya* If you remember that the lamp-posts that you observe number one more than the spaces between them, you will readily understand the use of **lat**:

> **lat satu,** every second, every other; **lat dua,** every third; **lat tiga,** every fourth.

The word **jaraknya** denotes the space between objects, as in

> **jaraknya tiap-tiap satu kĕreta** the distance between each
>   vehicle

152. *Cuba, minta* Both of these words can contain an implicit 'please' as in:

> **Cuba baca sekali lagi** Please, read once again
> **Minta susu, encik** Please, pass the milk

Thus, **sila, tolong, cuba** and **minta** have been mentioned as words indicating 'please', each being a little more appropriate in certain contexts.

153. *Agaknya, nampaknya, rasanya, rupanya* The notes given in Lesson 13 can now be expanded to include **agaknya** and **rasanya**. All four expressions can be used for 'apparently', 'it seems', and 'I should say'; but context must decide which is most appropriate. There is no difficulty when the literal meaning is obvious, as with **rasa** in the following context:

117

Masam běnar buah mangga ini! Buah mangga awak apa rasanya? Manis! Buah mangga saya ini manis rasanya.
This mango is terribly sour! How does your mango taste? Sweet! My mango has a sweet taste.

But when the four terms are used to suggest a general impression that has been gained, each term tells us something different about the nature and certainty of the evidence for the impression. It is very difficult to find equivalent English phrases that will fit every context; but these suggested equivalents may help students to learn to differentiate between the Malay expressions:

agaknya, I should say at a guess; **nampaknya,** it looks to me, as I see it; **rasanya,** I feel that, I sense that; **rupanya,** it turns out.

Sometimes **agaknya** is used like 'I wonder'.

Kěmana dia pěrgi, agaknya? I wonder where he has gone?

154. *Pasal, fasal* This is one of a few words (mainly borrowed from Arabic) which can be pronounced with a '*p*' or '*f*'. Because the '*f*' sound is not natural to Malay speech, '*p*' is used more often in this book when there is a choice.

EXERCISES

Read and translate:

A. 1. Sějauh dua ratus batu. 2. Sělama lapan bělas jam. 3. Sěbanyak dua puluh pěti. 4. Itu jalan sěhala. 5. Dua orang itu sěbangsa. 6. Dua orang budak itu sěmur. 7. Bikin kěrja itu sěmula. 8. Bělikan saya dua hělai baju sěwarna. 9. Rumah saya bukan sěběsar ini. 10. Janganlah duduk sětěmpat. 11. Janganlah ganggu sěmasa saya běkěrja. 12. Sěisi rumah dia kěna sakit. 13. Sětahu saya dia duduk di situ lagi. 14. Di sěpanjang sungai ada hutan bakau. 15. Měreka kěrja di sawah padi sěpanjang hari. 16. Dia tinggal di pulau itu sěumur hidup. 17. Městi ada sěkurang-kurangnya sěpuluh orang. 18. Těntulah ada sěhabis-habis banyak dua puluh orang dalam bas. 19. Dia sělalu cuba sěboleh-bolehnya. 20. Kěrja ini městi habis sělewat-lewatnya dua hari lagi. 21. Isikan minyak sěběrapa pěnuh. 22. Bawa barang-barang sěběrapa cukup saja. 23. Mari kita běrjalan sěběrapa cěpat. 24. Mari kita běrsiap sěběrapa lěkas.

25. Mĕreka tunggu bĕrsama-sama di tĕpi-tĕpi sungai. 26. Mĕreka bĕkĕrja bĕrsama-sama di satu bilik. 27. Mari kita tarik sĕkali sĕbĕrapa kuat. 28. Cuci lantai itu sĕhabis-habis bĕrsih. 29. Pĕriksa kawasan ini sĕhabis-habis luas. 30. Dalam masa itu dia boleh bĕrjalan sĕhabis-habis jauh dua batu. 31. Awak mĕsti bĕli sĕhabis-habis mahal sĕratus ringgit. 32. Awak mĕsti bayar wang sĕhabis-habis sikit sĕpuluh ringgit. 33. Lat satu minggu kami dapat gaji. 34. Lat dua orang sudah dipĕriksa doktor. 35. Lat tiga minggu saya bĕkĕrja di ibu pĕjabat. 36. Lat ĕmpat hari dia bĕrtugas malam. 37. Tĕntukan jaraknya tiap-tiap satu meja tak lĕbih dari ĕmpat kaki. 38. Tĕntukan jaraknya dua batang bĕsi itu tak lĕbih dari sĕmbilan inci. 39. Ambillah wang ini sĕbagai ganti. 40. Pinjamlah kĕreta ini sĕbagai ganti.

B. 1. Apa pasal awak bĕlajar sĕorang diri? 2. Apa pasal awak ditinggalkan sĕorang diri saja. 3. Cuba sĕnangkan diri awak. 4. Dia hilangkan diri dari kapal sĕlama tiga hari. 5. Dia lĕpaskan diri dari tangan polis. 6. Saya ganggu mesin itu tak sĕngaja. 7. Dia tak sĕngaja masuk bilik yang salah itu. 8. Sĕngaja dia ikut jalan yang salah. 9. Istĕrinya bĕrbangsa Cina tĕtapi pandai cakap Mĕlayu. 10. Sungai itu tak sĕbĕrapa dalam. Bolehlah menyĕbĕrangnya. 11. Lain kĕreta tak ada, saya kĕna pakai kĕreta sĕndiri. 12. Tali ini tak sĕbĕrapa kuat; tĕntu putus nanti. 13. Siapkan kĕrja ini sĕbĕrapa cĕpat yang boleh. 14. Hari sudah gĕlap, sĕboleh-bolehnya dia nak pulang juga. Tak mahu bĕrmalam di sini. 15. Jangan ganggu dia bĕrmain di situ, nanti bĕrgaduh. 16. Dia suka baca buku sĕmasa baring di tĕmpat tidur. 17. Bila istĕri tak sĕnang, saya sĕndiri cuci baju. 18. Istĕrinya kĕ pasar lat dua hari sĕkali, sĕbab pasar itu agak jauh. 19. Orang itu sĕngaja langgarkan kĕretanya kĕ pokok itu, pasal kĕretanya 'dah lama sangat. 20. Awak mĕsti makan ubat ini sĕkurang-kurangnya dua kali sĕhari. 21. Dia sĕlalu silap masuk jalan itu. Jalan itu 'dah jadi jalan sĕhala. 22. Tayar ini tak boleh tahan lama. Janganlah pakai. 23. Sĕlĕpas bĕrlanggar, kĕretanya ditahan polis untuk dipĕriksa. 24. Pĕrĕmpuan itu cĕpat tarik anaknya. Kalau tidak, tĕntu jatuh kĕ dalam sungai. 25. Kalau nak masuk, tolaklah pintu itu kuat sadikit pasal pintu itu baru dipasang. 26. Pasal apa orang itu bawa payung? Hari nampaknya tak hujan. 27. Sĕkali pun umurnya sudah lima puluh tahun, nampaknya macam orang muda lagi. 28. Saya rasa saya kĕnal bĕnar kĕpada orang putih itu. Siapa dia agaknya? Dimana dan bilakah saya sudah bĕrjumpa dĕngannya? 29. Hari dĕkat nak malam, sĕjuk rasanya. 30. Bĕrguna juga rupanya barang-barang lama yang awak simpan itu, Omar. 31. Ĕmak bapa lambat sĕdikit balik malam ini. Sĕcĕpat-cĕpatnya pukul lapan nanti, barulah sampai kĕ rumah. 32. Sĕkĕjap lagi ĕmak pĕrgi mĕsyuarat Pĕrsatuan Wanita. Sĕcĕpat-cĕpatnya pukul ĕnam pĕtang nanti, baru dia balik. 33. Mĕsyuarat pĕrsatuan itu diadakan sĕbulan sĕkali.

Substitute in the following exercises:

C. *pattern:* Saya **pun** tak **suka**.
pun, tahu; pun, boleh; pun, mahu; sĕndiri, suka; sĕndiri, tahu; sĕndiri, sĕmpat; sĕndiri pun, boleh; sĕndiri pun, tahu; sĕndiri pun, sĕmpat

D. *pattern:* Awak sĕorang saja yang **sĕmpat**.
cukup pandai; cukup dĕkat; bĕlum kahwin lagi; tak pĕrnah kĕ sana; bĕlum pĕrnah buat bĕgitu; pĕrnah nampak

E. *pattern:* Sĕkarang ini pun **makanan itu** bĕlum **cukup** lagi.
wang itu, cukup; pagar itu, cukup tinggi; kawasan itu, cukup luas; jaraknya, cukup; waktunya, sampai; halanya, bĕtul; silapnya, habis-habis; mesin, dicuba

F. *pattern:* Cuba **tengok** sĕkali lagi.
pĕriksa; baca; tanya; tolak; tarik; balik; bĕrjalan; panggil

G. *pattern:* Minta **wang, Ahmad**.
rokok sĕbatang, Hassan; lalu, ĕncik; api, Kadir; maaf, tuan; susu. Cik Hasnah; tolong, ĕncik

H. *pattern:* Sĕkali pun dia **sakit, dia habiskan kĕrjanya juga**.
marah, 'tapi dia tolong juga; luka, dia boleh tahan juga; suka, dia tak ditĕrima juga; bawa kĕreta itu, sudah rosak; masuk hutan, sudah sĕsat jalan; silap, sudah kĕna hukum.

Lesson Nineteen

The prefix *tĕr*; the implications of *pula*; *biar* and *biarkan*.

VOCABULARY

baldi bucket
biar let, leave, allow
bilang count, say
bising noise, row, racket
buruk worn out, dilapidated
dapur stove, oven
duri thorn
hutan rimba primary jungle
lewat late
lupa forget
mabuk intoxicated
padam extinguish, put out
paksa compel, force
paku nail

pĕcah broken, shattered
pijak tread on
pinggang waist
pula (see notes)
rapat close, tight
sĕmak undergrowth
sĕrah submit, hand over, surrender
tajam sharp, sharp-witted
tawa laugh (see notes)
tĕrtĕntu certain, definite, limited
tiang post, pillar, mast
ular bisa poisonous snake

PHRASES

Tĕrpulang kĕpada awak That's up to you, please yourself
Tĕrpulanglah! It all depends!
Itu saya punya pasal That is my concern
kahwin paksa forced marriage
kahwin suka sama suka a love-match

dapur minyak oil-stove
bilik dapur kitchen
boleh jadi perhaps, it could be that
tali pinggang waist-belt
takut kalau in case, lest, for fear that
mabuk laut sea-sick
kawat duri barbed wire
tĕrdiri dari composed of

121

155. *Těr* As in English, certain affixes are used regularly on some stem words. Although **tawa** is given in the Vocabulary, **kětawa** and **těrtawa** are commonly used for 'laugh'. This may give rise to difficulty in using dictionaries, which contain words listed alphabetically according to the letters in stem words. Students must learn to recognise words like **těrjěmahkan** (translate) in which the **těr** is not a prefix. This lesson's Vocabulary contains **těrtěntu** as an example of common use of the prefix giving us numerous synonyms in various contexts in English. The linking of **těrtěntu** and **dulu** in the following example indicates once again how much flexibility is required for translation into English and how basic thinking is needed for translation into Malay:

> **pada waktu dan těmpat yang těrtěntu dulu**
> at a previously determined time and place

The following separation of the functions of **těr** does not mean that they are mutually exclusive; the prefix may be employed for different implications simultaneously.

1. *Passive:* The passive nature of the verb is stressed less than with **di**, and other implications of **těr** are probably included.

> **Banyak orang těrbunuh di jalanraya** Many people are killed on the roads

2. *Accidental completion:* By implying that the action of the stem was accidental, this function contrasts with the deliberate intention suggested by **kan**.

> **těrděngar**, to overhear, catch the sound of; **těrpijak**, accidentally tread on; **těrlupa**, forget, slip one's mind; **těrtidur**, drop off to sleep.

3. *State:* Here **těr** does the work of the 'a' to be found in many English nautical expressions—adrift, afloat, aloft, aboard—and other terms such as 'alive' and 'asleep', and can be seen as 'in a state of'.

> **těrbuka**, open; **těrtutup**, shut; **těrmasuk**, included, including; **těrtidur**, asle.. (compare with note 2); **těrbalik**, upside down, back to front, inside out, capsize (in reverse order).

4. *Degree:* It is used on adjectives and adverbs to suggest 'too' or 'extremely', and it may be used for the superlative degree.

tĕrlewat, too late, very late; **tĕrlambat,** too slow, very slow; **yang tĕrtinggi,** the highest.

The words **tĕrlampau** and **tĕrlalu** are often used for 'too, extremely'.

5. *Inability to complete:* Here the **tĕr** is preceded by **tidak** to give the meaning of 'unable to be'.

tidak tĕrbayar, unable to be paid; **tidak tĕrkira,** beyond count; **tidak tĕrkata,** indescribable.

156. *Bilang* In colloquial Malay this word is often used for 'say'.

157. *Pula* The English words for **pula** vary considerably according to context. First, it is essential to recognise two elements in **pula**:

1. Consternation or surprise, where the **pula** has the force of 'on earth', particularly after questioning words (**kĕnapa pula,** why on earth); *and*

2. Completion or extension of a sequence, which is seen most clearly when **pula** links with a **nanti** (saying 'otherwise') and gives the idea of 'as a result':

Lĕkaslah habiskan kĕrja itu, nanti kita tĕrlewat pula.
Hurry up and finish the job, otherwise we'll be too late.

Thus, the numerous terms suitable for **pula**—too, to boot, then, next, in turn, moreover, *etc.*—are too many to be included in a simple vocabulary list.

158. *Biar, biarkan* Notice how these contain the two different ideas of 'leave', (1) permit, give leave to, and (2) ignore, leave alone, leave out.

EXERCISES

Read and translate:

A. 1. Agaknya Mat tĕrtidur. Cuba awak panggil dia kuat-kuat. Kalau panggil dia pĕlan-pĕlan, dia tak tĕrdĕngar. 2. Wang sĕpuluh sen memanglah susah hĕndak nampak kalau tĕrjatuh kĕ tĕmpat macam ini. 3. Kalau nak buat kĕrja ini, biarlah bĕtulbetul. 4. Boleh jadi mĕreka tĕrlupa nak tutupkan pintu malam tadi. 5. Parang itu tĕrlalu tumpul, biarlah saja. 6. Kakinya luka apa? Tĕrpijak botol yang pĕcah. 7. Kalau bĕrjalan janganlah tĕrlampau cĕpat, nanti tĕrjatuh pula. 8. Jangan lupa padamkan api rokok itu, nanti tĕrbakar pula kĕrusi meja dalam sĕtor itu. 9. Buka dapur, pusing nombor ĕmpat. Biarkan daging itu sampai masak—kira-kira sĕtĕngah jam. 10. Siapa yang biarkan pintu pagar itu tĕrbuka lebar-lebar? 11. Kĕnapa awak ini tĕrtawa tak tĕntu pasal? 12. Awak bĕrdua sudah tĕrbiasa bĕrgaduh saja. Diam, sĕkarang. Jangan tĕrtawakan dia lagi, Ahmad. 13. Biarlah nasi itu sĕjuk; saya bĕlum mahu makan lagi. 14. Biarlah dia pĕrgi cuti sĕkarang; kĕrja tak ada. 15. Biarlah lambat, nanti kita sampai juga. 16. Biarkanlah api itu padam; tak ada gunanya lagi. 17. Biarkanlah kĕrbau itu makan rumput; di sini panjang. 18. Biarkanlah monyet itu makan pisang ini sampai habis. 19. Biarlah hari hujan; sudah lama panas. 20. Malas bĕtul budak itu! Pukul sĕpuluh ini dia masih tĕrtidur lagi.

B. 1. Barang-barang itu masih tĕrsimpan dalam pĕtinya. 2. Kapaltĕrbang 'dah bĕrlĕpas; dia masih tĕrtunggu-tunggu lagi. 3. Tuan pĕngurus bĕlum sampai; pintu opis masih tĕrkunci lagi. 4. Orang-orang di kampung bĕlum bangun; lampu-lampu rumah bĕlum di pasang lagi. 5. Sudah bĕbĕrapa kali dia bilang kotak itu, masih tĕrsilap lagi. 6. Kĕnapa dia bĕlum datang-datang lagi? Boleh jadi dia tĕrlupa. 7. Dia datang ikut jalan bĕlakang, kĕnapa? Boleh jadi dia tĕrsalah simpang. 8. Kĕnapa dia tiba-tiba naik marah bĕgitu? Boleh jadi dia tĕrkĕjut bila dĕngar bising. 9. Tutup kotak itu rapat-rapat, nanti masuk pula sĕmut. 10. Istĕri saya sĕlalu tĕrkĕjut bila kapaltĕrbang lalu di atas. 11. Hal itu tĕrpulang kĕpada tuan pĕngurus; bukan saya punya pasal lagi. 12. Bila awak isikan kotak-kotak dalam pĕti itu, biarlah bĕtul-bĕtul. 13. Orang tua itu tĕrlalu pĕnat. Biarlah dia bĕrehat sikit. 14. Jaraknya satu-satu orang ini tĕrlampau jauh. Rapat-rapat sikit. 15. Biar saya tengok dalam laci itu dulu. Boleh jadi ada pisau tajam di dalamnya. 16. Sĕbab tak ada makanan di sana, dia orang tĕrpaksa bĕrpindah kĕ kawasan lain. 17. Kalau isi minyak, janganlah tĕrlampau pĕnuh, nanti tong buruk itu tĕrbalik pula. 18. Kĕnapa pula dia mahu bĕrkahwin dĕngan pĕrĕmpuan tua itu? Bukankah dia orang muda dan kaya pula? 19. Ada orang yang sukakan hujan dan ada pula orang yang sukakan panas. 20. Ali kĕna buang kĕrja, kĕnapa? Boleh jadi

124

dia tĕrtidur sĕmasa dalam bĕrtugas. 21. Kĕnapa kĕretanya habis rosak bĕgini? Boleh jadi tĕrlanggar tiang lampu. 22. Janganlah buang kulit pisang di mana-mana saja. Kalau tidak kita yang tĕrpijak kulit pisang itu, orang lain pula yang kĕna nanti.

Substitute in the following exercises:

C. *pattern:* **pada hari** yang tĕrtĕntu saja.
pada waktu; di tĕmpat; di kawasan; ikut jalan; untuk jarak; untuk bilangan orang.

D. *pattern:* **Budak itu** biar **dia tidur** dulu, jangan **kĕjutkan.**
barang itu, di luar, bawa masuk; orang itu, di luar, beri dia masuk; kotak itu, di dalam pĕti, kĕluarkan; baldi itu, di situ, cuci; tali pinggang itu, di situ, pakai.

E. *pattern:* Tiba-tiba **dia** tĕrjatuh **masuk air.**
dia, jumpa ular bisa di sĕmak-sĕmak; dia, nampak sĕekur bĕruang di hutan rimba; dia orang, kĕjut bila dipanggil dari bĕlakang; kapaltĕrbang itu, bakar tĕrus melĕtup; dia, langgar tiang lampu tĕrus jatuh; tangannya, kĕna pisau tĕrus bĕrdarah.

F. *pattern:* **Bawalah kĕreta pĕlan-pĕlan** takut kalau tĕr**langgar budak sĕkolah** nanti.
ikatlah barang itu kuat-kuat sikit, balik; taruh buku kira-kira itu dalam opis, hilang; simpan ubat itu baik-baik, makan budak-budak; ambillah tali yang baru, putus; sĕmbunyikan gula-gula itu, nampak anak.

G. *pattern:* **Kaki**nya luka tĕr**pijak paku.**
kaki, pijak batu tajam; kaki, pijak gĕlas pĕcah; kĕpala, kĕna pintu; pinggang, kĕna kawat duri; muka, kĕna duri.

H. *pattern:* **Lĕkaslah pasang tali kipas itu** nanti **kita** tĕr**lambat** pula.
bĕrhati-hati, buat kĕrja itu, awak, silap; cĕpat, bĕrjalan, awak, tinggal; duduk, diam-diam, pĕrahu ini, balik; jangan, bising-bising, orang sĕbĕlah, ganggu; jangan, bĕli kĕreta yang mahal-mahal, awak tidak, bayar; jangan, bĕrlari-lari di tĕpi sungai, awak, jatuh; jangan, masuk sĕmak-sĕmak ini, awak, pijak ular; jangan, tĕrlalu jauh, awak, sĕsat jalan; jangan, minum bir tĕrlalu banyak, awak, kena sakit pĕrut dan mabuk.

I. Read these questions then insert **pula** after each questioning word or phrase:

125

Pasal apa dia datang balik?
Apa gunanya pisau yang tumpul ini?
Bila awak nak gantikan dapur yang buruk itu?
Di mana dia ada sĕkarang?
Kĕ mana awak nak pĕrgi malam-malam bĕgini?
Kĕnapa dia orang bĕrjalan rapat-rapat?

Lesson Twenty

The tense indicators *sĕdang*, *tĕngah* and *akan*;
forms and uses of the *mĕ* and *pĕ* prefixes; *makin*
in related changes (a form of comparison).

Vocabulary

akan (see notes)
balai hall, station
gali dig
hilir downstream, lower
  waters of river
hormat honour, respect
hulu (ulu) upper waters,
  hilt, handle
kayuh to paddle, pedal
kĕbakaran fire (out of
  control)
kĕjar pursue, chase
kĕlakuan behaviour
lapur to report
lubang hole, aperture
makin increasingly, getting
mĕngaku admit, confess

mĕngalir to flow
pĕngaruh influence
pangkalan jetty, quay, base
pĕrintah command,
  government
rakit raft, dinghy
ramai crowd, crowded,
  numerous (of people)
sapu wipe, sweep
sĕdang in the process of,
  while
tak payah there's no need
  to, don't bother
tak usah there's no point in,
  don't
udara air, atmosphere

Phrases

bĕri hormat pay respect,
  salute
di bawah pĕrintah under the
  command of
matahari the sun

makin mĕnjadi ⎫ proliferate,
mĕnjadi-jadi ⎬ get worse
  ⎭ (disease,
  etc.)

mĕngaku salah plead guilty,
  admit guilt
orang ramai the public
ramai orang many people,
  crowd
pĕgawai pĕmĕrintah
  commanding officer
rakit pĕnyĕlamat life-raft

kapal pĕnyĕlamat salvage ship

sĕbaik-baik as soon as, as well as possible

sĕbaik-baik sĕmpat just as, no sooner had

mĕngikut lapuran according to a report

balai polis police station

pĕmbĕsar nĕgĕri state dignitary

Lesson Notes

159. *Sĕdang, tĕngah, akan* These words are tense indicators. By saying 'in the process of', **sĕdang** and **tĕngah** are used like the continuous present and past tenses in English, though not so often. In speech both are used, but in written Malay only **sĕdang** is used. Their position in this case is between the pronoun and the verb; but, if **sĕdang** precedes the pronoun, it takes on the meaning of 'while'.

> **Dia sĕdang mĕmbaca suratkhabar** He is reading a newspaper
>
> **Sĕdang dia mĕmbaca suratkhabar** While he was reading a newspaper

The word **akan** was mentioned in the notes on the **kan** suffix (Lesson 9). Used as a tense indicator it gives a definite 'will/shall' that contrasts with the unstressed future implied by **nanti**.

160. *Prefix mĕ* Whether this prefix takes the form **mĕ, mĕm, mĕn, mĕng** or **mĕny** depends on the initial letter of the root word. As can be seen from the examples in the following table, when the initial letter is either 'p', 't', 'k' or 's', it is dropped from the **mĕ** form of the verb (the letters in brackets are rare as initial letters):

verbs beginning with					take	for example:
l	m n r	(w y)			Mĕ	mĕlahirkan, mĕminta, mĕnanti
		b	p		Mĕm	mĕmbaca, mĕmakai (pakai)
(z) c d j			t		Mĕn	mĕncari, mĕndapat, mĕnulis (tulis)
vowels g h			k		Mĕng	mĕngambil, mĕnghisap, mĕngira (kira)
			s		Mĕny	mĕnyimpan (simpan), mĕnyapu (sapu)

Students may observe exceptions to these rules, as in *mĕn*tadbirkan (manage, administer), *mĕn*tĕrjĕmahkan (translate), *mĕn*tĕrtawakan (laugh at), *mĕn*sifatkan (describe)—but such occasions are few.

128

Some very common verbs, like **makan**, **minum** and **pĕrgi**, never carry the **mĕ** prefix, whereas others, such as **mĕlawat**, **mĕngalir** and **mĕnangis** (to weep), are rarely heard without it. The few verbs like **mĕninggal** (from **tinggal**) which take on a particular meaning must be learnt individually. Some nouns take on a verbal form when prefixed with **mĕ**—as with **mĕrotan** (to cane) and **mĕrokok** (to smoke). Another word for 'why' is **mĕngapa**, which loses its verbal form in translation here but is restored again in **Itu tak mĕngapa** (That doesn't matter) and in **mĕngapakan**, meaning 'to do something to someone':

> **Saya tak mĕngapakan dia**   I didn't do anything to him.

Students must learn to guard against making certain false assumptions, particularly in the use of the dictionary. A word like **mĕreka** (they) can become so familiar that it is easily confused with the **mĕ** form of **reka** (invent). One may suffer disappointment looking for the root word of **mĕnganga** (gape) under **anga** and **kanga**, forgetting that it could be **nganga**.

Some intransitive verbs (verbs whose action is not carried out on someone or something) are created by appending an appropriate form of this prefix:

> **mĕndalam**, take root, deep-rooted (of influence *etc.*);
> **mĕndĕkat**, draw near; **mĕluas**, spread; **mĕninggi (tinggi)**, rise,
> go higher; **mĕnjauh**, go further away; **mĕnghilir**, go upstream;
> **mĕngganas**, engage in a reign of terror.

161.   *Uses of mĕ*   Words bearing this prefix are best considered as verbal nouns or gerunds, though one must be careful when fitting the grammar of one language over another language. In the phrase **tĕmpat mĕnyimpan barang-barang** (store, dump), **mĕnyimpan (simpan)** is a verbal noun, as can be seen in the literal translation 'a place for *the keeping* of things'. This helps to explain why the **mĕ** derivative is used so commonly after other verbs or words which encourage the formation of a noun from a verb. Examples of such words are

> **tĕmpat, pandai, usah, payah, untuk, suka, hĕndak, mahu, tahu,
> akan, sĕdang, sudah, tĕlah, dalam, dĕngan.**

Many other verbs function similarly as the preceding verb in coupled actions, as in

129

Dia datang měncari awak   He came looking for you
Dia pěrgi měnangkap ikan   He went fishing.

In other sentences the actions may be separated:

Saya nampak dia tadi měngayuh basikal
I've just seen him peddling a bicycle.

(Those who note the participial rather than the gerundive nature of the prefixed verbs in the translations should not believe that their grammatical function in the Malay has changed.)

Use of the **mě** prefix can help to place emphasis on the performer of an action.

Dia měmběritahu say   He informed me

To give even greater stress to the doer of the action **lah** and **yang** can be included:

Dialah yang měmběritahu saya   It was he who informed me.

Use of the prefix can also indicate the repetitive nature of an action or the fact that a long period is required for its implementation. It is, therefore, particularly suitable for verbs like **měnangis** (weep) and **měnari** (dance), verbs which are rarely heard without the prefix. These last two points, stress and continuity, are observable in **ada yang . . . ada yang . . .** (some were . . . some were . . .):

Ada yang měmbaca buku, ada yang měnulis surat
Some were reading, others were writing.

Occasionally the prefix is put on nouns to make comparisons; it then does the work of **macam**. From **babi buta** (blind pig), **laut** and **batu**, we get **měmbabi buta** (act recklessly, rush blindly), **mělaut luasnya** (sea-like in extent), and **měmbatu** (become as hard as rock).

162.   *Reduplication with mě*   The purposes of reduplication do not change but the forms vary. Readers will observe that in most cases the stem word is repeated:

mělambai-lambaikan   wave something continuously (**lambai**, wave)
měmburuk-burukkan   denigrate, disparage
měngada-ada   show off, fantasise

mĕncuba-cuba   attempt, have a try at
mĕncuri-curi   secretly, stealthily
mĕlĕbih-lĕbihkan   exaggerate

But, when a letter has been excluded in forming the derivative, the letters after mĕ are repeated:

(pandai) mĕmandai-mandai   show off cleverness, be too clever
(tunggu) mĕnunggu-nunggu   wait long for, look forward to
(kĕjut) mĕngĕjut-ngĕjut   jerking, jerkily
(kira) mĕngira-ngira   guess, estimate
(kata) mĕngata-ngata   vilify, dispraise
(soal) mĕnyoal-nyoal   question repeatedly, interrogate

In another kind of reduplication the mĕ prefix appears in the latter half. Variety and continuity can be expressed in this way.

sĕbĕlah-mĕnyĕbĕlah   both sides, opposite sides
kĕna-mĕngĕna   connection, relation
tĕrus-mĕnĕrus   continuously
kira-mĕngira   calculating, computing
pandang-mĕmandang   exchange glances
tĕmbak-mĕnembak   shooting, firing
tari-mĕnari   dancing
surat-mĕnyurat   correspond, correspondence

163.   *pĕ prefix*   The forms of this prefix are similar to those of mĕ. The variants are pĕ, pĕm, pĕn, pĕng, and pĕny; and the same letters (p, t, k, s) are dropped from the stem. The prefix is used to make agents or instruments like those carrying the suffixes 'er' and 'or' in English, such as 'player', 'writer', 'actor', 'cooker' and 'accelerator'. One example that has already been used in exercises is **pĕngurus** from **urus** (mengurus—organise, arrange, manage); and **pĕnghulu**, introduced in this lesson, is derived from **hulu**.

pĕnulis writer
pĕmbaca reader
pĕlaut seaman
pĕlawat visitor
pĕlari runner (not to be confused with **pĕlarian**, refugee),
pĕnjaga guard
pĕmbunuh killer, murderer

pĕnyapu broom, brush, wiper
pĕnolong assistant
pĕngayuh a paddle, pedal
pĕrompak robber
pĕncuri thief
pĕnakut coward
pĕngarah director
pĕmalas loafer
pĕnanam padi rice planter

131

pĕnggali spade	**pĕsakit** sick person
pĕmbuka opener	**pĕmuda** male youth
pĕnyakit disease	**pĕmudi** female youth

From **bĕkĕrja** and **bĕlajar,** which were quoted as exceptions to the **bĕr** derivatives, we get **pĕngajar** (instructor), **pĕlajar** (student), and **pĕkĕrja** (worker). **Pĕngaruh** is now treated as a stem word although it was derived from **aruh,** and so we get **bĕrpĕngaruh** (influential) and **tĕrpĕngaruh** (influenced). It is difficult to see why **pĕndapat** (opinion) was obtained from **dapat. Pĕkĕdai** is another word which does not drop the 'k'.

164. *Makin* Sometimes this word carries **sĕ** for emphasis, but without change of meaning. These examples show how it is used:

Dia makin tua makin bodoh He gets sillier as he gets older
Tanah ini makin lama makin tinggi The ground gets higher
and higher (*i.e.* as
time of walking goes
on)
Pĕnyakit itu sĕmakin mĕnjadi The disease is spreading.

165. *Ramai, banyak* In written Malay **ramai** replaces **banyak** in describing people.

166. *Kĕlakuan* This word and **kĕbakaran** are examples of affixation studied in the next lesson. The stem of **kĕlakuan** is **laku,** which is broadly concerned with the acceptability of things for sale, money, and actions.

Buah nanas ini ĕncik boleh ambil; tak ada lakunya.
You can have these pineapples; there's no demand for them.
Wang itu tak laku lagi di nĕgĕri ini.
That money is no longer accepted in this country.

From the stem are derived **bĕrlaku** (to happen), **mĕlakukan** (carry out, effect, perform; stimulate demand), and **sĕlaku** (as, like).

EXERCISES

At this stage students are advised to buy a Malay-English English-Malay dictionary using the system of spelling agreed between Malaysia and Indonesia. Those who are going to study old publications will also require eventually a dictionary in the old spelling. The main aim of these exercises is to give practice in using the **mě** and **pě** prefixes, and the sentence structures are of secondary importance.

A.

Write the root words of the following:

měněrima, měnyuruh, měninggalkan, měnyělamatkan, měnolong, měnutup, měmadamkan, měngirimkan, měnguning (turn yellow), měngěcilkan, měngěnakan, měmakai, měngěluarkan, měnyěbabkan, měmanjangkan, měmukul, měnunggu, měnengok, měngěnalkan, měngějutkan, měnyěmbunyikan, měnanam, měngurangkan, měnangkap, měnyalahkan, měnembak, měnyěrang, měnguatkan, měnunjukkan, měnyimpan, měngumpulkan, měmindahkan, měněntukan, měnipu, měngěmaskan, měmotong, měnyěntuh, měnahankan, měměriksa, měnakutkan, měngatakan, měnyamarkan, měnarik, měmasang, měnolak, měměrintah, měnyiram, měnumbuhkan, měmendekkan, měnyimpan, měmaksa.

B.

Give the **me** forms of:

langgar, baca, cari, ambil, baikkan, adakan, curi, lawan, adu, běri, cuci, luaskan, ěrti, cantikkan, lompat, bawa, dapat, gigit, masukkan, bayar, datangkan, gulungkan, mainkan, ubatkan, gunakan, bunuh, gantikan, habiskan, jatuhkan, naikkan, gosok, hisap, ikat, jalankan, ganggu, jual, hidupkan, rěbus, jaga, ikut, belok, ringankan, ingatkan, hukumkan, jadikan, gali, lapurkan, nanti, rugikan, rompak, elokkan, hilangkan, isikan, jumpa, ikat, minta, namakan, warnakan, wayangkan.

C.

Give the **pě** forms of:

padam, tolong, sapu, pěrintah, tanam, jaga, pukul, tembak, curi, malas, kayuh, arah, běsar, bunuh, jual, duduk, ganas, ikut, bayar, jahat, lari, kěrusi, lawat, gali, baca, tulis, main, dapat, malu, muda, tipu, ajar (2), sakit (2).

Substitute in the following exercises:

D. *pattern:* untuk **mě**mbelok kanan (Choose the appropriate form of **mě**).
panggil talipun; potong kayu; tanam padi; jěmur kain; kěmaskan barang-barang; cuci kěreta; gali lubang; angkat pěti besar;

masukkan barang-barang; padamkan api rokok; pĕriksa injin; cari pĕnghulu; ubatkan orang kampung; sĕkolahkan anak; panjangkan cuti; bayar wang; mĕmbĕri hormat kĕpada pĕmbĕsar-pĕmbĕsar nĕgĕri.

E. *pattern:* Dia tĕngah **mĕmbaca buku.**
tulis surat; kĕmaskan biliknya; siram pokok-pokok; pĕriksa fail-fail; kira wang; buat pondok; gosok kasut; bawa kĕreta baru; cari kawan; tolong ĕmaknya.

F. *pattern:* Dia orang sĕdang **mĕnengok wayang.**
padamkan kebakaran; pĕriksa hal itu; pasang radio; tanam padi; tutup lubang di jalan; tahan orang ramai; sapu lantai; tangkap ikan; cari rumah kawan.

G. *pattern:* Tak payahlah **mĕnanti di sini lagi.**
mĕnjaga kĕreta; mĕmbayar banyak wang; mĕngĕjutkan mĕreka sĕkarang; mĕncari dia lagi; mĕngubatkan dia lagi; mĕnunjukkan dia, dia sudah pun tahu; mĕnyimpan barang-barang buruk itu.

H. *pattern:* Ada yang **mĕnjual,** ada yang **mĕmbĕli pula.**
mĕmasak, mĕncuci kain pula; mĕnolong, mĕngganggu saja; mĕngangkat tangan, tidak mĕngĕrti pula; mĕnengok saja, mĕnyĕntuh pula; mĕngaku salah, mĕnyalahkan orang lain; mĕlarikan diri, bĕrtahan diri.

I. *pattern:* Sĕbaik-baik sĕmpat saya **masuk, wayang gambar** pun **mulai.**
kĕluar dari kĕdai, pintu, dikunci; habis makan, lampu, padam; habis mandi, air, ditutup; pulang kĕ rumah, hujan, turun; naik, bas, bĕrjalan.

J. *pattern:* Sĕbaik-baik **sampai di rumah** saja, dia **mulai mĕmasak.**
masuk bilik, mĕmbuka talivisyun; hari gĕlap, mĕnutup sĕmua pintu; sampai di kampung, mĕlawat kĕ rumah pĕnghulu; air dibuka, mĕncuci pakaian; makanan itu masak, mĕnaruhnya kĕdalam almari.

K. *pattern:* **Pokok kĕlapa itu** makin **lama** makin **tinggi.**
budak itu, lama, bĕsar; sungai itu, mĕnghilir, mĕndalam; monyet itu, lama, mĕngikut kata; tanah itu, lama, mĕnurun; bukit itu, tinggi, sĕjuk udara; kĕlakuannya, tua, baik.

L. *pattern:* Dia dipĕrintah **mĕnolong abangnya di kĕbun.**
mĕmbayar balik wang itu; mĕnjaga adiknya; mĕmbuat kĕrja itu sĕmula; mĕlapurkan diri kĕ balai polis; mĕncari kĕrani bĕsar.

134

M. Find the correct position for **makin** in each sentence.

1. Matahari měninggi. 2. Pěnyakit itu měnjadi-jadi. 3. Rakit pěnyělamat měnděkat. 4. Kěbun kělapa itu měluas. 5. Air sungai itu cěpat měngalir. 6. Pěngaruh komunis měndalam di kampung itu.

N. Use the **mě** prefix on the second verb in each sentence.

1. Dia duduk baca buku. 2. Dia pěrgi tangkap ikan. 3. Dia duduk mainkan těrompet. 4. Dia pěrgi hantar orang kě pangkalan laut. 5. Apa hal awak datang cari saya? 6. Saya nampak dia tadi taruh kěreta di bělakang.

Lesson Twenty-one

The suffix *i*; the prefixes *kĕ* and *pĕr*; the affix
combinations *pĕr...an, pĕ...an*, and *kĕ...an*;
the appellative tag *Si*; using *hati*; more uses
of *ada*; *takkan* and *sungguh*.

Vocabulary

bahawa   that (conjunction)
bĕnar   true, valid, quite,
   really
bohong   lie, falsehood
daerah   district
dĕmam   fever
ĕntah   (see notes)
harap   hope
harus   should, ought
hati   liver, 'heart'
jawab   to answer
kĕmudian   afterwards, and
   then
kĕnal   know (a person)
khidmat   obedience, duty
kura   spleen
lulus   approve, pass
   (exam, application)

malang   unfortunate
mĕntĕri   minister
mustahak   essential,
   important
nasihat   advice
nyata   clear, evident
palsu   false, counterfeit
pandu   drive, pilot, guide
panggung   theatre, cinema
pikir (fikir)   think
puas   satisfied, have more
   than enough of (action)
sungguh   genuine(ly), real(ly)
sungguhpun   although
supaya   to, so that
taun   cholera
wabak   epidemic

Derivatives:

mĕmbĕnarkan   permit, allow,
   confirm
sĕbĕnarnya   in actual fact
bĕnar-bĕnar   truly, indeed
harapan   a hope
mĕngharapkan   rely on, trust

bĕrhati-hati   take care, pay
   attention
jawapan   an answer
bĕrkhidmat (dĕngan)   serve
   (in)
pĕmbohong   liar

136

malangnya unfortunately	pěmandu driver, pilot
pěnasihat adviser	pikiran opinion, idea
měnasihatkan to advise	měmikirkan think about
měnyatakan explain, state	měněrangkan clarify, explain
panduan exemplar, guide	

PHRASES

kěmalangan jalanraya road accident

surat kěběnaran letter of credential/authority, a pass

pěnyakit taun cholera

cakap těrus těrang speak frankly/openly

pikir-pikir dulu think twice, consider first

tukar pikiran change one's mind

těrang bulan moonlight

rumahtangga homestead, home

děmam kura malaria

děmam panas high fever

sama ada whether

měnarik hati interesting

supaya jangan not to (after commands, advice, warnings etc.)

LESSON NOTES

167. *Suffix 'i'* This affix has already been used in **mulai**. Sometimes **kan** is employed in speech where dictionaries will only quote derivates bearing **i**—as with **měmbaikkan/měmbaiki** and **měmbaharukan/měmbaharui**—and there is no difference in meaning. But, when both suffixes are admitted as applicable to one stem in written Malay, there is a change of meaning.

> **měnjalankan kursus latihan** run a training course
> **měnjalani kursus latihan** undergo a training course

Seeing the **i** as a kind of preposition helps us to understand many of the words to which it is attached, because English verbs with associated prepositions can often be found for the translations. (In fact, a historical link is suggested with **di**.)

měnyěbělahi to side with

měnaiki travel on/by

mělalui go through, via, along

měngatasi to overcome, surmount

měndapati find out, discover

měngakui acknowledge, confess

měngěnai come into contact with, concerning

mělěbihi exceed, surpass

137

mĕmpĕngaruhi to influence
mĕmpunyai to own, possess
mĕndĕkati to approach
mĕnyĕbĕrangi to cross over
mĕmasuki enter, join
mĕngikuti accompany, follow

mĕnjumpai meet with, find
mĕngĕnali recognise, know, identify
mĕnghormati to respect, honour
mĕnghargai appreciate, value

(Notice that the **p** is not dropped from either **mĕmpĕngaruhi** or **mĕmpunyai**.)

168. *Prefix 'kĕ'* You have already met this affix (notes of Lessons 10 and 17, and in **kĕtua** and **kĕtawa**). When it is included in verbs (which are few in number) the **k** is dropped in the **mĕ** form.

> **Kĕtuai (mĕngĕtuai)**, to head, preside over; **kĕtahui (mĕngĕtahui)**, **kĕmukakan (mĕngĕmukakan)**, put forward, propose; **kĕbumikan (mĕngĕbumikan)**, bury, inter (**bumi**: earth); **kĕhĕndaki (mĕnghĕndaki**—**kĕ** has been dropped—but **bĕrkĕhĕndakkan** is more common), need, require.

169. *Prefix 'pĕr'* This is used to form fractions other than those you have already met (half, quarters). As with **bĕr** the **r** is dropped when this letter begins the stem word:

> **Dua pĕrtiga** (two-thirds); **tiga pĕrlima** (three-fifths); **sĕmbilan puluh pĕratus** (ninety per cent).

Used in verbs, the **p** is not dropped when preceded by the prefix **mĕm**. Sometimes the effect of **pĕr** is like that of the causative **kan**; sometimes it suggests extension of the duration of the verb; sometimes it is used to present a meaning different from that of another form of the verb; and other times, I suspect, it is used to arrange a pleasant-sounding juxtaposition of syllables.

mĕmpĕrbuatkan make, build
mĕmpĕrhatikan observe, pay attention to
mĕmpĕrkuatkan strengthen
mĕmpĕrkĕnalkan introduce
mĕmpĕrelokkan beautify, decorate

mĕmpĕrkatakan discuss, talk about
mĕmpĕrolehi obtain
mĕmpĕruntukkan allocate, vote (money)

138

That use of reduplication to produce metaphorical meaning, as in **anak-abak** (doll), is paralleled in:

mĕmpĕrmainkan make fun of   **mĕmpĕrlĕmbukan** make an
                                                              ass of

170. *Affixes 'pĕr·. . . an'* The word pĕrpuluhan is used in decimals:

    lima pĕrpuluhan sĕmbilan 5.9
    satu pĕrpuluhan dua dua 1.22

Nouns are formed with this combination of affixes.

pĕrkhidmatan service
pĕraduan competition
pĕrtolongan help, assistance
pĕrmainan game, match
pĕrmintaan application, request
pĕringatan remembrance, reminder
pĕrbuatan action, deed, verb
pĕrgaduhan quarrel
pĕrsamaan similarity, comparison

pĕrbualan conversation
pĕrhatian attention, interest
pĕrkahwinan marriage
pĕrkataan a word
pĕrsaudaraan kinship, relationship
pĕrhubungan communication, relations
pĕrdagangan trade
pĕrhĕntian kĕretapi railway station

171. *Affixes 'pĕ . . . an'* There is no sure way of distinguishing which root words will form nouns with this pair of affixes or the previous pair. We can note, however, that the last group comprises words from stems that usually take **bĕr**; and for this reason **pĕrasaan** (feeling, sensation, spirit), having probably dropped an **r**, should be in the last group, though in effect the category matters little. The form of the **pĕ** in this group is usually determined once again by the initial letter of the root word; but **kĕrja** once again produces an exception in **pĕkĕrjaan** (occupation, work), and at other times different derivatives are required for different meanings:

pĕpĕriksaan examination (academic)
pĕmĕriksaan inspection

pĕlajaran education, lesson
pĕngajaran instruction

The previously affixed **kĕ** and **pĕr** may now function as part of the stem and so decide the form of the **pĕ**:

pĕngĕtahuan knowledge

pĕmĕrhatian observation, scrutiny

The other examples are quite straightforward:

pĕlabuhan harbour, anchorage, docks

pĕmbangunan development

pĕmbĕlian a purchase, purchasing

pĕnjualan sale, selling

pĕmbunuhan killing, murder

pĕndapatan income, earnings

pĕngĕrtian understanding, interpretation

pĕnghabisan end, conclusion

(**yang pĕnghabisan** the last)

pĕngĕluaran issue, production

pĕlanggaran collision

pĕngakuan confession, admission

pĕngaduan complaint

pĕmĕrintahan rule by government

pĕnyampaian presentation

pĕnangkapan arrest, the catching of

172. *Affixes 'kĕ . . . an'* In most cases, abstract nouns are formed with these affixes but some derivatives function as verbs, some as adjectives, and others as adverbs. The different effects of unlike affixes are seen most clearly when they share one root word. It can be seen in these examples that the **pĕ . . . an** combination is more concerned with the carrying out of an action:

kĕbĕrsihan cleanliness

pĕmbĕrsihan the cleansing of

kĕtĕrangan evidence, explanation

pĕnĕrangan briefing, clarifying of

1. Sometimes the **kĕ . . . an** combination is used like **kĕna**.

   Dia kĕhilangan rumahtangga dalam kĕbakaran itu.
   He suffered the loss of his home in the fire.

2. In **kĕdĕngaran** and **kĕlihatan** (**lihat:** 'see') the affixes resemble 'ible' in 'audible' and 'visible'.

   Bising kapaltĕrbang itu tidak kĕdĕngaran lagi.
   The noise of the aeroplane could no longer be heard.

140

3. The word **kĕbĕtulan** is obviously linked with **kĕna bĕtul** (hitting exactly) and functions adverbially as 'coincidentally' or 'as it so happened'.

4. Reduplication of the root word gives the 'ish' effect noted previously (notes, Lesson 16, vagueness) in spoken Malay.

    kĕbudak-budakan, childish; **kĕkuning-kuningan,** yellowish

Other derivatives are:

kĕbangsaan national	**kĕrajinan** diligence, industriousness
kĕbanyakan majority	
kĕbĕnaran truth, permission	**kĕsakitan** illness, painfulness
kĕbĕratan burden/load, diffident, reluctant	**kĕsihatan** health
	kĕsĕjukan coldness, affected by the cold
kĕbiasaan customary practice	
	kĕsĕmpatan opportunity
kĕbodohan stupidity	**kĕsilapan** error, mistake
kĕadaan state, situation	**kĕtinggalan** get left behind
kĕbolehan ability	**kĕturunan** descent, extraction
kĕbĕranian bravery	**kĕmiskinan** poverty
kĕcurian theft, suffer theft	**kĕkurangan** shortage
kĕkuatan power, strength	**kĕhilangan** loss, deficiency, suffer loss
kĕdatangan arrival	
kĕhabisan use up, exhaust	**kĕjadian** happening, incident
kĕhidupan livelihood, living	
kĕhormatan respect, honour	**kĕsĕlamatan** safety, security
kĕhutanan forestry	**kĕsukaan** pleasure, happiness
kĕpandaian cleverness, skill	**kĕsusahan** difficulty, trouble
kĕpunyaan property of, owned by	**kĕsulitan** hardship, difficult problem
kĕputusan decision	**kĕlulusan** qualifications
kĕrajaan government	

This completes the notes on the affixes you must know for an understanding of written Malay. In conversational Malay the use of **tah** and **Si** may baffle students who are unprepared for them. The following notes should be of help.

173. *Tah* This is attached to interrogative words and is quite like **kah** but no answer is expected to the question; that is to say that it is used in rhetorical questions and exclamations.

    Apatah lagi? Wanglah. What else but money?

174.   *Si*   This term denotes familiarity that ranges from endearment to contempt. There is no exact equivalent in English, though in some contexts it is akin to 'old' (as used in 'old bean') and in others is used like 'our', 'your' and the 'y' in nicknames. Context will decide how it should be translated, but the following are possible examples:

Si Nasir, their Nasir; **Si Ali,** our Ali; **Si Mat,** old Mat; **Si Panjang,** Lanky

175.   *Ĕntah*   This word expresses doubt and verbally represents a shrug of the shoulders. It may say 'maybe' or 'don't know' if used singly, but, if repeated in a balance of alternatives, it often says 'whether . . . or . . . '.

Ĕntah jauh ĕntah dekat, mana tahu?
Whether near or far, how is one to know?

176.   *Harap*   This is another word that can express 'please'. It is sometimes used this way (preceding **jangan**) in notices to the public.

Harap jangan mĕrokok   Please don't smoke.

177.   *Hati*   The anatomical meaning of 'heart' is **jantung** but **hati** is used for the metaphorical sense.

puas hati, satisfied; **susah hati,** unhappy, troubled; **suka hati,** pleased; **sĕnang hati,** contented; **panas hati,** angry, cross; **hati kĕcil,** inner self, conscience.

178.   *Jawab*   Only a few words end with **b** and those that can take a suffix change the **b** to **p** when they do so.

jawapan, an answer; **wajib,** obligatory; **kĕwajipan,** obligation, responsibility

179.   *Ada*   When followed by a verb **ada** can either
(*a*) Stress affirmatively (as **bukan** does negatively):

Dia ada mĕnjawab   He did answer   *or*

(*b*) Show continuity of action, like **sĕdang:**

Orang di sana ada mĕmbaiki jalan   The people over there are repairing the road.

142

In accordance with the notes on the **mĕ** prefix, the verb usually carries **mĕ** and its gerundive nature can be seen even when **ada juga** (which can be used for 'sometimes') precedes the verb.

> **Di kĕdai makan orang Islam itu rupanya ada juga mĕnjual minuman keras.**
> Apparently hard liquor is sometimes sold in that Muslim restaurant. (The selling of hard liquor)

180. *Takkan*   This is a shortened form of **tak akan** and when used before the pronoun, it means 'it's unlikely'.

> **Dia tak akan datang**   He won't come
> **Takkanlah dia datang**   It's unlikely that he'll come.

181. *Sungguh*   Both this word and **bĕnar** are used for 'truly, genuinely, really' but **sungguh** comes before, and **bĕnar** after, the word it modifies.

> **sungguh sakit**
> **sakit bĕnar**   } really ill

In speech **sungguhpun** (although) is often balanced with **tĕtapi** as the first word of the second half of the sentence. If we think of the more literal interpretation 'true enough' for **sungguhpun,** the need for the **tĕtapi** is more apparent.

> **Sungguhpun saya kĕnal namanya tĕtapi dia kĕnalkan dirinya juga.**
> Although I knew his name, he still introduced himself.

In written Malay the use of **tĕtapi** like this is much rarer.

EXERCISES

Read and translate:

A. 1. Puas saya mĕncari rumah ini. Sudah sĕtĕngah jam lamanya saya mĕncari. Sĕkarang baru bĕrjumpa.   2. Bila awak pĕrgi kĕ kampung Mĕlayu, awak harus bĕrjumpa pĕnghulu dulu.   3. Siapa-siapa yang bĕrbaik hati haruslah dihormati.   4. Dia sangat suka hati mĕnĕngok kĕpandaian anaknya.   5. Dia nak minta cuti pasal kĕsusahan di kampung.   6. Bagaimana kĕadaan di pĕlabuhan sĕkarang? Sĕmuanya baik, ĕncik. Orang buruh di sana sudah pun puas hati.   7. Kĕbanyakan orang kampung

susah hati sĕkarang. Rupanya ada dua tiga rumah hilang dalam
kĕbakaran dan bĕbĕrapa ekor lĕmbu mati pula. 8. Sudah tiga
jam dia pĕrgi kĕ jabatan itu. Haraplah dia dapat pulang sĕbĕlum
matahari masuk. 9. Harap jangan mĕrokok dalam panggung
ini. 10. Pĕrmainan bola itu akan diadakan pada hujung minggu
ini. Ramai orang akan mĕnengok. 11. Takkanlah dia bĕrcakap
bohong. Bukankah dia pĕgawai daerah? 12. Bĕrhati-hatilah
supaya jangan mĕlanggar budak-budak sĕkolah. 13. Bĕbĕrapa
orang tĕlah kĕhilangan rumahtangganya dalam kĕbakaran di
daerah itu. 14. Surat pĕrmintaan ĕncik untuk mĕmbuat rumah
itu bĕlum diluluskan lagi. Tunggulah sampai hujung bulan ini.
15. Jalan ini bĕlum dibaiki lagi. Sĕlalu tĕrjadi kĕmalangan jalanraya di sini. Bĕrhati-hatilah mĕmandu kĕreta. 16. Mĕngikut
kĕnyataan yang dikĕluarkan dari pĕjabat pĕngarah kĕsihatan
dan pĕrubatan nĕgĕri daerah itu tĕlah mĕnjadi kawasan wabak
taun. 17. Kĕtua polis daerah tĕlah mĕnasihatkan orangramai
supaya jangan mĕmbĕri pĕrtolongan kĕpada orang yang tidak
dikĕnalinya. 18. Kalau dia berkata nak tiba kira-kira pukul
lima, takkanlah pukul lima bĕtul dia nak sampai. Ĕntah kĕrĕ-
tanya rosak di tĕngah jalan. Ĕntah dia bĕrjumpa dĕngan kawan.
Mana kita tahu? 19. Kĕrajaan nĕgĕri tĕlah mĕluluskan pĕrun-
tukan sĕbanyak dua puluh lima ribu ringgit untuk mĕmpĕrbĕsar-
kan jalanraya di daerah ini. 20. Mĕntĕri Pĕrdagangan dan
Pĕrindustrian tĕlah mĕnyatakan bahawa untuk mĕngatasi
kĕkurangan simen di Sarawak kĕrajaan tĕlah mĕluluskan sĕbuah
kilang simen didirikan di sana. 21. Mĕntĕri Pĕlajaran hari ini
bĕrkata bahawa kĕrajaan bĕrpuas hati dĕngan bilangan sĕkolah
baharu yang tĕlah dibuka tahun lalu dan bilangan guru-guru
adalah mĕncukupi. 22. Bĕrhati-hatilah supaya jangan mĕngganggu pĕmandu-pĕmandu kĕreta di jalanraya. 23. Kĕputusan
pĕpĕriksaan bahasa kĕbangsaan akan diposkan kĕpada sĕmua
pĕlajar pada hujung bulan ini. 24. Dalam lapuran radio
Mĕntĕri Bĕsar tĕlah mĕngatakan bahawa kĕrajaan akan mĕmĕ-
nuhi pĕrmintaan untuk mĕngadakan tanggagaji baharu bagi
sĕmua orang buruh di pĕlabuhan. 25. Sĕdang polis mĕngambil
kĕtĕrangan mĕngĕnai kĕcurian wang itu, tiba-tiba kĕlihatan si
pĕncuri bĕrjalan arah kĕ pĕrhĕntian kĕrĕtapi. 26. Bagaimana
sĕorang budak sĕkolah dapat menyimpan wang sĕbanyak itu,
ĕntahlah. 27. Bĕnarlah kata-kata orang tua 'Ayam hitam
tĕrbang malam' ia-itu pĕkĕrjaan yang jahat sĕlalu dijalankan
dalam gĕlap. 28. Kalau pĕgawai kĕrajaan lĕbih pandai mĕngambil hati anak-anak nĕgĕri tĕntulah pĕngikut-pĕngikut komunis itu

144

tukar pikiran měnyěbělahi kěrajaan nanti. 29. Apa yang dapat dilakukan oleh orangramai dalam kawasan wabak taun ialah děngan měngikut nasihat dari pěgawai-pěgawai kěsihatan, iaitu supaya sětiap orang měmasak dahulu air sěbelum diminum dan měnjaga kěběrsihan kawasan kampung. 30. Hal-hal macam ini těntu měnarik hati, tětapi kalau saya těrlambat balik, macam mana pikiran istěri saya nanti? Těntu dia panas hati pula. Tinggallah dulu.

Substitute in the following exercises:

B. *pattern:* Ěntah **jauh,** ěntah **děkat,** mana tahu?
mahal, murah; sěnang, susah; lama, sěkějap; tua, muda; bětul, tidak; palsu, tidak; mustahak, tidak

C. *pattern:* **Surat sulit itu ditaruh dalam pějabat.** Ěntah **dimana,** tak tahulah saya.
Dia sakit hati kěpada orang, siapa.
Pěrkhidmatannya tak bolen dipanjangkan, pasal apa.
Dia sudah pěrgi cuti dua minggu, kěmana.
Dia pěrgi měngadukan hal kěpada polis, pasal apa.
Sěmua pěpěriksaan dia dapat lulus, macam mana.

D. *pattern:* Puas sudah saya **měncari dia.**
měnděngar bohongnya; měnděngar jawapan bodoh ini; měněrangkan kěpadanya; měmbaiki paip gětah ini; měnděngar kětěrangan palsu ini; měnunggu di sini.

E. *pattern:* Takkanlah dia nak **běli baju** yang běgitu **murah.**
měminjamkan pěrkakas, mahal; pakai kasut, buruk; běrbaik děngan orang, jahat; měngharapkan orang, bodoh; běrjalan kaki, jauh; mandi dalam air, kotor.

F. *pattern:* **Buku** itu **měnarik hati.** Haruslah awak **měmbacanya.**
makanan, kotor, měmbuangnya; buah, sědap, měrasanya; basikal, rosak, měmbaikinya; jam, lambat, měmbětulkannya; budak, jahat, měmarahkannya; dapur, lama, měnggantikannya.

G. *pattern:* Sěbělum **ambil kěputusan,** pikir-pikirlah dulu.
měngharapkan dia; masuk pěraduan itu; měngikut nasihatnya; měmběri kětěrangan; běrkahwin; měminta kěběnaran.

H. *pattern:* Sebaliknya dia ada **měnjawab děngan benar.**
měněrima nasihat saya; měngambil pěpěriksaan itu; běrhěnti

dari pĕrkhidmatannya; bĕradu dalam pĕraduan itu; mĕmbĕri jawapannya; mĕmbĕri kĕputusannya.

I. *pattern:* Sungguhpun dia **kaya** tĕtapi dia sĕlalu **bĕkĕrja**.
sakit, bĕkĕrja; salah, lĕpas; tua, bĕlajar; kaya, pinjam wang; bĕristĕri, buat kĕrja rumah.

Lesson Twenty-two

Samples of newspaper Malay and recommendations in further study.

At this stage students should seek as much practice as possible in conversation and reading, and the aim of the rest of this book is to facilitate self-progress. Intelligent observation and planning will achieve much better and quicker results than haphazard attempts to assimilate large amounts of new vocabulary and idiom.

The pattern of conversation with new acquaintances is fairly predictable and repetitive, and so one's questions and answers concerning identity, place of origin, family, work, and similar subjects, can be rehearsed. At a different level one can direct conversations to some extent with questions like, 'What is your opinion about — ?'. If there is time, the different answers of various individuals can be written down and compared and the meaning of new vocabulary checked. The scripts of plays are excellent sources of conversational Malay for the student who wants to ponder over sentence structure and meaning at leisure. Having made one's self familiar with a script, the stage presentation is not difficult to follow and one can concentrate on cadence, rhythm and timing.

Paradoxically, despite the use of complicated affixes, student progress in written Malay is usually much faster at this stage because it does not require the interest and patience of listeners. Intelligent observation and frequent use of the dictionary are required. It is difficult to travel far into Malaysia from Singapore without realising that **utara** means 'north'. (Though the writer has heard of several matrimonial squabbles resulting from the fact that wife-navigators could not find it on the map!) Notices abound which are written in both English and Malay. The two versions are worth the student's attention. And if you really do want to know how to translate, 'Let's go, boys, and head them

147

off at the canyon', dubbed or subtitled television film will provide the answer.

The purpose of this lesson is to illustrate a good method of tackling newspaper Malay. Since journalese tends to be repetitive, students should at first simply identify the subjects of short news items and then collect clippings under various headings such as 'Soccer' and 'Disaster'. The following exercises for translation are typical of newspaper crime reports; and, needless to say, all persons and events are entirely fictitious.

A. KOTA HARIMAU, 20 Julai—Dawai-dawai talipon bĕrnilai $1,800 untuk dipasangkan pada sĕmbilan batang tiang talipon di Jalan Kĕindahan Alam di sini tĕlah dilapurkan hilang sĕmalam.

dawai wire   **nilai** value, worth

B. KAMPUNG AIR MERAH, 14 Disember—Pĕncuri tĕlah mĕmĕcah atap gĕnting rumah sĕorang kĕrani di Jalan Bahagia di sini malam tadi dan mĕlarikan wang dan barang kĕmas bĕrjumlah lĕbih $3,000.

Mĕnurut jurucakap polis, Ĕncik Ahmad bin Yunus, 41 tahun, tidak ada di rumah bila kĕjadian itu bĕrlaku.

gĕnting thin, narrow, tense	**jumlah** total
atap gĕnting tiled roof	**turut** join in, follow
barang kĕmas jewellery	**mĕnurut** according to

C. PEKAN KĔTAM, 6 Januari—Sĕorang lĕlaki yang mĕmpunyai dua kĕsalahan sĕbĕlum ini hari ini dipĕnjarakan 5 tahun dan didĕnda $4,000 atau 3 tahun lagi pĕnjara oleh Mahkamah Tĕngah di sini kĕrana mĕmiliki pistol dan pĕluru.

Kuan Yu Seng, 28, mĕngaku salah atas tiga tuduhan mĕmiliki dua pucuk pistol bĕrjĕnis Biretta.

Kuan juga mĕngaku salah mĕmiliki 2 butir pĕluru .32 dan 8 butir .22. Ia didapati mĕmiliki sĕnjata dan pĕluru itu di sĕbuah rumah Jalan Tanjung pada jam 8.00 malam 12 Jun lalu.

Kuan dihukum 5 tahun pĕnjara atas kĕsalahan pĕrtama, didĕnda $2,500 atau dua tahun pĕnjara atas kĕsalahan kĕdua dan $1,500 atau sĕtahun pĕnjara atas kĕsalahan kĕtiga.

pĕnjara prison	**pĕluru** bullet, ammunition
mahkamah court	**tuduh** accuse
milik property	**butir** (numerical coefficient)
mĕmiliki possess	**butir-butir** details
kĕrana because, on account of	

D. SUNGAI BATU, 18 Mac—Dua orang lĕlaki hari ini dihu-kum pĕnjara sĕjumlah 14 tahun dan disĕbat 8 rotan oleh Mah-kamah Tĕngah di sini kĕrana mĕrompak wang tunai $7,353.40 sen.

Ah Kim Wan, 30, dipĕnjarakan 3 tahun dan didĕnda $1,000 atau sĕtahun lagi pĕnjara sĕmĕntara Tan Choong Foo, 29, dipĕnjarakan lima tahun dan didĕnda $5,000 atau 5 tahun lagi pĕnjara.

Ah Kim Wan dipĕrintahkan supaya disĕbat 2 rotan sĕmĕntara Tan yang mĕngaku mĕmpunyai ĕmpat kĕsalahan sĕbĕlum ini tĕrmasuk mĕrompak dihukum sĕbat 6 rotan.

Mĕreka mĕngaku salah mĕrompak sĕorang pĕniaga barang kĕreta wang tunai $7,353.40 sen dĕngan mĕnggunakan sĕpucuk pistol di Kĕdai Auto Spares, Jalan Pasar Bĕsar, kira-kira jam 4.20 pĕtang 30 Januari lalu.

Mahkamah dibĕritahu bahawa mĕreka tĕlah masuk kĕ kĕdai tĕrsĕbut hari itu bĕrlagak sĕbagai orang hĕndak bĕli barang, tĕtapi Tan tĕlah mĕngĕluarkan pistol dan mĕlakukan rompakan itu.

sĕbat whip, 'birch'	**sĕbut** mention, pronounce
wang tunai cash	**tĕrsĕbut** aforementioned
sĕmĕntara while, temporary	**lagak** pose, swank
sĕmĕntara itu meanwhile	

E. ULU JURANG, 9 Mei—Sĕorang pĕkĕdai basikal, Ĕncik Abdul Wahab bin Yusuf, 42 tahun, dirompak wang tunai bĕrjumlah $300 oleh dua orang pĕrompak yang masuk kĕ kĕdainya di Jalan Kĕliling di sini malam tadi.

Jurucakap polis mĕmbĕritahu kĕjadian itu bĕrlaku kira-kira jam 9 malam tadi kĕtika pĕkĕdai itu hĕndak mĕnutup kĕdainya. Tiba-tiba dua orang pĕmuda, sĕorangnya bĕrpistol, mĕnyĕrbu masuk kĕ dalam. Salah sĕorang dari pĕrompak tĕlah mĕmĕrintah sĕmua kĕluarga pĕkĕdai itu masuk kĕ dalam bilik bĕlakang kĕdai.

Tĕtapi salah sĕorang anak gadis pĕkĕdai itu yang sĕdang mĕmbaca buku di bahagian dapur kĕdai mĕnyĕdari kĕjadian itu lalu lari kĕluar dari pintu bĕlakang dan bĕrteriak mĕmanggil orang.

Kĕdua-dua pĕrompak itu sĕmpat mĕlarikan wang tunai $300 yang diambil dari laci meja kĕdai sĕbelum mĕninggalkan tĕmpat tĕrsĕbut.

kĕtika at the time when	**bahagian** part, division
sĕrbu rush	**sĕdar** aware, conscious
salah se- one (or other) of	**mĕnyĕdari** become aware of
bahagi divide	**tĕriak** yell, shout

F. KUALA LUMPUR, 22 Nov.—Polis sĕdang mĕncari ĕmpat orang dari satu kumpulan yang dipĕrcayai bĕrtanggungjawab kĕ atas bĕbĕrapa pĕcah rumah dàn kĕcurian di sĕkitar bandaraya yang mĕlibatkan barang-barang bĕrnilai $70,000.

Timbalan Kĕtua CID Bandaraya, Timbalan Pĕnguasa D. Kurindam, bĕrkata tiga daripada mĕreka bĕrasal dari Pulau Pinang dan sĕorang lagi bĕrasal dari Perak.

Ĕncik Kurindam bĕrkata kumpulan ini tĕlah mĕlakukan lĕbih 12 kes pĕcah rumah dan kĕcurian.

Katanya, orangramai yang mĕngĕtahui di mana orang-orang ini bolĕh bĕrhubung dĕngan balai polis yang bĕrhampiran.

pĕrcaya believe, trust	**timbalan** deputy
tanggung support, bear	**kuasa** power, authority
tanggungjawab responsibility	**pĕnguasa** superintendent
di sĕkitar in and around	**asal** origin, provided that
bandaraya chief city, capital	**hampir** near, nearly
libat involve	

G. KOTA SĔJAHTĔRA, 16 Ogos—Sĕorang pĕmuda, Ismail bin Mansor, 21, tĕlah dihukum sĕmbilan bulan pĕnjara kĕrana kĕsalahan mĕncuri 23 hĕlai baju kanak-kanak dan dua hĕlai baju panas lĕlaki bĕrharga $67.00.

Hukuman itu dijatuhkan oleh Pĕngadil Mahkamah Rĕndah, Ĕncik Abdul Ghani bin Yakob, dalam pĕrbicaraan kĕ atas yang dituduh di sini hari ini.

Yang dituduh mengaku salah mĕlakukan pĕrbuatan itu bĕrsama-sama sĕorang rakannya pada jam 4.50 pagi 28 Julai tahun ini di satu tĕmpat dĕkat Jalan Pĕmancar Radio di sini.

Rakannya, Ali Mohamad bin Naib, 19, tĕlah dikĕnakan ikat jamin sĕbanyak $400.00 dĕngan bĕrkelakuan baik sĕlama sĕtahun atas tuduhan yang sama.

Inspektor Abdullah bin Zaini yang bĕrtindak sĕbagai Pĕgawai Pĕndakwa mĕmbĕritahu mahkamah kĕdua-dua orang yang dituduh tĕlah ditangkap oleh mata-mata gĕlap Harun bin Yaman kĕtika sĕdang mĕmbawa pakaian curi itu di tĕmpat kĕjadian.

Tambah bĕliau, kĕdua-duanya tidak dapat mĕnĕrangkan siapa

tuan sěběnar pakaian itu dan di mana měreka ambil apabila disoal oleh mata-mata gělap Harun.

Bagaimanapun, katanya, sětělah dibawa kě balai polis didapati pakaian itu tělah dilapurkan hilang dari sěbuah kědai kěpunyaan Ling Soon Kee, 48, di Jalan Kěrbau di sini yang dipěcah orang sěbělumnya.

kanak-kanak children
baju panas sweat-shirt
adil fair, just
pěngadil magistrate
bicara discuss
pěrbicaraan court, trial
rakan pal, friend
jamin guarantee, surety
ikat jamin pledge surety,
  accept bail

běrtindak act, take action
dakwa claim, assert
pěndakwa prosecutor
mata-mata gělap plain-
  clothes policeman
tambah add, increase
běliau he, she (respectful)
bagaimanapun nevertheless

Lesson Twenty-three

PĚRIBAHASA

The literal meaning of **pĕribahasa** is 'fine language', and it covers a range of habitual expressions called **simpulan bahasa, ibarat, pĕrumpamaan, bidalan, pĕpatah** and **tĕlabai,** which has an equivalent range of terms in English with 'idiom', 'proverb', 'adage', 'aphorism', 'maxim' and 'dictum'. Most of the Malay sayings have figurative meanings, and there are several books devoted solely to explaining them. What may surprise students is the delight Malays take in employing them to embellish and drive home the point they are making. They savour the neat, balanced saying that is so brief at times as to take on the nature of a conundrum; there is little hint of the weariness associated with hackneyed expressions. Sometimes the sayings are partly quoted— just as we might say, 'Too many cooks', it being assumed that the listeners can complete them. Not only is a knowledge of Malay sayings necessary for further progress in the language, it is essential for the understanding of Malay thought and culture.

To enable students to absorb the new vocabulary more easily these sample sayings are divided into three main groups. The idioms given first are accompanied by their meanings; interpretation of the other sayings is given in the Keys for Exercises so that students can use them for translation practice.

VOCABULARY (A.)

ajak invite, persuade
bunga flower, interest (on money), design, pattern
buta blind
cucuk pierce, vaccinate
darat land (not sea)
hidung nose

huruf letter (a, b, c)
kais scratch the ground (of fowl)
kaki addicted to (secondary meaning)
katak frog
kĕra long-tailed monkey

kĕtam crab, plane (wood)	**sĕkam** chaff, rice-husk
kucing cat	**sĕpĕrti** like, as
mulut mouth	**talam** metal tray
pahat chisel	**tanduk** horns (of animal)
pasir sand	**tĕmpurung** coconut-shell
pĕmukul hammer, striker	**tikus** rat, mouse
sagu sago	**tongkat** walking-stick
salak to bark	**tulang** bone

1.

ajak-ajak ayam, insincere invitation; **anak bulan,** new moon; **nĕgĕri-nĕgĕri di bawah angin,** countries south-east of India (reached from the west by monsoon winds previously); **bĕrat mulut,** close-lipped; **bĕrat tulang,** lazy; **bĕrkaki ayam,** bare-footed, **bolih tahan,** can last out, can manage, will do; **buah mulut,** the talk of the town; **buat bodoh,** pretend stupidity; **buaya darat,** confidence trickster; **bukan main,** extraordinarily (ain't 'arf); **buta huruf,** illiterate; **cĕpat tangan,** light-fingered, thievish; **cĕpat kiri,** left-handed; **harga mati,** fixed price; **jual mahal,** play hard to get; **kaki minum (kaki botol),** addicted to drink; **khabar angin,** rumour; **makan gaji,** do paid work (not self-employed); **mata angin,** points of the compass; **minta diri,** excuse one's self (in taking leave); **naik angin,** get angry; **orang tĕngah,** middle-man, conciliator; **raja sĕhari,** bridegroom; **ringan tulang,** hard-working; **(hadiah) sagu hati,** consolation (prize); **tidur-tidur ayam,** only half-asleep.

2.

1. Sĕpĕrti anjing mĕnyalak bukit.
2. Sĕpĕrti ayam, kais pagi makan pagi, kais pĕtang makan pĕtang.
3. Sĕpĕrti katak di bawah tĕmpurung.
4. Sĕpĕrti kĕra mĕndapat bunga.
5. Sĕpĕrti kĕtam mĕnyuruh anaknya bĕrjalan bĕtul.
6. Sĕpĕrti pagar makan padi.
7. Sĕpĕrti pahat dĕngan pĕmukul.
8. Bagai anjing dĕngan kucing.
9. Bagai api di dalam sĕkam.
10. Bagai Si Buta kĕhilangan tongkat.
11. Bagai talam dua muka.
12. Bagai tĕlur di hujung tanduk.
13. Bagai tikus jatuh kĕ bĕras.

14. Bagai hujan jatuh kě pasir.
15. Bagai kěrbau dicucuk hidung.

VOCABULARY (B.)

acuan matrix, mould
akar root
alang-alang if you're going to
bebek bleat, quack
bubur gruel, porridge
burung bird
ěnggang hornbill
gajah elephant
galah punt-pole
harimau tiger
jong a junk
juang struggle, fight
kambing goat
kandang enclosure, pen
kěnyang satisfied (after
  eating)

kuak, měnguak bellow, croak
lada pepper
patah snap, fracture
pělanduk mouse-deer
pipis grind, mash
pipit sparrow
ranting twig
sambil while, engaged in
sělam submerge, dive
suluh torch
timpa strike (downward),
  fall on
tinggi rěndah uneven
udang prawn
yu (ikan yu) shark
(tiada=tidak ada)

1. Ada gula ada sěmut.
2. Ada udang di sěbalik batu.
3. Alang-alang mandi biarlah basah.
4. Bagaimana acuan běgitulah kuihnya.
5. Běrgalah kě hilir těrtawa buaya, běrsuluh di bulan těrang
   těrtawa harimau.
6. Burung těrbang dipipiskan lada.
7. Bumi mana yang tak kěna hujan?
8. Ěnggang lalu ranting patah.
9. Ěnggang sama ěnggang, pipit sama pipit.
10. Gajah sama gajah běrjuang, pělanduk mati di těngah.
11. Jong pěcah yu kěnyang.
12. Masuk kandang kambing měmbebek, masuk kandang kěrbau
    měnguak.
13. Nasi sudah měnjadi bubur.
14. Rumah sudah, pahat běrbunyi.
15. Sambil měnyělam sambil minum air.
16. Sudah jatuh ditimpa tangga.
17. Takkan pisang běrbuah dua kali.
18. Tak tahu měnari dikatakan tanah tinggi rěndah.

154

19. Tĕrlĕpas daripada mulut harimau masuk kĕ mulut buaya.
20. Tiada rotan akar pun jadi.

Vocabulary (C.)

alah (kalah) defeated, beaten
balas return, counter
  (-punch, etc.)
bisa venom
dĕras swift
hanyut adrift
indah beautiful

mĕnang win
pangkal starting-point,
  beginning
tĕgal because
usul bearing, demeanour;
  proposal

1. Ada hujan ada panas; ada hari boleh balas.
2. Ada padi sĕmua kĕrja jadi; ada bĕras sĕmua kĕrja dĕras.
3. Alah bisa tĕgal biasa.
4. Alah mĕmbeli mĕnang mĕmakai.
5. Usul mĕnunjukkan asal; bahasa mĕnunjukkan bangsa.
6. Biar lambat asal sĕlamat.
7. Biar putih tulang, jangan putih mata.
8. Biar sakit dahulu sĕnang kĕmudian.
9. Hati hĕndak, sĕmua jadi.
10. Indah khabar dari rupa.
11. Malu bĕrkayuh pĕrahu hanyut; malu bĕrtanya sĕsat jalan.
12. Rambut sama hitam, hati lain-lain.
13. Sĕdikit-sĕdikit, lama-lama mĕnjadi bukit.
14. Sĕsat di hujung jalan, balik kĕ pangkal jalan.
15. Takut kĕrana salah, bĕrani kĕrana bĕnar.

Points for Further Study

The purpose of this section is to encourage further study of Malay language and literature and to give pointers to the possible direction of further progress. No answers or explanations are provided elsewhere in this book to the questions and words which arise. It is hoped that students will be stimulated to go to reference books and Malays (who are invariably delighted to help students of their language) for the information that is lacking.

THE OLD SYSTEM OF SPELLING

Those whose reading takes them into the old system should find little difficulty in adapting to it. In the present system, **c** has replaced **ch**, and **sy** is now used for **sh**. Those words which contained **dh, dz** and **th** now have **d, z** and **s** respectively.

There have been vowel changes in some words so that **i** has often replaced the complete **e** and **o** has become **u** in some cases.

Particles and prepositions which were joined by hyphen to the word to which they related have been joined to or separated completely from the word. Other composite words joined by hyphen have become complete.

Where previously a '2' was used to indicate reduplication, now the phrase is written in full with a hyphen.

All of these points are illustrated in the following examples, with the new method given first:

consonants	**cari, chari; syarat, sharat; zalim, dzalim; darurat, dharurat; salji, thalji**
vowels	**kasih, kaseh; masuk, masok**
particles	**apakah, apa-kah; marilah, mari-lah; bilakah, bila-kah**
prefix sě	**sěorang, sa-orang**
composites	**suratkhabar, surat-khabar**
prepositions	**di kěbun, di-kěbun; kě bandar, ka-bandar**

passive	**diběri, di-běri**
reduplication	**běrkali-kali, běrkali2**

This is an incomplete description of the changes but it is sufficient for its purpose.

RHYMING REDUPLICATION

This is not an exact expression because the repetition it describes is sometimes merely alliterative. You may, however, have already reached the conclusion that Malays enjoy the repetition of sounds. A kind of rhyming repetition has been developed which some have likened to Cockney rhyming slang, but to the Malays these expressions are **'bunga bahasa'** rather than slang. Here are some examples which may form the basis of a collection, and which require your research for interpretation:

> **kaya-raya; jungkang-jungkit; gotong-royong; alang-kěpalang; běramah-tamah; lintang-putang; hutang-piutang; běrulang-aling; běli-bělah; tunggang-langgang; sěrta-měrta; bukitbukau.**

MORE ON AFFIXATION

The male suffixes **man** and **wan**, and the female **wati** have become increasingly popular.

> **jutawan,** millionaire; **angkasawan,** astronaut; **sěniman,** actor; **sěniwati,** actress; **pěragawati,** model, mannequin

In fact, **sěni** itself is an affix indicating 'concerned with the fine arts', as in **sěnilukis** (painting).

There is also an increasing use of **tidak** in derivatives:

> **kěadilan** justice   **kětidakadilan** injustice.

OLDER MALAY LITERATURE

To the interested student Malay books written in the traditional style can provide valuable insight into the historical background and cultural roots of the Malays. It is a great pity that many who grow to love Malay culture shun standard literary works, particularly when it is found that their objections are directed against

157

a handful of words that dominate the style. The mistake lies in taking the words too seriously and seeking meaning in them that does not exist. They are simply introductory words to ideas, words that bridge ideas, or the past equivalents for punctuation marks. Holding in mind traditional biblical words and phrases like 'Now it came to pass that', 'Thus it was that', 'then', 'moreover', and 'and', when they are used to introduce, carry on, and join ideas, it is not difficult to learn to ignore them for apparent meaninglessness and yet appreciate the functions they perform.

The most common of these words is **maka.** It usually does the work of a comma or semi-colon though sometimes you may use 'and', 'then' or 'so' in its place. Other words used to introduce paragraphs or sentences, and provide a transitional phrase in narrative, are:

> **hatta, arakian, kalakian, shahadan, bahawa, ada pun, adanya, bĕrmula, sa-bĕrmula.**

If you must translate them, choose the English most appropriate for the context from words and phrases like 'and so', 'now', 'now it happened that' and 'furthermore'.

Beginners in this field of study usually find '*Hikayat Abdullah*' to be a fascinating account of life and events in the late eighteenth and early nineteenth centuries.

SOME TASKS FOR STUDENTS

1. The general notion of **tumpang** is 'to take advantage of a service that is, or may be, available'. Find out its particular meaning in these:

   (a) **tumpang di hotel**   (b) **minta tumpang kĕreta kawannya**
   (c) **Saya tumpang bĕrtanya.**

2. How does **mĕlainkan** differ from **kĕcuali**?
3. Look up **bĕkas** to find out how 'finger-prints' may be linked with 'ex-minister'.
4. The word **pihak** is given in some dictionaries as 'side'. Find out how it differs from **sĕbĕlah** and how it may translate simply 'the'.
5. Compare and contrast the uses of **kaji** and **ilmu.**
6. Find the difference in meaning between **haram** and **halal.**
7. The words **bongsu, sulung, angkat, yatim** and **ipar** denote what in family relationships?

8. Find out the origin, usage and meaning of **pakcik** and **makcik.**
9. What do the abbreviations 'T.M.' and 'T.H.' mean with regard to dates?
10. What do the words **mĕndiang, arwah** and **almarhum** have in common?
11. How do the Malays distinguish in speech between 'fingers' and 'toes' and between 'thumb' and 'big toe'?
12. The words **adat** and **pantang** are very important in Malay culture. Find out all you can about them.
13. Can you find any difference between **pĕndidikan** and **pĕla-jaran**?
14. Seek all the uses of **sĕrba** and the context in which **sĕrba satu** might be used.
15. How is it that **cium** can be used for both 'kiss' and 'sniff'?
16. Find as many different words as you can for 'father' and 'mother'.
17. Learn to distinguish where necessary between **nasib, nyawa, kĕhidupan, riwayat** and **hikayat.**
18. The words **sayang, kasih, cinta, bĕrahi** and **asyik,** may indicate 'love', but how do they differ?
19. Find out what the terms for 'north-east' and 'north-west' are and suggest a reason for the use of **laut.**
20. What is a **pantun**? What is its form? When is it used?

Bĕrkĕnaan Dĕngan Orang-orang Mĕlayu

Melayu adalah satu bangsa yang terbesar bilangannya di antara penduduk-penduduk yang menduduki tenggara Asia, khasnya di Tanah Melayu.

Ugama yang dianutinya ialah Islam. Mengikuti ajaran ugama Islam orang Melayu mesti bersembahyang lima kali dalam sehari. Sembahyang Jumaat dikhaskan untuk orang-orang lelaki sahaja. Jika mampu, orang Melayu juga sebagai umat Islam dimestikan pergi ke Mekah menunaikan Fardu Haji, dan (kecuali ada sebab-sebab yang menghalang) berpuasa dalam bulan Ramadan. Koran adalah satu kitab ugama yang sangat ditakuti dan apabila orang-orang Melayu memegang Koran hendaklah dia bersih dari segala-segalanya dan mesti meletakkan Koran tempat yang lebih tinggi dari tempat duduk biasa. Sebagai orang yang berugama Islam orang Melayu dilarang memakan daging babi dan minum minuman keras.

Orang Melayu adalah satu bangsa yang tinggi budi-pekertinya

serta bersopan-santun sesama manusia dan orang Melayu juga penuh diselimuti oleh adat-adat lama yang dipesakai sejak turun-temurun. Pakaian untuk perempuan ialah baju kurung dan tudung; untuk laki-laki ialah baju kurung, kain samping dan songkok, manakala senjata tradisinya ialah keris. Perempuan-perempuan yang masih memegang adat dan patuh akan kelihatan memakai tudung barang ke mana mereka pergi. Gulungan rendah (yang dimaksudkan budak-budak serta orang-orang muda) mesti menghormati orang-orang yang tua darinya. Tidak boleh membantah kata orang tua-tua. Anak-anak gadis tidak dibebaskan kesana kemari dan bercampur serta bercakap dengan orang lelaki terutama orang-orang muda. Orang Melayu pantang usik kepalanya dan kaki tidak boleh duduk lebih tinggi dari tempat sebenarnya. Kalau memanggil orang Melayu hendak-lah dilambai dengan jari tangan ke bawah dan tidak dengan jari ke atas dikuitkan. Apabila seseorang berkunjung ke rumah rakannya atau seseorang yang sama berugama Islam dia akan memberi salam terlebih dahulu sebelum masuk ke rumah dan membuka kasut. Jika seseorang Melayu dalam kampung mendapat kesusahan atau mengadakan keramaian, semua orang-orang kampung akan datang ke rumahnya. Apabila seseorang Melayu mati, hartabendanya akan turun kepada anaknya.

Orang-orang Melayu di kampung suka bercucuk tanam untuk menyara hidupnya setiap hari. Kebanyakannya bekerja sebagai penoreh getah, bersawah padi dan menangkap ikan. Orang Melayu, terutama di kampung-kampung, suka bekerja bergotong-royong dalam membina sesuatu untuk kebaikan orang ramai, misalnya membina mesjid, membina jambatan dan sebagainya.

Hari kebesarannya dalam setahun ialah dua kali — Hari Raya Puasa dan Hari Raya Haji. Ada banyak lagi hari sambutan kebesaran bagi ugama bagi mereka, seperti menyambut hari lahir Nabi Muhammad, hari Turun Alkoran dan sebagainya. Selain dari upacara-upacara dan sambutan yang tertentu ada juga pesta-pesta dan upacara-upacara meriah yang berlainan dilakukan pada setiap negeri dan daerah, seperti Pesta Mandi Safar di Melaka dan Pesta Puja Pantai di Kelantan. Malam Jumaat adalah malam beramal atau malam ibadat bagi orang-orang Melayu.

Orang-orang Melayu masih kuat memegang kepada kesenian dan kebudayaannya. Tarian-tarian dan lagu-lagu Melayu asli masih lagi dinyanyi dan ditarikan oleh penari-penari dan penyanyi-penyanyi Melayu asli. Negeri-negeri seperti Kelantan dan Terengganu mempunyai aliran kebudayaan dan kesenian yang tertentu. Orang-orang di sana suka kepada seni-seni pahat dan ukir-mengukir.

Běrkěnaan děngan Adat Perkahwinan Orang Mělayu

Perkahwinan adalah satu masa yang ditunggu-tunggu oleh setiap anak gadis dan teruna. Maka segala tanggungjawab ini adalah diurus dan diselenggarakan oleh ibubapa sendiri.

Apabila seseorang anak lelaki itu telah remaja maka ia dirisik-andaikan, dengan tujuan mengintip akan kehendak hatinya. Pada masa dahulu, terutama di kampung-kampung, gadis atau teruna yang hendak berkahwin akan menurut segala kata ibubapanya, walau gadis atau teruna mana yang akan menjadi pasangan hidupnya tidak menjadi soalan, tetapi, kalau dia membantah kata-kata orang tuanya, dikira anak yang menderhaka. Pada masa ini kebanyakan gadis dan teruna kahwin dengan persetujuan mereka sendiri (atau 'suka sama suka'). Ini pada pendapat mereka akan lebih menjamin hidup berumah-tangga. Umur yang biasa seseorang gadis dan teruna itu kahwin dalam kalangan orang-orang Melayu ialah antara 15 dan 20 tahun; ada kalanya lebih dari itu dan ada kalanya kurang dari itu.

Adat perkahwinan orang-orang Melayu (atau selalunya juga disebut 'adat nikah-kahwin') adalah berlainan di antara satu negeri dengan satu negeri, dan kadangkala dalam sebuah negeri itu pula adat nikah-kahwinnya berbeza di antara satu daerah dengan yang lainnya. Perbezaan yang terdapat antara negeri dan daerah itu ialah menurut adat atau keturunan asal orang-orang yang mendiaminya. Di Negeri Sembilan misalnya adat nikah-kahwin dilakukan menurut adat Minangkabau lama sementara di Melaka adatnya banyak yang mengikut cara-cara adat Cina, dan begitu juga di negeri-negeri yang lain. Namun begitu, tidaklah pula bererti adat nikah-kahwin yang dipesakai sejak zaman berzaman itu terus mengikut alirannya dari sejak dahulu—tetapi kini telah dimodenkan mengikut peredaran zaman.

Walau bagaimana pun berasingannya yang terdapat di antara negeri dan daerah, ada pula yang disebut 'adat biasa' atau 'adat lumrah' yang biasanya dilakukan bagi keseluruhan adat nikah-kahwin orang Melayu. Oleh kerana perbezaan yang terdapat sungguh kecil, boleh dikatakan adat ini sama sahaja.

Menurut dari segi ugama Islam, orang Melayu boleh berkahwin sampai empat orang; ini jika orang itu mampu dan mendapat persetujuan daripada isteri yang tua (atau isteri yang pertama). Seringkali berlaku penceraian dalam masyarakat orang Melayu. Apabila Si Suami menceraikan isterinya (kerana suami berhak menceraikan Si Isteri dan tidak sebaliknya) dia terpaksa menjatuhkan 'talak', samada satu, dua atau tiga. Maksud talak satu ialah Si Suami itu boleh kahwin dengan isterinya itu kembali kalau dia mahu, dan begitu juga talak dua; tetapi kalau talak tiga telah dijatuhkan, Si Suamai tidak boleh mengahwini bekas isterinya itu kecuali kalau bekas isterinya itu menikah terlebih dahulu dengan orang lain, baru bercerai dan kahwin kembali dengannya. Perbuatan ini dinamakan 'Cina buta'.

Ada teruna dan gadis kahwin lari dari kampungnya. Dia nikah di tempat lain dengan tidak tahu ibubapa kedua-dua belah pihak. Kahwin serupa ini dinamakan 'kahwin cowboy'.

Adat Melayu tidak membenarkan seorang perempuan dan seorang lelaki duduk atau kesana kemari dengan mesra kalau tidak menjadi suami isteri. Mereka yang berbuat demikian akan ditangkap oleh pegawai-pegawai ugama (tangkapan ini dinamakan 'tangkap basah') dan mereka akan dinikahkan.

Seseorang suami tidak boleh meninggalkan isterinya selama enam bulan atau lebih dengan tidak memberikan berita tentang dirinya, samada dia bertugas di luar negeri atau sebagainya. Nafkah lahir dan batin akan diselenggarakan oleh pehak suami setelah berkahwin, kerana sudah menjadi tanggungjawab Si Suami. Kalau Si Suami tidak balik-balik begitu lama, isteri boleh minta cerai dengan tuan Imam atau Kadi.

CARA MĚNGURUSKAN KĚMATIAN

Di kampung, apabila seorang telah meninggal dunia, semua dalam kampung itu diberitahu, semada dengan mulut atau pun dengan memukul kentung yang ada di mesjid dan di surau-surau.

Orang kampung datang melawat ke rumah orang mati itu. Ada yang membaca ayat-ayat suci dan ada yang menuruskan perkebumian dengan membuat dan menyediakan papan keranda dan sebagainya. Mayat orang mati itu dimandikan terlebih dahulu oleh Imam kemudian dikapankan dengan menggunakan kain putih. Setelah selesai mayat itu dikapankan, mayat itu pun dimasukkan ke dalam usungan untuk diusung ke perkuburan.

Sebelum mayat itu turun dari rumah, semua saudara-mara atau anak beranak Si Mati itu meminta agar sesiapa yang ada berhutang atau pun jika Si Mati itu membuat salah dengan sesiapa sekali pun yang ada itu diminta diampunkan dosanya dan dihalalkan segala yang termakan dan terminum.

Kemudian barulah usungan mayat itu dibawa ke perkuburan Setelah sampai, mayat itu pun dikebumikan mengikut saluran ugama Islam. Setelah selesai Imam pun membaca doa dan talkin, barulah mereka yang pergi itu bersurai dan kembali ke rumah masing-masing.

Kebiasaannya sebelah malam di rumah orang kematian itu diadakan kenduri arwah dengan membaca doa dan menjamu orang-orang kampung itu; sesudah itu ada pula yang membaca Koran hingga ke larut malam.

Kaum keluarga Si Mati membuat kenduri arwah bagi Si Mati pada hari ketiga, ketujuh, keseratus, dan menziarahi kubur Si Mati tiap-tiap tahun pada hara raya.

Keys for Exercises

Lesson Two

A. 1. Here's a letter. 2. That's rice. 3. This is bread. 4. Here's some water. 5. Is that tea? Yes, it's tea. 6. Is this the shirt? Yes, that's the shirt. 7. Is this his hat? No, this is his hat. 8. Is that your pencil? Yes, it's my pencil. 9. Are those your books? No, these are my books. 10. Are these their hats? Yes, those are their hats. 11. What's that? It's my pen. 12. What's this? It's our coffee. 13. What's this? It's Mr Smith's newspaper. 14. What are those? Those are their writing-books.

B. 1. I am British. 2. He is Chinese. 3. Are you a Malay? Yes I'm a Malay. 4. Are you soldiers? No, we're civilians. 5. Are those Indians civilians? No, they are soldiers. 6. Who is that woman? She's an Indonesian. 7. Are those Malays civilians? No, they are police recruits. 8. Who is that Chinese? That's Mr Lim.

C. 1. Close the door. 2. Please, switch off the light. 3. Take off your hat. 4. Don't put the light on. 5. Read these letters. 6. Don't wear that blouse. 7. Drink this water (liquid). 8. Don't eat that rice. 9. What's he reading? He's reading a newspaper. 10. What are you doing? I'm writing a note. 11. What's that woman doing? She's getting a newspaper. 12. What are those British soldiers wearing? They are wearing military uniform. 13. What are the policemen doing? They are helping us. 14. Who took the drinking water? Meriam did. 15. Please, give him this shirt. 16. Please, give me that exercise book.

D. 1. We didn't receive your letter. 2. They didn't read my letter. 3. We mustn't open those doors. 4. She doesn't help us. 5. You mustn't let him come in. 6. He didn't join the army; he joined the police. 7. Whose shirt is this? Dollah's. 8. Whose book is that? Osman's. 9. What book is that? An English book. 10. What sort of blouse is that? A police blouse.

11. Did you give him the book or not? 12. Did they get the newspapers (or not)? 13. I didn't receive any mail this morning. 14. They don't eat bread; they eat rice.

E. Is this your *shirt*? No, that is my *shirt*.
F. What are *you* doing this morning?
G. Don't *write any letters* this evening.
H. Please, give him this *pen*.
I. I didn't *take a pen;* (*I took*) *a pencil*.
J. Whose *book* is this? It's *my book*.
K. What *book* did he *read*?

Lesson Three

A. 1. This is old bread. 2. That's hot-tasting food. 3. Here is some hot food. 4. That's a new house. 5. These are clean clothes. 6. This is the main market. 7. That's a small car. 8. That is cold tea. 9. That is dirty water. 10. Those are small cars. 11. Here is some hot tea. 12. Is this the entrance gate? 13. Is this the main road? 14. Is that drinking water? 15. Is that the police camp? 16. Is this a new shop?

B. 1. That rice tastes hot. 2. This coffee is cold. 3. This office is small. 4. Those books are dirty. 5. That market is big. 6. This water is hot. 7. The village is new. 8. This room is small. 9. My car is old. 10. His shop is new. 11. Their office is large. 12. My house is hot. 13. His clothes are dirty. 14. Is your village large? 15. Is my shirt dirty? 16. Is his room clean?

C. 1. Drink this cold water. 2. Go into the main road. 3. Drive this small vehicle. 4. Take that clean blouse. 5. Sit in the old office. 6. Buy the big hat. 7. Send these small letters. 8. Don't eat this dirty food (rice). 9. Don't come in this clean room. 10. Don't take the old lorry. 11. Don't use this hot water. 12. You mustn't open the entrance door. 13. He mustn't shut the main door. 14. They mustn't go to that coffee shop.

D. 1. She is going to go shopping for some bread. 2. He went to the market to buy a shirt. 3. He is going to the shop to buy a writing-book. 4. They went to the village to buy an old car. 5. What are you going to do, sir? I'm going to buy a book. 6. Where do you live? 7. Where do they live? 8. Where are you sending those letters to? 9. Where do you come from, sir? From London. 10. From whom did he buy that old vehicle? 11. To whom did you give those new shirts? 12. I've just received a letter from Kadir. 13. They have only just got to work. 14. We stayed a long time in the restaurant. 15. Where are you going to, Mat? To Encik Daud's house in that village. 16. He served a long time in the army. 17. Where's Encik Hassan? In the dining room. 18. He didn't work here long. 19. I gave the big hat to Zainal. 20. I took the dirty clothes from the small room. 21. Which road goes to Muar? 22. Which car are you going to take? 23. I came to the main door but couldn't get in. 24. They couldn't get to the market. 25. What's Encik Ahmad going to do? He's going to do some work in the office. 26. What are you going to do? Eat. 27. They want to drink but don't want anything to eat. 28. I don't want to join the army; I wish to go into the police. 29. What are you going to do? I'm taking somebody to Labis. 30. Mr Jones has gone to Kuala Lumpur to see somebody off to London.

E. 1. dari mana 2. di mana 3. ke mana 4. dari mana 5. di mana 6. ke mana.

F. The final negative sentences are translated:
1. She didn't work in that office for long. 2. They didn't spend much time eating in the restaurant. 3. He hasn't been driving for long. 4. You didn't take long to write the letter. 5. We soon did the job. 6. He didn't take long to get here.

G. 1. I've only just finished writing the big letter. 2. She has only just brought that cold water. 3. Kadir has just shut the main gate. 4. Hasan has just closed the small door. 5. Ahmad has only just bought that new hat. 6. I've only just read the new book.

H. Where are *you* off to, *Mat*? To *Muar*.

I. Have you worked here long?

J. Here is some clean water. That water is dirty.

K. Which room? The dirty room.

L. Encik Mat couldn't come to work.

M. Ahmad went to the shop to buy a newspaper.
Husain came from the office to get the small book.
Corporal Osman sat in the classroom writing a letter to Encik Kadir.
Ali went to the village to get his book from Husain.

166

Lesson Four

A. 1. Have you a car? Yes. Where is the car? It's on the road outside the office. 2. Have you any children, Zainal? Yes. Where are the children now? They're at school. 3. Isn't Osman coming to work today? No, he is taking his wife home. Where is his wife's village? On Batu Road. 4. Are you married, sir? Not yet. Have you a house? No, I stay in a hotel. 5. Let's go to town. I don't want to go now. Have you some work to do? It isn't much. Wait for me in the coffee shop. 6. This drinking-water is cold. Yes, I've just taken it from the fridge. Is it a big fridge? Yes, it is.

B. 1. There were a lot of people in town last night. 2. Put that file away in the drawer of my desk. 3. Whom were you waiting for at the main door just now? I was waiting for my wife coming from the village. 4. Please, put this letter in the post-box. 5. There were a lot of files in the cupboard (cabinet). 6. There are a lot of men in the lorry. 7. If there's no food in the house, go and buy some at the market. 8. Go and get the chair from the back of the room. 9. Just this morning I put the file on the desk. Now it's in the filing cabinet. 10. There are many cars in front of the school. 11. If the doctor isn't at home, look for him in the village. 12. That's a big lorry in front of that shop. 13. Her husband has just gone out of the house to look for the child on top of the hill. 14. Take the new shoes out of the box. 15. Today he is working in the town but tomorrow he'll be working in the village. 16. There still aren't many letters in the file. 17. There's an old car under the house. 18. Many villagers intend going into town today. 19. He has just put his shoes on to go out of the house. 20. Did you work long in the office last night? 21. Is the furniture in the office new? 22. Where are his wife and children now? 23. Did you take a letter from the drawer just now, sir? 24. Where are you taking your wife and children this afternoon? 25. My child starts school today. 26. I don't want to use that small box. Put it at the back of the shop. 27. Is Mr Ali in? Not yet, he's going to the bank this morning. 28. Do you live in a rural area? 29. The shop-keeper hasn't come this morning. 30. She didn't close the door of the filing cabinet yesterday afternoon. 31. Who is the person in the big car? 32. Are her children grown up now? 33. Couldn't he get in?

C. There are a lot of *people* in the *shop*.

D. If *Hasan* isn't in the *office*, look for him in the *dining-room*.

E. Don't you want to go to the *office this morning*?

F. Is the *house* in *front* of the school *new*?

G. The *water* in the *glass* is *cold*.

H. Where is the *car*? It's on *the road*.

I. Haven't you *eaten* yet?

Lesson Five

A. 1. When are you going back (home)? When I've finished my work, then I can go. 2. I want to take this rice back to the shop. 3. They learn English at a school in the town. 4. What did he say just now? He wanted to know the way to the hospital. 5. There aren't enough chairs in this office. 6. Rice used to be cheap in the market but now it's dear. 7. When did you last go to the hospital? 8. You go ahead. I have a little work in the office. 9. Ahmad has taken a bus to Malacca to see a police officer. 10. We are going by ship but how are we coming back? By road. 11. Yesterday afternoon I had to go to the hospital. 12. Does one have to drive on the left of the road? Yes. 13. What's it like working in that office? Fine. 14. Why does she want to go back early? Because her child is ill. 15. He's just got on the ferry-boat. Where is he off to? To Batu Pahat. 16. The Malay school is on the right of the river. 17. You can wait for the bus there. 18. My wife still isn't a good English speaker. 19. How long did you work in that town. 20. The job is finished so let's take a taxi to Encik Rahman's house.

B. 1. Do you want to see me, sir? Yes. 2. Can we come in now? Yes. 3. Do you know where he lives now? Yes. 4. Has Osman taken his wife back yet, or not? Not yet. 5. Are your children grown up now? Yes, they are. 6. Does their child like studying English at school? Yes, he does. 7. Is the doctor's house far from here? Not far. 8. Are the clothes in that shop cheap? No, very expensive. 9. Why didn't he come to work today? Because he's ill (of course). 10. Does your child have to stay in the hospital? Yes, she does.

C. 1. His wife isn't a good driver yet. 2. Encik Rahman's house in the new village isn't finished yet. 3. Her child is now able to read. 4. The boat is now far away, and they are just arriving. 5. When our children have grown we are going to send them to study in Kuala Lumpur. 6. When we saw him in the hospital, he still couldn't speak. 7. I don't want this car; it isn't big enough. 8. How do you know? My next-door neighbour told me. 9. The shopkeeper told me that there is enough rice in the town now. 10. There are still few people in that village who can speak English. 11. There is an ambulance by your house, did you know? 12. On which side of the road are you going to wait? 13. Open the top surface of the box. 14. On which side was the drawer he put the file in just now? The right. 15. There are Malay villages on both sides of the river. 16. The hill is on the far side of the town. 17. Why didn't he come to school this morning? Because the river has risen. 18. He used to be able to speak Malay, how about now? 19. You weren't very good at that job before, how are you now? 20. Do I have to turn right now? Not yet. 21. How are you, Encik Daud? Fine, sir. 22. Cik Zuraidah likes to go to the market in the afternoon.

D. Because the *vehicle* isn't *big* enough.
E. Why did she *come here*?
F. Which (side) *house* has he just *gone in*? The one on *the right*.
G. When did you last *see Mat*?
H. on the *right* side of the *road*
I. On which side of the *town* does he *live*?
J. You *go* ahead/first/for now.
K. The *child* is now *well grown*.
L. 1. mahu 2. suka 3. sudah 4. tahu 5. boleh 6. mesti
M. This morning Omar took a taxi to the town because he wanted to see a customs official. Hassan waited in front of the bank to catch a bus to go to Malacca. Roslan took a taxi to the market to buy rice because rice is now expensive in the village shop.

Lesson Six

A. tiga; ĕnam; ĕmpat; lima; lapan; satu; tujuh; dua; sĕpuluh; ĕmpat bĕlas; ĕnam bĕlas; dua puluh tiga; dua puluh lima; dua puluh tujuh; lapan puluh sĕmbilan; ĕnam puluh ĕmpat; tiga puluh tiga; lima puluh ĕmpat; sĕratus satu; sĕratus ĕmpat puluh ĕnam; dua ratus sĕbĕlas; tiga ratus ĕmpat puluh ĕnam; ĕmpat ratus lapan puluh ĕnam; sĕmbilan ratus ĕmpat bĕlas; lima ratus dua puluh dua; sĕribu ĕnam puluh sĕmbilan; tujuh ribu lima ratus tiga puluh tujuh; lapan ribu tujuh ratus dua bĕlas; ĕmpat ribu ĕnam ratus; sĕjuta dua puluh ribu sĕratus dua puluh lapan; lapan juta lima ratus tujuh puluh tiga ribu dua ratus sĕpuluh.

B. 1. His wages are fifteen dollars a day. 2. They take thirty days' leave per year. 3. I gave them fifty cents each. 4. One must drive here at thirty miles per hour. 5. The rice is two dollars a gantang. 6. How much are these shirts? Nine dollars each. 7. These trousers have gone up in price to twenty-eight dollars a pair. 8. This sort of watch is a good two hundred dollars (each). 9. She goes twice a week to the hospital. 10. The people in this firm are paid once a month. 11. Aeroplanes land there three times a day. 12. How many clerks work in this warehouse? There is only one. 13. How many wives does he have? 14. The river isn't very wide. 15. My home isn't very many miles from here. 16. The hill on the other side of the river isn't very many feet in height. 17. How many dollars did those new shoes cost? 18. How many times does he get leave per year? It used to be once, now it's twice. 19. How many times has Ismail been on leave this year (so far)? 20. How long have they been waiting there? A good hour.

C. 1. My father sold his car two months ago. He hasn't yet bought another. 2. Last week he went into the army again. 3. His parents want to come to Malaysia in four months time. 4. This money isn't enough. Give me another five dollars. 5. In another five days Ismail will be back from home leave. 6. When does your child have to go into hospital again. 7. How many more people can get on the boat? Another eight will be enough. 8. That rice is scarcely sufficient? Do you want some more? 9. You've just taken ten days' leave. What more do you want? 10. The car is very cheap. What more (can you want)? Buy it. 11. That civilian has worked for three weeks but still not received any pay yet. 12. How much further have we got to go? Exactly four miles. 13. The price of rice has risen by fifty cents a gantang. 14. My wife's mother goes to market three times a week. 15. Give them this money, fifteen dollars each. 16. What speed can one drive on this road? 17. How much did you pay for those books? A dollar seventy each. 18. Because his wife was ill, he had to spend yesterday (or 'a night') in the village. 19. What is the depth of the water? A good six feet now. 20. At which milestone is his house? At the thirty-first milestone, Ipoh Road. 21. How much longer before you go home? Another forty minutes then I can go. 22. How long will it take you to get to the market? 23. I've been in this hospital a good two weeks. 24. The river is wide enough but the water isn't yet deep enough.

25. He works long hours each day but his wages are low. 26.
This shirt is only small but the price is high.

D. How much did *you* pay for *the car*?
E. *The vehicle* isn't very *big*.
F. When are you *going to school* again?
G. How many *miles* further does he want to *go*?
H. There is a *policeman* in the *car*.
I. I still haven't *met him*.
J. He has *known how to drive* for a long time.
K. It is a long time since we *met*.
L. How long have you been *waiting here*?

M. Mr Ali in Mr Mat's Shop

Mat—Good morning, Cik Ali.
Ali —Good morning, Cik Mat.
Mat—How are you?
Ali —Fine, thank you.
Mat—Aren't you working today, Cik Ali?
Ali —No, I'm free today.
Mat—How many days off do you have a week, Cik Ali?
Ali —I have one free day a week.
Mat—What do you want to buy today, Cik Ali?
Ali —I want three gantangs of rice and a kati of coffee.
Mat—Why do you buy so little rice, Cik Ali?
Ali —I buy rice twice a month. There isn't much coffee in the
       shop, Cik Mat.
Mat—The coffee comes once a month, Cik Ali, it's due next
       week.
Ali —How much is a gantang of rice, Cik Mat?
Mat—It's cheap now at two dollars ten cents a gantang. It was
       two dollars forty cents.
Ali —How much is the coffee and rice, Cik Mat?
Mat—Not much, eight dollars ninety cents, Cik Ali.
Ali —Here's the money, Cik Mat.
Mat—Thank you. Here are the rice and coffee.
Ali —I'm going to the market now.
Mat—Aren't you driving?
Ali —No, the market isn't very far, Cik Mat.
Mat—Goodbye, Cik Ali.
Ali —Goodbye, Cik Mat.

A. 1. What day is it today? Today is Saturday. 2. What day is it tomorrow? Tomorrow is Sunday. 3. What day are you setting off for Singapore, sir? Monday morning. 4. Next week we get paid on Thursday. 5. All of the staff are free on Fridays. 6. What days of the week don't you work? Every Friday and Sunday. 7. He goes to see a film show each Wednesday. 8. Omar is on duty at the air-field this Tuesday. 9. This Thursday my father retires from work at the factory. 10. The Japanese football team arrived by aeroplane on Monday night. 11. What night does your wife want to go to the cinema? Sunday night. 12. What time is it now? It's twenty minutes to seven. 13. What time do you get up in the morning? At a quarter to six. 14. What time did Ěncik Zainal telephone just now? At ten o'clock exactly. 15. Wake me up at half-past five tomorrow morning. 16. My children get up at seven o'clock to go to school. 17. The Japanese ship will dock at about 5.00 p.m. 18. We go to Friday prayers at ten past twelve. 19. What time does the show start this evening? At about 7.15. 20. We can break our fast at about six in the evening. 21. Ěncik Harun went to the mosque at eleven o'clock and still isn't back yet. 22. In the fasting month we work between eight and twelve o'clock and from one o'clock to half-past three in the afternoon. 23. Omar has walked from the four and a half milestone to the nine and a quarter milestone. 24. All the staff have lunch between twelve and one o'clock. 25. My father likes to have an afternoon sleep between two and three o'clock.

B. 1. How much did Mat pay for the two wrist-watches? 2. Bring another ten stones here. 3. He went to the market and bought thirty eggs. They were twenty cents each. 4. Yesterday I found a new songkok in that box. 5. At which milestone do Omar's parents live? At the $5\frac{1}{2}$. How far is their home? About $\frac{1}{2}$ mile. 6. How many miles is it to the Western Assurance building? About $6\frac{3}{4}$. 7. How many hours do you work a day? Approximately seven hours. 8. At what time do you shave in the morning? At seven o'clock each working day. 9. He is wearing two watches, one on the left hand, and one on the right. 10. His father stopped working a year and a half ago. 11. They were waiting for the bus but it didn't stop. 12. I have telephoned three times to Muar and still not yet managed to speak to Ěncik Kadim. 13. I read in the newspaper that the firm wants another six drivers. 14. Tell Ěncik Hashem that he can take his leave between Tuesday and Friday. 15. There are many houses on both sides of the road from the fifth to the seventh milestones. 16. Where's Zainal? He has gone to buy a newspaper to look for work vacancies. 17. The building isn't quite two hundred yards from my office. 18. The rice in the box is just less than three and a half gantangs. 19. The apples cost a dollar twenty for five. Would you like to buy some? 20. All vehicles must stop at the main road. 21. They started playing football at six o'clock and finished at half-past seven. 22. On Monday Ěncik Karim started work with the police force in Muar. 23. How many more miles is it to the mosque from here? (3 versions).

C. *two* and a half *dollars*
D. approximately *three* more *years*
E. between *one o'clock* and *two o'clock*
F. from 7.00 *a.m.* till 3.00 *p.m.*
G. not quite *five yards*
H. What is the number of your *taxi*?
I. At what time do you *have breakfast*?
J. What day are you *going back to your village*?

Lesson Eight

A. 1. How many pairs of shoes are missing from the godown? About fifty pairs. 2. How many cigarettes do you smoke a day? Nowadays only ten. 3. There are two schools there, a Malay and an English. 4. In the afternoon I want to go to the village and buy two hens. 5. Put those three shirts in the wardrobe. This shirt I'm going to wear. 6. How much poultry does his father have now? Altogether sixty head. Last week he bought another five. 7. How many blades are there in a packet of razor blades? In this small packet, five. 8. They saw several animals near the river. Didn't manage to catch one. 9. The animal is very big and has a long tail. 10. What work has Hashim just been doing in the garden? He was planting three coconut trees. ('batang' indicates they are trees not coconuts) 11. She went and bought fruit at the market this morning, and now she wants to buy another two coconuts. 12. I have just bought two tickets, and now they are missing. 13. The four boats are now far away out of sight. 14. Near the river there are several villages. Do Europeans like to live near rivers? 15. That letter is missing.

Send another one. 16. Which letter were you looking for just now? Those two in the file. 17. Put the two pairs of swimming-trunks in a bag. 18. I had only two slices of bread for breakfast. Let's go and eat at Long's cafe. 19. He bought two cheap houses and sold them at high prices. 20. How many dollars does a white shirt cost? 21. How many dollars is a pound of beef? 22. That meat isn't enough. Take another piece. 23. All soldiers carry a rifle and a parang when they go into the jungle. 24. Ahmad succeeded in catching six fish in the river last night.

B. 1. Whose is the car outside that big building? It's mine. 2. Whose is the poultry in the plantation? It all belongs to Hashim. 3. What's the name of the owner of those two (adjacent) shops? His name is Long. 4. There are several cars yonder. Which is Ĕncik Karim's? The white car is his. 5. Which ship have you just come off? It's called 'ss. Bahagia'. 6. What's the name of the Chinese restaurant on the right side of this road? 7. What are the names of those two European women? I don't yet know their names. Their husbands work on two rubber estates near Kota Tinggi. 8. Omar's father died last year but his mother is still alive. 9. It's nearly seven o'clock and only now is he going to put the lights on in the house. 10. I can't go back yet. I have to fix my car engine first. 11. I love to bathe when the tide is coming in. 12. Are you going to buy a brick house in the town? I can't because they are too expensive. 13. These cigarettes aren't enough. Give me another packet, please. 14. Why did the police go into the warehouse this afternoon? Somebody has stolen something. 15. All those goods have fixed prices. 16. Don't go into the next road. It's a dead-end. 17. I parked your car in the cul-de-sac on the left of this road. There it will be quite safe. 18. This parang is too long. Pass me a knife, please. 19. Go and tell Ĕncik Harun there's an ox in his garden. 20. Ali has sold his boat. Is he going to buy a new one? No, he wants to invest his money.

C. He loves *working in the garden*.

D. I don't care for *working in the garden*.

E. That can't be, because *the hill* is too *high*.

F. three *lorries* only

(*Use:* batang, bilah, buah, ekor, biji, pasang, biji (batang, for trees), buah, ekor, helai, keping, orang)

G. How many *ducks* are there?
(biji, laras/pucuk, batang/buah, buah/pintu, helai, orang, pucuk, batang, ekor, (none), biji, keping)

H. those two *shirts*
(ekor, bilah, orang, pucuk, ekor, biji/batang, batang, buah, buah, bilah, pucuk, buah)

I. These *books* aren't sufficient. Give me another *one*.
(biji, bilah, biji, batang, ekor, buah, helai, keping, keping, buah)

J. 'This is Hashim's car' becomes 'This car is Hashim's'.

K. All the people of this village work in Cik Harun's plantation.
(Semuanya after these: ini, saya, kopi, kampung, sini)

L. 1-3; 2-5; 3-4; 4-2; 5-1; 6-6.

Lesson Nine

A. (Here **bulan** is not repeated and numerals replace the names of the months)
1. dua puluh satu haribulan tiga.   2. sepuluh haribulan sebelas.
3. empat haribulan dua.   4. dua puluh dua haribulan enam.
5. tujuh belas haribulan sepuluh.   6. tiga puluh haribulan empat.
7. lima belas haribulan tujuh.   8. sebelas haribulan lima.   9. tiga haribulan sembilan.   10. sembilan haribulan lapan.   11. enam haribulan dua belas.   12. satu haribulan satu.   13. tahun seribu sembilan ratus tiga puluh tiga.   14. tahun sembilan belas lima puluh sembilan.   15. tahun enam puluh lima.   16. tahun seribu sembilan ratus tujuh puluh enam.   17. sepuluh haribulan sebelas tahun sembilan belas enam puluh sembilan.   18. empat belas haribulan lima tahun empat puluh empat.   19. dua belas haribulan sembilan tahun seribu sembilan ratus empat puluh sembilan.   20. sepuluh haribulan tiga tahun sembilan belas tujuh puluh tiga.

B. 1. This licence expired on the twenty-first of this month.
2. My elder sister is going to marry on the sixteenth of next month.   3. The course finishes on 10th October.   4. My elder brother joined the army on 22nd September last year.   5. Ěncik Salim became head of the office on 1st January this year.   6. In which year were you born? In 1953.   7. On what date did he move house? On the eighteenth of last month.   8. My younger brother is going to change school on 7th September.   9. In which month is the ship sailing back here? I don't know yet. It could be August.   10. How many months are you going to spend on the course? It's for a month only.   11. Which year did

you start working here? 1960.   12. How many more years is it before you can retire, sir? Another 3 years.   13. On what date did you marry your wife? On 28th July 1965.   14. Date of birth? 11th July 1953.   15. How old is your younger sister? She has just turned nine years old, that's all.   16. In which month is the firm going to move to Kuala Lumpur? Maybe this month.   17. Why did Dollah ask for a day off? He wants to move house on the tenth of this month.   18. On what day of the month did he start getting the marriage allowance? From the eighth.   19. How many years have you worked as a clerk? It's now twenty and a half years.   20. The amah (servant) says she wants to go back home on the second of next month.

C.   1. Zainal wants to extend his leave by another two days. 2. All drivers must stop at the main road.   3. Tell someone to go and clean the floor of the warehouse.   4. Before going home you must finish off that job first.   5. Show them how to fill in those forms.   6. Having entered the hospital, she immediately gave birth to the child.   7. Where did you leave the money before it was missing?   8. I left the lorry at the 6th milestone on Jalan Muar.   9. When I tell you, quickly hoist up the bin.   10. Detail two men to go and help the mechanic today.   11. Wrap up those small things and put them in the bin.   12. The man in the shop said he could enlarge the photograph after Wednesday.   13. That clock is a little slow. Please, put it on five minutes.   14. After his father died, he ran through all his money.   15. The amah has bathed and put the children to bed.   16. Before you can telephone, you must put the money in first.   17. In this week's leave Ahmad wants to renovate his house in the village. 18. Please get me my newspaper from the office.   19. Go to the shop and buy me two packets of cigarettes.   20. Tell him to make our coffee now.   21. Can you show me which road goes to Kampung Danau?   22. Hashim can draw my pay for me this week.   23. After the evening meal I read a book to my young(est) child.   24. All the offices close at five o'clock so I must hurry back to town.   25. I took a bus as far as Johor Bahru then walked from there.   26. The car can't turn here, sir. You must reverse a little first.   27. Go past the side of the market, and there is Ěncik Ali's house near the telephone box.   28. This letter won't do. Tell him to write it once again.   29. How many brothers and sisters have you? Altogether six, two elder brothers, an elder sister, a younger brother and a younger sister. (See notes.)

30. Are your father's brothers and sisters still alive? His elder brother is dead, and there are only two elder sisters and a younger brother left.

D. How many years did you *work as a mechanic*?
E. In which year did he *become village chief*?
F. In which month are you *going to Kuantan* again?
G. How old are *you*? Over *twenty-three*.

H.
Osman—How are you, Cik Aziz?
Aziz — I'm fine.
Osman—It's a long time since I've seen you. Where have you been?
Aziz — I've moved to Kampung Sentosa, and as soon as I moved I went on leave. That's why you haven't seen me in the office.
Osman—What's it like living in a new house now, Cik Aziz?
Aziz — My new house is like the old house in Jalan Padang Bola but the rooms are a little bigger. There are four rooms in all.
Osman—Very nice, Cik Aziz. I found out from the villagers that you are going to marry off your daughter. Is this right, Cik Aziz?
Aziz — That's right. It was because of that we were in a hurry to move. The new house will be able to hold quite a few more people when the date for it arrives.
Osman—When are you going to arrange the wedding?
Aziz — I still don't know the date of it yet, 'Man. His folk want to wait till he has finished his training. After that he is going to take a course in Johor. He works in the police.
Osman—Police work is very good, Cik Aziz. The pay is good, and they get marriage allowance and a house.
Aziz — But 'Man, one can't get a police house straight away.
Osman—Why is that?
Aziz — There are many police still haven't got houses. A newly married policeman has to fill in forms and wait till there is a house vacant.
Osman—Right, Cik Aziz, I'm late now. Today's my son's birthday. He's now reached seven.
Aziz — Okay, good-bye.

A. 1. I can remember the first day he came to work here. 2. On what matter have you come to see the manager this morning? 3. He isn't a Malay, he's Chinese. 4. What is the name of the owner of the second shop? 5. If the articles are so heavy, how can he carry all of them? 6. That thin man has just come out of hospital. 7. Omar isn't as fat as that. 8. If the food isn't tasty, don't buy it. 9. Mr Nasir lives in a fine house. It's situated two miles from here. 10. When the manager orders, all the clerks quickly obey. That's how things are in that company. 11. Remind Ěncik Salim I want to see him before he goes to the education office. 12. The fourth lesson is easy, not hard like the sixth. 13. You can get to his house along this narrow way. 14. Tie the animal tightly with this rope. 15. I want you to cut that strong rope short like this. 16. Put the heavy things underneath and the light things on top. 17. He used not to be as heavy as he is nowadays. 18. What's the body weight of your car? Over three tons. If that's the case, you can't go over that narrow bridge ahead. 19. Don't worry. I can speak to the manager about the matter. 20. I don't know about the matter because I was at home ill yesterday. 21. When important personages arrived at the field everyone stood up. 22. In that village women do the easy jobs only. 23. What weight are you? Only 150 pounds. 24. I can't bring this thing in. If so, can I just put it here.

B. 1. Now my father lives comfortably in the village, not in difficulty as before in the town. 2. That sturdily-built man is called Wahid, isn't he? 3. What are you worrying about? It isn't important. You can do it quite easily. 4. His watch was lost in the river. It'll be difficult to find such a small thing. 5. I think the goods are worth $1000. They aren't that dear. 6. We don't want to cross the river. We want to fish. 7. When I'm at leisure like this, I like to stay at home with my wife and children. 8. Who was it standing at the office door just now? I don't know his name. I think he was looking for work. 9. Which meat do you prefer, beef or chicken? 10. At present there are a lot of people looking for work in the towns because the wages there are high. 11. There are a lot of vehicles ahead; we'll be late in getting to the office this morning. If that's so, we'd better take a short cut here. 12. You can come with me and eat at my house this evening, what do you say? That's fine, thank you very much. 13. This coconut-milk is really nice. Isn't that so, Cik Kadir? 14. Ěncik Harun will be going back soon. We'd better just wait for him here. 15. The crate he is carrying isn't heavy; it's only light. 16. It's now afternoon. We'd better set off immediately. 17. I remember the first time he came to my house three years ago. 18. Wrap up all of these small things, then tie them with string. 19. If you want to live in a government house, fill in this form. 20. His lunch was just a piece of cake. He'd better go and see the doctor in the evening.

C. That is a *good book*.

D. It was he who *told* me.

E. Who was the one *writing a letter*?

F. Which one, *this* one or *that* one?

G. It wasn't *I* who *told him*.

H. He *drives an old car*, doesn't he?

I. That *stout* man's name is *Ali*.

J. It'll be difficult to *go up* such a *high hill*.

K. The *house* he *bought* isn't all that *big*.

L. What are you *looking at*?

Lesson Eleven

A. 1. What colour was the blouse that she bought? A white blouse. 2. Yesterday he wore grey trousers. 3. What make of car did Omar buy? A Toyota. 4. The labourers in the government department are of Chinese race. 5. Why is the old man walking shoeless? 6. Those black shoes are very expensive. 7. His wife entered the maternity hospital at a quarter past two this morning. 8. His car is damaged after colliding with a lorry. 9. Many lads like to wear chocolate-coloured trousers. 10. The labour officer is called Ěncik Karim. 11. What does he want? He wants to contact the chief clerk in the labour department. 12. How old is the typist in the front office, do you know? I think she is about nineteen. 13. He went straight from the office to the swimming pool. 14. On arrival at the swimming pool he immediately put on his trunks and went into the water. 15. When the police came looking for him, he went straight into hiding. 16. Tell all the staff to get together in my office. 17. Arrange all the furniture as before. After that tell all the labourers to line up for their pay. 18. The young man is well-mannered but he still isn't married yet. 19. The cashier wants to see the manager this morning to ask for unpaid leave. 20. When his car broke down, he walked immediately to the village to ask for help. 21. When the traffic lights have changed to green, you can then drive on. 22. How long did you stay in the training school? I trained there for six months.

B. 1. In the break period Ishak went home to change his clothes because the ones he was wearing had got dirty. 2. If you intend changing a tyre, I can help you. 3. Before the youths can get into Singapore they must get a hair-cut first. 4. What's to be done? The vehicle has broken down and we can't go now. 5. How can he come to work today if he was very ill yesterday? 6. If you aren't tall enough, how can you join the police? 7. Ĕncik Ahmad's cattle got free and crossed the road. That was why the two cars collided. 8. The police on duty at the door of the bank have to be armed. 9. My elder brother is a rice-planter in Kedah and my younger brother is at school there. 10. He took a day off last month and daren't ask for any more leave. 11. If he went to a night-club last night, I bet he'll be late to work this morning. 12. If those drums are now empty, stack them outside the warehouse. 13. What can I do? I want to buy cigarettes but the shops are closed. 14. They used to quarrel a lot, but now they are on good terms. 15. Youngsters like that aren't brave enough to spend the night in the jungle. 16. The missing article was valueless. Don't worry. 17. On arriving at the foot of the hill they went straight to the top. 18. You mustn't stop. Carry on working till it's all finished. Then you can rest for a quarter of an hour. 19. The Chinese merchant's son wants to continue his education in England. 20. When he came that day, the head of department shook hands with all our people. 21. Hashim used to work as a barber, but now he sells cars in the town. 22. He met a lot of Japanese merchants after he had become a member of the golf club.

C. What colour *car* does he use?
D. *The holiday* is finished now, so what's to be done?
E. The *child* has no *money*.
F. He went from *home* straight to the *hospital*.
G. Arriving *home*, we immediately *went to bed*.

Lesson Twelve

A. 1. Her car was stolen last night. She has just gone to report the matter to the police. 2. Harun's hand was cut on a knife and

180

bled. His shirt was stained with the blood. 3. Last night my child was bitten by mosquitoes. 4. Your shoes are dirty with oil. 5. The post office in Jalan Swettenham was robbed last week. 6. Encik Dollah was charged by the police because he parked his car on this side of the road. 7. This is the spot where two policemen were killed by communists. 8. Hamzah was ordered to go and see the manager. 9. My wife has to cook at 3.00 a.m. in the fasting month. 10. He was called in to the manager because he didn't come to work on Monday. 11. They were fined two hundred dollars each. 12. He has to keep his money at home because his house is a long way from the bank. 13. I had to look after the children last night because my wife fell ill. 14. That merchant has to pay two thousand dollars in tax. 15. The restaurant was robbed by two armed men. 16. When he was deceived by the woman, he immediately got angry. 17. Last year a lot of labourers were sacked. 18. His father was transferred to Kuala Lipis last month. 19. Because there wasn't a bridge, they had to swim across the river. 20. If he wants further promotion, he has to study English. 21. The people who stole the foodstuff have been caught by the police. 22. The policeman fired but missed. 23. He fired at the animal and hit it in the stomach. 24. I have to work every Saturday this month.

B. 1. Don't keep your money at home; save it in the bank. If it's at home, it's bound to be stolen. 2. He didn't pay the duty. He is bound to be fined some time. 3. Put that stack of cartons right, otherwise they'll fall. 4. Make sure all the barrels contain oil. 5. Many people who live outside London come into work by rail each day. 6. Husin, you delight in being naughty. Anyone who is naughty is bound to be caned. How can you ever be proficient if you don't study properly? 7. When he arrives, take the money and give him this letter (receipt). 8. The police still haven't arrested the head of the gang that killed the owner of the shop. 9. The low-ranking official was reprimanded by the head of department. 10. Is the stranger asking for help? No, he only wants a light for his cigarette. 11. Tell that lad not to play with fire, otherwise he'll burn his clothes. 12. If that's the case, we must complain to the police. 13. A schoolboy died in hospital after being attacked by an animal near his village. 14. Don't worry. The chief clerk will be here in a minute. Perhaps he'll be able to help. 15. The gardener was sentenced to six months' hard labour. 16. This isn't the first time he has broken the law. 17.

The men who robbed the radio shop didn't dare leave their hiding-place.   18. It's now five o'clock. Let's go home. Wait a second, I want to finish this job first.   19. Yusuf has won the lottery. That's why he wants to retire now.   20. Be careful when crossing the road yonder. If you don't, you'll be knocked down.   21. What matter did you want to tell me about, Yusuf? Say it now! If the bus comes, you will no longer have a chance to speak to me. 22. There isn't much petrol in the tank. You had better stop at the nearest petrol station.   23. The school headmaster was slightly injured when his car ran into a tree.   24. If you take a few pains over it, this lesson isn't all that difficult.

C.   His *car* is *damaged* from what? From *collision with a bus*.

D.   For that reason they were *charged*.

E.   It isn't *you* who *are* wrong, *I am*.

F.   In *half an hour's* time he'll be *setting off*.

G.   If I had known the *car* was so *cheap,* I would certainly have *bought it*.

H.   Whether he wants to or not, he has to *go into hospital* nevertheless.

Lesson Thirteen

A.   1. Check that all the classrooms are tidy. The headmaster will be coming to inspect them.   2. If they don't carry a map, they are sure to get lost in that area.   3. During his visit to Kuala Lumpur he went to Friday prayers in the National Mosque.   4. I thought the girl had died but, it seems, she's still alive.   5. If it rains heavily, it will be hard to find the way.   6. Perhaps some day we can go and visit the National Museum.   7. They could only travel slowly because it rained heavily.   8. The area of the field is two and a half acres. It belongs to one of my relations. 9. We shall have to widen the area before we can make a football pitch.   10. Before going home, tidy up this office.   11. If he doesn't know how to read a map, how can he find the right road? 12. Drive a little slower. I want to read that road-sign.   13. Why can't he go into that area? It appears the military are going to do training there.   14. That spot is very dangerous. Many cars have crashed there.   15. Please, stack these things neatly.   16. Have a look at this book. The pictures in it are really beautiful.   17. Why did she put this file in the drawer, do you know? I don't know, sir. I'll be able to tell you later.   18. That lad is incredibly silly. Heavy rain like this and he wants to swim in the river.   19. Look out! Snakes of that colour are dangerous. 20. Don't send that letter before the manager puts his signature on it. 21. My cousin wants to go and study overseas. 22. He went abroad last year and is coming back next year. 23. I was born in Negeri Sembilan in 1957. 24. Why was he dismissed from work? For being idle. 25. Soldiers certainly know how to dress smartly.

B. 1. He looks like an Indian but his parents are Thai. 2. Bring the file to my office. I want to look through all the letters. 3. Is Omar working in the field? No, he's just gone to look for a water-buffalo, and will be back soon. 4. I don't know where he is now. Perhaps he has gone to his uncle's house. 5. Of course he's tired. He's had to work nights for a week. 6. When coming down the hill, go slowly, or you'll slip. 7. Start the engine when I tell you. Then set the car going slowly. 8. That bin doesn't seem to be in the right place. We must move it. 9. Why isn't he back from leave yet? Apparently he is ill after his fall yesterday. 10. Excuse me, please. There are so many people here that it's difficult to walk. 11. He came to ask for help, didn't he? It would appear so. 12. Ahmad has gone to telephone; it seems his wife is near to giving birth. 13. He is bound to want to buy such a beautiful picture. 14. I'm too idle to clear the table now. 15. I can't be bothered to write a letter now. Tomorrow will do. 16. That young woman is no longer a girl. She's married. 17. Kids who live near the main roads are bound to live with danger. 18. That lad is a terrific runner. He got there in no time. 19. Stop there to buy petrol. The petrol is nearly finished. 20. When it's nearly time to stop work, tell that lad to clear up these things. 21. The battery is nearly finished; it's sure to be difficult to start the engine tomorrow. 22. They have almost finished, yet we have barely started. 23. I still haven't received my pay and I have nearly run out of money. 24. It's nearly night-time; we'll just stop here for evening meal. 25. It's about to rain heavily and yet he's gone to look for rattan in the jungle.

C. *He* looks like a *Japanese*.

D. He *went to the village*, it appears, to *visit a relation*.

E. It seems *the patient* is *eating* a lot today.

F. Perhaps they *are coming back here*.

G. He has obviously *lost his way*.

H. Check that *the battery water is sufficient*.

I. See if *the battery water is sufficient*.

J. Such *pretty things* are sure to be *expensive*.

K. That *young woman* is extremely *fat*.

L. That *sign* isn't in the right place.

A. 1. Your watch is just like mine. How much did you pay for it? 2. This blanket isn't much good. Give me a thicker one. 3. Jungle fruit is sourer than garden fruit. 4. The hill is very high and getting up it is extremely difficult. 5. Who is the tallest man in the firm? I don't know, but I think Omar is the tallest. 6. Which is the biggest airport in Singapore? I reckon Seletar airport is the biggest. 7. The aeroplane is arriving in twenty minutes. 8. Why did the driver take the narrow road? Because the road is a short cut to the airport. 9. That new clothing shop is bigger than the old one. 10. Which is sweeter, pineapple or durian? Pineapple is certainly sweeter. 11. Don't take the fruit now. If it is (left to become) fully ripe, it will be much sweeter. 12. This wood is very hard and difficult to cut. 13. The price of these sheets is higher in Kuala Lumpur. It would be better to buy here. 14. He isn't very good at it now but he practises a lot and is sure to get better. 15. He is the same age as my child. Why can't he finish school? 16. I'm not as well-off as Mr Mahmud, so I can't buy such an expensive car. 17. They'll have to travel faster if they want to get there early. 18. This is a nice mirror, but that mirror is even better. 19. Those monkeys are very fierce; don't go near them. 20. If the patient hasn't eaten for two days, he must be extremely hungry now. 21. Of all the clerks in the office Zainal is the most hard-working. That's why he was rapidly promoted. 22. Last week I was very ill, and now I'm still weak. 23. Vehicles have difficulty in running on this soft ground. Look for a firmer spot. 24. Which is the most open area of land? The most open, I think, is between the hill and the river. 25. It's right that he is well now, but if he takes two days holiday he'll be even stronger. 26. Your sarong today is very pretty, Kadir. Is it a new sarong? 27. What drink do you like? The one I like best is milk. 28. Today I'm going to buy some new and pretty curtain material. 29. The windows here are bigger than the windows in the next room. Make sure the material for them is longer. 30. Put the letter back in its envelope. 31. Who is weaker, Jalil or Mahmud? I think Mahmud is weaker than Jalil. 32. Which are more vicious, bears or monkeys? I reckon bears are more vicious than monkeys. 33. Which is harder, the ground here or yonder? I think it's harder here.   34. Of all the men, who is the most proficient? The best is Ěncik Yusuf.   35. I think your book is better than mine. Let's exchange.   36. This clothing is of high quality. Buy now at low prices!

B.   This *watch* is just like that *watch*.
C.   *This fruit* isn't as *sweet* as *pineapple*.
D.   The *house* isn't very *tall*.
E.   Which is *tasti*er, *Malay food* or *Chinese food*?
F.   That *pineapple* isn't very good, take a *sweet*er one.
G.   They have to *travel* even *far*ther.
H.   Who is the *old*est of all the *men*?

Lesson Fifteen

A.   1. We must always help people in trouble regardless of whether they are poor or rich.   2. My eldest child is fed up with studying. He doesn't want to go to school any more.   3. How much fried banana have you still got? There are eight pieces left. Wrap them all up.   4. Let's go back now. It's already evening. When the night is here, it'll be difficult to find the way back to the house. 5. I used to be an idle student. Only now do I know how useful school education is.   6. Every morning and evening we spray all the trees with water. If there is grass beneath the trees, we get rid of it all. That way our trees are always healthy.   7. Make sure the bin is full of clean water.   8. Use this towel, that one is wringing-wet.   9. He always goes to the sea's edge when the tide is coming in.   10. Don't throw litter all around. Put it in the rubbish-bin. 11. Don't throw the rope away, there may be a use for it.   12. The meal is ready, let's eat or the food will get cold.   13. If your hands are wet, don't touch the electric points.   14. It's time to take your medicine again.   15. Please, put up a wire between the trees in the garden to dry clothes.   16. That patient needs immediate treatment.   17. This wet wood is difficult to burn. Look to see if there is some dry.   18. People are forbidden to kill animals in this area of jungle.   19. There's a button missing from this shirt. 20. When she was washing the floor of the house, I was washing the car at the kerbside.   21. We had better take an umbrella; it looks like rain again.   22. Yellow umbrellas are always reserved for sultans and rajas.

B.   1. Get those two rolls of wire from the lorry. They are to be fixed here.   2. All these clothes are wet; apparently they are to be put out to dry. 3. How are your wife and children back home? Quite well. 4. They have had to wait quite a long time for the aeroplane. 5. He went out of the back door to look for Zainal, but at that very moment Zainal was coming in the front door. 6. Ěncik Omar went on leave on Wednesday, but he was asked to return quickly that same day. 7. I used to live in this area, but now I'm no longer familiar with these roads. 8. Usually he sunbathes on the beach in the afternoons, but not today. 9. I thought he was a private but, it appears, he's an officer. 10. This device has many uses. It isn't to be moved. 11. When my daughter comes back from school, she always prepares her work for the following day. 12. If there is no telephone, he can be contacted again by telegram. 13. Who knows but that at some time in the future these old things can all be used again. 14. These things are of high value; the cartons are not to be pressed. 15. The air in this room is too hot because the air-conditioner needs to be adjusted. 16. I'm not hungry, a piece of toast will be enough. 17. The road between the hills isn't very straight. 18. Now one can travel by air-conditioned coach to Thailand. 19. I met Ěncik Lim just now. He says he wants to deal in dried coconut. 20. The engine isn't running properly and I haven't the tools to put it right. 21. What use is his car if it still isn't registered. 22. Go and say to Ěncik Ahmad that there is someone wanting to see him.

C. That *grass* needs *cutting*.

D. This *paper* isn't to be *got rid of*.

E. No one is allowed *to smoke* here.

F. Usually he *goes on holiday to Singapore*, but not this time.

G. That *medicine* is of no further use; it can be *thrown out*.

H. What further use is that *file, burn it*.

I. Those *pills* should be very useful in future.

J. It is time to *set off*.

K. He isn't used to this *work*.

L. He isn't accustomed to *spending the night in the jungle*.

M. I always *prepare a meal* at *that* time.

Lesson Sixteen

A. 1. Put them straight (in a straight line). 2. Go quickly. 3. Walk properly. 4. Take good care of the car. 5. Put the letter safely away. 6. Store the fruit in the right way or it will go bad. 7. Count the money accurately. 8. Don't pay too high a price. 9. Don't talk too long. 10. Come a little nearer. 11. Better to go a little slower.   12. You'd better tie the mooring rope fairly tight.   13. Cut the string up into short pieces.   14. He goes to work very early in the morning and comes back late in the evening.   15. If we are going to cross the swamp, we must set off early.   16. The film show is excellent. The tickets were soon sold out.   17. In future don't ever do that again.   18. Usually she doesn't eat boiled eggs but now and again she does.   19. Don't go into the jungle alone. If you were to be lost, who would know?   20. Suddenly the rope snapped because the wind was blowing very strongly.   21. Look at this key. Sometimes it will open, sometimes it won't. It would be better just to get another.   22. Whenever he is free, he likes to walk in the vicinity of the palace.   23. Make sure nobody takes this thin material.   24. The meat has been eaten by a dog.   25. The long grass has been cut by the gardener.   26. The broken fan-belt is to be replaced by the shopkeeper.   27. Ensure that the soldiers don't neglect their duties.   28. See that the job isn't done by an ordinary clerk.   29. Make sure that nobody takes the file.   30. Sometimes I sleep with the fan on.   31. Sometimes they go to the market-town by boat.   32. Be careful in that very deep water.   33. Watch your step in that thickish jungle.   34. The radio in the house next door can be heard far away.   35. Why didn't Omar come out into town? He's reading. What is he reading? A book he bought yesterday.

B.   1. The eggs that have just been boiled are still not hard yet.   2. He mended the broken fence yesterday.   3. When he was caught by the wind, he fell straight into a drain.   4. What else is there to wait for? Isn't it night (late) already.   5. If the sapling had been looked after carefully, it wouldn't have died like this.   6. The vegetables he bought yesterday have been eaten up by the cattle.   7. If you always come so late, you are sure to be fired.   8. His father, who was bitten by a dog three weeks ago, still hasn't come out of hospital yet.   9. If the door is locked as it is left, no one will be able to get in.   10. Put those wet things to dry outside the room.   11. Put the lights on a little earlier. It's getting dark.   12. You can come to my house any time you are free.   13. It's all right. He's not playing too near the kerbside.   14. Let's wait together till they come.   15. Don't be too shy. If you don't eat, you'll be hungry.   16. The dogs next door look very fierce.   17. It's time we cut that very thick lalang (long grass).   18. Instead of suffering the cold like this, put on some clothes that are a little thicker.   19. If he got up early in the morning, he'd be able to help his mother. 20. When they had only just arrived, they were always getting lost in the capital. 21. How can he rest very long if people come visiting him every day. 22. Why was the Chinese arrested by the police without any warning at all? 23. What else is he looking for at this late hour? Tomorrow will do! 24. Sometimes the lad is beaten by his mother till he's black and blue. 25. Whenever he is free, he takes his children for a break by the sea. 26. I didn't notice when he came; suddenly he was there in his office. 27. With little further delay, Ali tied the box tightly with the string. 28. Cut the bread rather thinly, then it can be toasted. 29. This is the kind of wide, open land that he is looking for to build a house. 30. If each job is done properly, difficult things become easy. (A fairly common saying.) 31. Of all the many fruits I prefer bananas. You too? 32. In pouring rain like this, why aren't you wearing a hat? 33. Why wasn't this rotten fruit got rid of? 34. If you are as scared as this, why do you live on your own? 35. Why doesn't Hassan want to go to the river? He's afraid. What is he afraid of? The crocodiles people have come across there.

C. He walked in the direction of the *mosque*.
D. He's *asleep*; hasn't *got up* even yet. (Would you believe it, he's still asleep!)
E. Don't *go to the town* so *late at night*, or you'll *lose your way*.
F. Use **jangan-jangan** in 1, 4, 6, and 7.
Use 'in time' for **dulu** in 2.

Lesson Seventeen

A. 1. My elder sister has long been married but my elder brother is still single. 2. The coconut is a type of plant that is very useful to man. 3. Tea-plants grow well on hills in hot countries. 4. Lift the crate carefully. The contents are fine glassware that are easily broken. 5. It is indeed true what you said before, that elderly folk like to chat. 6. Ali didn't sell at high prices to the villagers. He took only a little profit. 7. When the teacher asked who knew the house of the sick pupil, Salim put his hand up quickly. 8. When you have finished that other job, put these ironed things in the wardrobe. 9. If it isn't lost, where is my money? Come and help me look for it. With a bit of luck I'll find it again. 10. How much was the money that was lost? Not much. Only 50 cents. But even 50 cents is still money. 11. Even a thief is a human. 12. You wait here a while. But you mustn't go anywhere, see? 13. Here on the beach I don't feel tired, and don't feel anything at all—not like at home. If I'm in the house, I always feel hungry. I feel just like you, Salmah. If I'm at home I always feel listless and tired. 14. If you want to return to the city, you must go back to the crossroads and turn left. 15. Malays say, 'If there is sugar, there are ants', that is to say: wherever there are beautiful females, there too there are males. 16. Not one of my friends has to work this Hari Raya. 17. It was quite right what he said, but this time it's a little different in that this brand of sweet is the same price as that brand. 18. This car is very different from any car I've ever used. 19. If possible, I'd like to change places with Mahmud because I haven't had a chance yet to visit the city. 20. I've never seen so many ants in one place. 21. He fishes just for pleasure, not thinking of profit. 22. Everybody has to pay the fare, no matter how much it is.

B. 1. We'd better turn at the end of this road. We just follow the small road on the left. 2. It looks as though all kinds of animals have stayed in that undergrowth. 3. If told to do anything, he does what he likes. That's the way of kids nowadays, wanting always just to listen to the radio and watch television. 4. If the red light is on, don't touch this button at all. 5. I didn't hear a single person in the classroom. The pupils were absolutely quiet there. 6. I was told to take him wherever he wanted to go, but, it turned out, he didn't want to go anywhere at all. 7. There is rubbish all over. Clean it up. 8. If the villagers co-operate with the government officials, the work will easily be carried out. 9. With sitting in one place so long, my left leg has got pins and needles. 10. Whoever wants to enter the swimming relay race, may do so. 11. That policeman likes to play about, always pretending to arrest his friends. 12. Shut that sugar bag tightly, otherwise ants will get in. 13. The pills you took before were sleeping tablets; these are different pills. 14. Don't use the car that's damaged. Use a different one. 15. All pupils in this school have to study Malay, English, arithmetic, etc. 16. I haven't time to discuss the matter now. Leave it till another time. 17. He did wrong in that he entered another person's house and, when questioned by the police, he just kept silent. 18. If you are going anywhere, let me know first. 19. Give me another book like this. If there aren't any, any other book will do. 20. Ensure that nobody at all smokes near this petrol point. 21. Not only was his car ruined but his friends were killed outright too. 22. Have you ever met a herd of animals in the middle of the jungle? 23. In the box there are sugar, sweets, salt, milk, and such things. 24. They work together in the same room. 25. The village chiefs always co-operate with the government. 26. He ran without stopping to the end of the road.

C. (The first group is given as an example):
1. If there is a person in the office, let me know. 2. If there is anyone in the shed, tell him to come out. 3. If there is anyone at all in the warehouse, call him here.

D. They didn't *say anything*, just *kept quiet*.

E. He has been (known to be) *ill* for *months on end*.

F. He is not only *silly* but *lazy* too.

G. What is the difference between '*co-operate*' and '*work together*'?

H. He didn't have time to *buy salt* before *the shop closed*.

Lesson Eighteen

A. 1. for (as far as) two hundred miles. 2. for eighteen hours. 3. as many as twenty boxes. 4. That's a one-way street. 5. Those two men are of the same race. 6. The two children are the same age. 7. Do the job again. 8. Buy me two shirts of the same colour. 9. My house isn't as big as this. 10. Don't sit together. 11. Don't bother me while I'm working. 12. All his household were ill. 13. As far as I know, she lives there still. 14. Along the river there is mangrove swamp. 15. They worked in the paddy-fields all day. 16. He lived on the island all his life. 17. There must be at least ten people. 18. There are, at most, twenty people on the bus. 19. He always tries to the best of his ability. 20. The job must be finished in two days time at the latest. 21. Fill it right up with petrol. 22. Just bring as many things as are needed. 23. Let's go as fast as possible. 24. Let's get ready as soon as possible. 25. They waited together fairly near the edge of the river. 26. They worked together in the same room. 27. Let's pull together as hard as we can. 28. Clean the floor till it's spotless. 29. Search every inch of the area. 30. Within that time he could travel at most two miles. 31. You must not pay more than a hundred dollars for it. 32. You must pay ten dollars at the very least. 33. We are paid every other week. 34. Every third person was examined by the doctor. 35. Every fourth week I work in the head office. 36. Every fifth day he does a night duty. 37. Make sure the distance between each table and the next is not more than four feet.   38. See that the metal bars are not more than nine inches apart.   39. Take this money in exchange.   40. Borrow this car in replacement.

B.   1. Why are you studying by yourself?   2. Why were you left all alone?   3. Please, make yourself at home. (or) Try and compose yourself.   4. He absented himself from his ship for three days.   5. He escaped from the hands of the police.   6. I accidentally interfered with the machine.   7. He unintentionally went into the wrong room.   8. He deliberately took the wrong road.   9. His wife is Chinese but she is a good Malay speaker.   10. The river isn't so deep. We can get across it.   11. If there is no other vehicle, I must use my own car.   12. This string isn't very strong; it's bound to snap.   13. Get the job prepared as fast as possible.   14. It's dark already yet he is fully determined to get back. He doesn't want to spend the night here.   15. Don't annoy him while he is playing there, or there'll be a row.   16. He enjoys reading while lying in bed.   17. When my wife is busy, I myself do the washing.   18. His wife goes to the market once every three days because it is rather a long way. 19. The man deliberately rammed the tree with his car because the car was too old. (Insurance?)   20. You must take this medicine at least twice a day.   21. He always goes into that road by mistake. It's now a one-way street.   22. This tyre can't last long. Don't use it.   23. After crashing, his car was held by the police for examination. 24. The woman quickly dragged her child back. If she hadn't, he would have fallen into the river.   25. If you are going in, give the door a little hard push because it's just been fitted.   26. Why is the man carrying an umbrella? It doesn't look like rain.   27. Even though he is now fifty, he still looks like a young man.   28. I feel I know that European well. I wonder who he is. Where and when have I seen him?   29. Night is coming on, and it feels cool. 30. It looks as though those old things you kept have been quite useful, Omar.   31. My parents will be home a little late tonight. The earliest they will arrive home is eight o'clock.   32. In a minute mother is going to a meeting of the Women's Institute. She'll be back at six o'clock this evening at the earliest.   33. The association get-togethers are held once a month.

C.   I don't *like* (it) (*either*).

D.   You are the only one who *has time to*.

E.   Even now *the food* still isn't *enough*.

F.   Try *looking* once again.

G. Have you any *money* on you, Ahmad, please? (I ask, please, for . . .)
H. Even though he *was ill, he still completed his work.*
(The exceptions are the last three:
He *drove the vehicle* just once and *it broke down.*)

Lesson Nineteen

A. 1. I should say Mat's asleep. Try calling him loudly. If you call softly, he won't hear. 2. It will obviously be hard to see ten cents if it happens to fall in a spot like this. 3. If (we) are going to do this job, it may as well be done properly. 4. Perhaps they forgot to shut the door last night. 5. That parang is too blunt, just leave it. 6. How was his foot hurt? He trod on a broken bottle. 7. When (If) you are going, don't go too fast, otherwise you will fall (slip/trip). 8. Don't forget to extinguish the cigarette, otherwise you'll set fire to the furniture in the store. 9. Switch on the oven, and turn to number four. Leave the meat to cook—about half an hour. 10. Who left the fence gate wide open? 11. Why are you laughing for no obvious reason? 12. You two do nothing but quarrel. Be quiet now. Don't laugh at (ridicule) him any more, Ahmad. 13. Let the rice (food) get cold; I don't want any more to eat yet. 14. Let him go on holiday now; there's no work. 15. Never mind being late, we'll still get there. 16. Let the fire go out; it's of no further use. 17. Leave the water-buffalo to eat the grass; it's long here. 18. Let the monkeys finish off these bananas. 19. Let it rain; it's long been hot. 20. He's terribly lazy that lad. It's ten o'clock and he is still sleeping.

B. 1. The things are still stored in their boxes. 2. The aeroplane has taken off; and he is still waiting around. 3. The manager hasn't arrived yet; his office door is still locked. 4. The people in the village haven't got up yet; the house lights still aren't on. 5. He has counted the cartons several times, and is still making mistakes. 6. Why is he still not here yet? It could have slipped his mind. 7. Why did he come along the back road? Perhaps he took a wrong turning. 8. Why did she get angry so suddenly? Perhaps she was startled when she heard the noise. 9. Close the carton tightly, otherwise the ants will get in. 10. My wife is always startled when aeroplanes fly overhead. 11. The matter is up to the manager; it is no longer my concern. 12. When you put the cartons in the crate, let's have it done properly. 13. The old man is extremely tired. Let him rest a while.   14. These men are too far apart from each other. Close them up a little.   15. Let me take a look in the drawer first. Perhaps there's a sharp knife inside.   16. Because there was no food there, they had to move to another area.   17. If you put oil in, don't fill it too full, otherwise the old drum will overturn.   18. Why on earth does he want to marry that old woman? Isn't he a young fellow, and rich too? 19. There are those who like the rain and there are those who prefer the heat.   20. Why was Ali fired? Perhaps he fell asleep on duty.   21. How was it his car was so completely damaged? Perhaps he happened to run into a lamp-post.   22. Don't throw banana-skins everywhere. If we don't step on them, then somebody else will.

C. only *on* certain *days*

D. Let the child sleep for now, don't wake her. (Use 'let' or 'leave').

E. Suddenly *he* happened *to fall into the water.*

F. *Drive slowly* in case *you hit a school-child.*

G. His *foot* is hurt through *stepping on a nail.*

H. *Quickly put the fan-belt on* or *we'll be* too *late.*

(There are other uses of **ter**)

I. Use **pula** after **apa, gunanya, bila, mana, mana,** and **kĕnapa.**

Lesson Twenty

A. tĕrima, suruh, tinggal, sĕlamat, tolong, tutup, padam, kirim, kuning, kĕcil, kĕna, pakai, kĕluar, sĕbab, panjang, pukul, tunggu, tengok, kĕnal, kĕjut, sĕmbunyi, tanam, kurang, tangkap, salah, tembak, sĕrang, kuat, tunjuk, simpam, kumpul, pindah, tĕntu, tipu, kĕmas, potong, sĕntuh, tahan, pĕriksa, takut, kata, samar, tarik, pasang, tolak, pĕrintah, siram, tumbuh, pendek, simpan, paksa.

B. mĕlanggar, mĕmbaca, mĕncari, mĕngambil, mĕmbaikkan, mĕngadakan, mĕncuri, mĕlawan, mĕngadu, mĕmbĕri, mĕncuci, mĕluaskan, mĕngĕrti, mĕncantikkan, mĕlompat, mĕmbawa, mĕndapat, mĕnggigit, mĕmasukkan, mĕmbayar, mĕndatangkan, mĕnggulungkan, mĕmainkan, mĕngubatkan, mĕnggunakan, mĕmbunuh, mĕnggantikan, mĕnghabiskan, mĕnjatuhkan, mĕnaikkan, mĕnggosok, mĕnghisap, mĕngikat, mĕnjalankan, mĕngganggu, mĕnjual, mĕnghidupkan, mĕrĕbus, mĕnjaga, mĕngikut, mĕmbelok, mĕringankan, mĕngingatkan, mĕnghu-kumkan, mĕnjadikan, mĕnggali, mĕlapurkan, mĕnanti,

193

měrugikan, měrompak, měngelokkan, měnghilangkan, měngisikan, měnjumpa, měngikat, měminta, měnamakan, měwarnakan, měwayangkan.

C. pěmadam, pěnolong, pěnyapu, pěměrintah, pěnanam, pěnjaga, pěmukul, pěnembak, pěncuri, pěmalas, pěngayuh, pěngarah, pěmběsar, pěmbunuh, pěnjual, pěnduduk, pěngganas, pěngikut, pěmbayar, pěnjahat, pělari, pěngěrusi, pělawat, pěnggali, pěmbaca, pěnulis, pěmain, pěndapat, pěmalu, pěmuda, pěnipu, pěngajar (instructor) and pělajar (student), pěnyakit (disease) and pěsakit (sick patient).

D. In order to *turn right*.
E. She is (in the process of) *reading a book*.
F. They are *watching a show*.
G. There's no need to *wait here any longer*.
H. Some *were selling*, some *were buying*.
I. As soon as I *went in, the show started*.
J. No sooner *did* (she) *arrive home* than she *started to cook*.
K. *The coconut-palm*, as *time went on*, grew *tall*er.
L. He was told to *help his elder brother in the plantation*.
M. 1. makin měninggi 2. makin měnjadi-jadi 3. makin měnděkat 4. makin měluas 5. makin cěpat 6. makin měndalam
N. 1. duduk měmbaca 2. pěrgi měnangkap 3. duduk měmainkan 4. pěrgi měnghantar 5. datang měncari 6. nặmpak dia tadi měnaruh

Lesson Twenty-one

A. 1. I'm tired of looking for this house. I've been searching for half an hour and only just found it. 2. When you go to a Malay village, you should see the village-chief first. 3. All good-hearted people ought to be respected. 4. He was very pleased to note his child's cleverness. 5. He is going to ask for leave because of a problem at home. 6. How are things in the docks now? Everything is fine. The labourers there are satisfied now. 7. Most of the villagers are unhappy now. It appears that two or three houses were lost in a fire and several head of cattle were lost too. 8. He has been away at the department for three hours. It's to be hoped he can get back before sunset. 9. Please don't smoke in this theatre. 10. The football-match will be held at the end of this week. A big crowd will see it. 11. It's unlikely he is telling lies. Isn't he the district officer? 12. Take care not to run into any schoolchildren. 13. Several people have lost their homes in fires in the district.   14. Your application to build the house still hasn't been approved. Wait till the end of this month.   15. This road still hasn't been repaired. Road-accidents are always happening here. Take care when driving.   16. According to a statement which was issued from the office of the state health and medical officer, the district has become a cholera-infected area.   17. The district chief of police has advised the public not to give aid to people they don't know.   18. If he said he would arrive about five o'clock, it's hardly likely he will arrive at exactly five o'clock. Perhaps his car has broken down in the middle of the road. Perhaps he's met a friend. How do we know?   19. The state government has passed an allotment of twenty-five thousand dollars to expand the public roads in this district.   20. The Minister of Trade and Industry explained that, to overcome the shortage of cement in Sarawak, the government has approved the building of a cement-factory there.   21. The Minister of Education today said that the government was satisfied with the number of new schools built last year and that the number of teachers was sufficient.   22. Watch that you don't hinder drivers on the road.   23. The results of the national language examination will be posted to all students at the end of this month.   24. In a radio report the Chief Minister said that the government will meet requests for the creation of new pay-scales for all dock-workers.   25. While the police were taking evidence concerning the theft of money, suddenly our thief was to be seen heading in the direction of the railway-station. 26. How a school-child could save that much money, I don't know.   27. It's true what the old people say, 'Black fowl fly at night', meaning that dirty deeds are always carried out in secret. 28. If government officers were more adept at influencing the native inhabitants, the followers of the communists would change their opinions and side with the government.   29. What can be done by the public in the cholera-infected areas is to follow the advice of the health officers; that is, for everyone to boil water before it is drunk and to keep the village areas clean.   30. Such matters are very interesting, but, if I'm late in getting home, what's my wife going to think? She's bound to be angry. Cheerio for now.

B.   Whether *a long way* or *near*, how is one to know?
C.   *The confidential letter is put away in the office.* Exactly *where*, I don't know.
D.   I'm tired of *looking for him.*

E. It's unlikely he would *buy* such *a cheap shirt*.
F. That *book* is *interesting*. You should *read it*.
G. Before *taking a decision*, think it over first.
H. On the contrary, he did *answer truthfully*.
I. Although he is *rich*, he is always *working*.

Lesson Twenty-two

A. KOTA HARIMAU, 20 July—Telephone wire valued at $1,800, to be fixed on nine telephone-poles in Jalan Keindahan Alam here, was reported missing yesterday.

B. KAMPUNG AIR MERAH 14 December—Thieves broke into the tiled roof of a clerk's house in Jalan Bahagia here last night and ran off with money and jewellery totalling more than $3,000.

According to a police spokesman, Mr Ahmad bin Yunus, 41, was not at home when the incident occurred.

C. PEKAM KETAM, 6 January—A man who had committed two previous offences was jailed today for five years and was fined $4,000, or three more years in jail, by the Middle Court here, for possessing pistols and ammunition.

Kuan Yu Seng, 28, pleaded guilty to three charges of being in possession of two Biretta pistols.

He also admitted having two .32 and eight .22 bullets. He was discovered to be in possession of the weapons and ammunition at a house in Jalan Tanjung at 8.00 p.m., 12th of last June.

Kuan was sentenced to five years in prison on the first offence, fined $2,500 or two years' jail on the second offence, and $1,500 or one year in prison on the third.

D. SUNGAI BATU, 18 March—Two men were today sentenced to a total of fourteen years imprisonment and eight strokes of the cane by the Middle Court here for robbery involving $7,353.40 cents in cash.

Ah Kim Wan, 30, was jailed for three years and fined $1,000 or another year in prison, while Tan Choong Foo, 29, was imprisoned for five years and fined $5,000 or five more years in jail.

Ah Kim Wan was ordered to be caned twice, while Tan, who admitted four previous offences including robbery, was sentenced to six strokes of the cane.

They pleaded guilty to robbing a dealer in car-parts of $7,353.40

cents in cash by employing a pistol in the Kĕdai Auto Spares, Jalan Pasar Bĕsar, at about 4.20 p.m., 30 January last.

The court was told that they had entered the shop that day, posing as potential customers, but Tan had brought out the pistol and effected the robbery.

E. ULU JURANG, 9 May—A keeper of a bicycle shop, Mr Abdul Wahab bin Yusuf, 42, was robbed of cash totalling $300 by two robbers who entered his shop in Jalan Kĕliling here last night.

A police spokesman said that the incident occurred at about nine o'clock last night when the shopkeeper was about to close his shop. Suddenly two youths, one of them carrying a pistol, rushed in. One of the robbers ordered all of the shopkeeper's family into the back room of the shop.

However, one of the shopkeeper's teenage daughters, who was reading in the cooking-area of the shop, became aware of what was happening and ran out of the rear door and shouted for someone.

Both the robbers had time to run off with $300 in cash which they took from a counter-drawer before they left the place.

F. KUALA LUMPUR, 22 Nov.—Police are looking for four members of a gang which is believed to be responsible for several cases of house-breaking and theft in and around the capital, which involve goods to the value of $70,000.

The Deputy-Chief of Metropolitan CID, Deputy-Superintendent D. Kurindam, said three of them originate from Penang and another comes from Perak.

Mr Kurindam said that this gang has carried out more than twelve cases of house-breaking and theft.

He said that the public who know where these men are can get in touch with the nearest police-station.

G. KOTA SĔJAHTĔRA, 16 August—A youth, Ismail bin Mansor, 21, was sentenced to nine months' imprisonment for the theft of 23 pieces of children's clothing and two sweat-shirts for males, valued at $67.00.

The sentence was passed by Magistrate of the Low Court, Mr Abdul Ghani bin Yakob, in a trial of the accused here today.

The accused pleaded guilty to carrying out the action in the company of a friend at 4.50 a.m. on 28th July, this year, at a place near Jalan Pemancar Radio here.

His accomplice, Ali Mohamad bin Naib, 19, on the same charge was bound over for good behaviour for one year on surety of $400.00.

Inspector Abdulla bin Zaini, who acted as prosecuting officer, told the court that both of the accused had been arrested by plain-clothes detective Harun bin Yaman while they were carrying the stolen clothing at the scene of the crime.

Neither of them, he continued, could explain, when questioned by plain-clothes policeman Harun, who the true owner of the clothing was nor where they had got it.

Nevertheless, he said, after they had been taken to the police-station, it was discovered that the clothing had been reported missing from a shop owned by Ling Soon Kee, 48, in Jalan Kĕrbau here and which had been broken into previously by someone.

Lesson Twenty-three

A. (2) 1. a completely ineffectual threat 2. living from hand to mouth. 3. extremely parochial and narrow-minded 4. unappreciative of the true value of something 5. not practising what one preaches (and, the blind leading the blind) 6. betraying a trust 7. the sluggard who has to be forced to work 8. always hostile to each other 9. trouble brewing unseen 10. helpless, floundering 11. two-faced 12. in a precarious position 13. a sudden stroke of luck, falling on one's feet 14. a waste of effort or expense 15. led by the nose

B. 1. flies around the honey-pot. 2. There's a catch somewhere. 3. In for a penny, in for a pound. (and, One may as well be hung for a sheep as for a lamb.) 4. Like father like son. 5. Anything patently absurd will be laughed at by the experts. 6. Counting one's chickens before they are hatched. 7. No one is perfect. 8. A dog with a bad name will be hanged on little evidence. 9. Birds of a feather flock together. 10. When powerful people fight, it is the ordinary man who suffers. 11. It's an ill wind that blows nobody any good. 12. When in Rome, do as the Romans. 13. It's no use crying over spilt milk. 14. Voicing criticism too late. 15. Killing two birds with one stone. 16. Suffering one misfortune after another. 17. Strike while the iron is hot. (and, Once bitten, twice shy.) 18. A poor workman blames his tools. 19. Out of the frying pan into the fire. 20. If what you want isn't available, a poorer substitute will do.

C. 1. The time for settling scores will come. 2. With the essentials much can be accomplished. 3. The worst of experiences can be endured if it becomes a common experience. 4. The high purchase price is justified by the long use obtained. 5. A man's nature indicates his ancestry; his behaviour indicates his background. 6. Speed matters less than safety. 7. Better death than dishonour. 8. Suffer present difficulties for future rewards. 9. Where there's a will, there's a way. 10. The reputation is better than reality. 11. The work-shy become drifters; the tongue-tied remain ignorant. 12. Outer resemblance hides the inner diversity of people. 13. Many a pickle makes a mickle. 14. When something has gone completely wrong, it is better to start afresh. 15. Fear springs from a bad conscience, courage from the truth.

Malay-English Vocabulary

The numbers in brackets refer to Lesson Notes associated with the words concerned.

abang elder brother (87)
acuan a mould
ada to be, present, situated; to have (35, 36, 37, 80, 179)
adik younger brother/sister (87)
adil fair, just
agak guess; rather, quite (153)
Ahad Sunday
ahli member, expert
air water, liquid
ajak invite
ajar
  belajar study
  mengajar teach
akan shall, will; to, for (85, 159, 180)
akar root
aku I (familiar)
  měngaku admit
alah (see **kalah**)
alat instrument, device
alang-alang if you're going to
alir flow
almari cupboard, wardrobe
amah female servant
ambil get, fetch, take
anak the young of, child (105, 136)
angin wind
angkat raise, lift

anjing dog
antara between, among
apa what; is it that (35)
api fire, flame
arah direction
asal origin, original
askar soldier, military
atap thatch
atas top, above
atau or
atur arrange
awak you, your
ayam chicken, fowl

B
baca read
badan body
bagai like
bagaimana how
bagaimanapun nevertheless
bagus excellent
bahagi divide, share
bahasa language, manners (104)
bahawa that
baik good, well (96)
baju shirt, blouse, jacket (18)
bakar burn
bakau mangrove
balai hall, station
balas return, respond

baldi   bucket
balik   return, back (46, 134)
bandar   city, town
bandaraya   capital city
bangun   rise, get up
bangsa   race, type
banyak   many, much (44, 118, 165)
bapa   father
barang   thing, article; —ever (75)
barangkali   perhaps
baring   lie down
baru/baharu   new, newly, only then (34, 54)
batang   numerical coefficient; stick, rod, bar
batu   mile, milestone; rock, stone (60)
basah   wet
bawa   take, lead, drive, carry
bawah   bottom, underneath
bayar   to pay
bebek   bleat, quack
bĕbĕrapa   several, some
bĕgini   like this, so, such (92)
bĕgitu   like that, so, such (92)
bĕlah   split (51, 77)
bĕlajar   (see ajar)
bĕlakang   rear, the back of
bĕlayar   (see layar)
bĕli   buy (64)
bĕliau   he/she (respectful)
belok   to wheel, turn
bĕlukar   secondary jungle
bĕlum   not yet (39, 62)
   sĕbĕlum   before
bĕnar   true, truly
bĕrani   brave, dare
bĕrapa   how much/many (57)
bĕras   uncooked rice

bĕrat   heavy, weight
bĕrdiri   (see diri)
bĕrĕnang   swim
bĕrhĕnti   to stop (78)
bĕri   give; allow
bĕritahu   tell, inform
bĕrjabat   grasp, shake (hands)
bĕrlabuh   (see labuh)
bĕrlaku   (see laku)
bĕrniaga   do business, trade
bĕrsih   clean
bĕruang   a bear
bĕsar   big, main, important
bĕsi   metal, iron
besok   tomorrow
bĕtul   correct
beza(nya)   difference
biar   let, allow, leave (158)
biasa   ordinary, usual (131)
bicara   discussion, debate
biji   numerical coefficient; pip, seed (70)
bikin   do, make (17)
bila   when
bilah   numerical coefficient; cutting edge
bilang   to count; say (156)
bilik   room
binatang   animal
biru   blue
bisa   venom
bising   noise, row
bodoh   foolish
boleh   cam, be able
bohong   lie, falsehood
borang   a form (of application)
buah   numerical coefficient; fruit
bual   chat, converse
buang   throw away, discard
buat   do, make, for

202

buaya   crocodile
bubur   porridge, gruel
budak   child (105)
bujang   single, unmarried
buka   open, switch on, take off (clothes)
bukan   no, not (91)
bulan   month, moon
bumi   ground, the Earth
bunga   flower, interest (on money), design
bungkus   wrap, parcel, packet
bunuh   kill, murder
buruh   labour
buruk   old, dilapidated
burung   bird
busuk   rotten, putrid
butang   button
butir   numerical coefficient; grain, particle

C

cadar   bed-sheet
cakap   speak, say
cantik   beautiful
cap   trade-brand
cari   seek, look for
cawan   cup (77)
cĕpat   quick, quickly
cĕrmin   mirror, window (124)
coklat   dark brown
cuba   try, test; please (152)
cuci   wash, rinse
cucuk   pierce, vaccinate
cukai   tax, duty
cukup   enough, very (47, 65)
cukur   shave
curi   steal
cuti   holiday, leave

D

daerah   district
daftar   register

dagang   trade
daging   meat, flesh (82)
dahulu/dulu   previously, ago, last (48, 54)
dakwa   prosecute
dalam   inside, interior, deep (43)
dapat   get, obtain, manage to
dan   and
dapur   stove, kitchen
darah   blood
darat   the land
darimana   from where, whence
daripada/dari   from (43)
datang   come
dawai   wire
dĕkat   near, nearby (117)
dĕmam   fever
dĕnda   court-fine
dĕngan   with, by (110, 121)
dĕngar   hear, listen
dĕpan   (see hadapan)
dĕras   swift
di   in, at (43)
dia/ia   he, she, it (24)
diam   to be silent
dingin   cold, chilly
diri   one's self (150)
   bĕrdiri   to stand
dua   two
duduk   sit, stay, live (4)
duit   money, coin, change
dulu   (see dahulu)
dunia   the world
duri   thorn
durian   a thorny fruit

E

ekor   numerical coefficient; tail
ela   yard (36 inches)

elaun allowance

elok fine, pretty; it would be better to (96)

ĕmak mother

ĕmpat four

ĕnam six

ĕncik form of address, Mr (2, 112)

ĕnggang hornbill

ĕngkau/kau you (familiar)

ĕntah perhaps, don't know (175)

ĕrti(nya) meaning (3)

esok (see besok)

F

fikir (see pikir)

faham (see paham)

fasal (see pasal)

G

gadis teenage girl (114)

gaduh quarrel

gajah elephant

gaji salary, pay

galah punting-pole

gali dig

gambar picture, photograph

ganas fierce, ferocious

ganggu annoy, disturb

gantang a unit of capacity

ganti substitute, change

garam salt

gĕlap dark, secret

gĕmuk fat, stout

gĕnting narrow, hill-pass, tense

gĕtah rubber

gigi teeth

gigit bite

goreng fry

gosok rub, polish, to iron

gula sugar

gulung roll up, a roll

guna use (132)

gunting clip, cut

guru teacher (112)

H

habis finished, completed, completely (142)

hadapan/dĕpan front, next (45)

hal matter, affair (95)

hala direction

halus delicate, refined

hampir nearly, near

hantar send, see someone off

hanyut adrift

harap to hope; please (176)

harga price, value (66)

hari day

harimau tiger

harus ought, should

hati liver, 'heart' (177)

hawa climate, air

hĕlai numerical coefficient; a fold

hĕndak/nak wish to, intend (28, 117, 129)

hĕnti (see bĕrhĕnti)

hidung nose

hidup alive, live

hijau green

hilang lost, missing (81)

hilir downstream

hisap suck

hitam black

hormat respect, honour

hubung connect, contact, communicate

hujan rain

hujung end, tip

204

hukum punish, law (113)
hulu/ulu upper waters, the interior
huruf letter (of alphabet)
hutan jungle

I

ia (see **dia**)
iaitu that is to say, in that
ialah to be
ibu mother (136)
ikan fish
ikat tie, fasten, secure
ikut obey, follow, via
ilmu the study of (126)
indah beautiful, fine
ini this, these, here is (20, 25, 42, 146)
ingat remember, think (97)
isi(nya) contents
Isnin Tuesday
istana palace
isteri wife
itik duck
itu that, those, the (20, 25, 42)

J

jabat (see **berjabat** and **jabatan**)
jabatan department
jadi become; happen, as, will do (90)
jaga guard, look after, alert, awake
jahat wicked
jalan road, way (5)
jam hour, clock, watch, o'clock (71)
jambatan bridge

jamin guarantee, surety
jangan don't, mustn't (22)
jantan male (of animals)
jarak distance between, space (151)
jatuh fall, drop
jauh far, a long way
jawab answer (178)
jĕmu bored, fed up, tired of
jĕmur to dry in the sun
jĕnis type, kind
jika if
jong a junk
jual sell
juang struggle, fight
juga also, nevertheless, quite (109, 130)
Jumaat Friday
jumlah total
jumpa meet, find (49)
juru expert, skilled worker (103)
juta million

K

kaca glass
kadang-kadang sometimes
kahwin marry
kain cloth, clothing (127)
kais scratch (the ground for food)
kakak elder sister
kaki foot, leg, 12 inches
kalah/alah defeated, lose
kalau if (100, 108)
kali time, occasion
kambing goat
kami we (exclusive) (21)
kampung village, home (33)
kanak-kanak children
kanan the right, senior (of rank)

kandang animal pen, stable
kapal ship, boat
kasi give (17)
kasih love, affection
kasut shoes
kata say, words (143)
katak frog
kati unit of weight (625 gr.)
kawan friend; herd, flock, shoal
kawasan an area
kawat wire
kaya rich
kayu wood, wooden
kayuh paddle
kĕbun garden, plantation
kĕcil small, little, young
kĕdai shop
kĕjut startle, waken
kĕlabu grey (not of hair)
kĕlapa coconut
kĕluar go out, come out
kĕmas neat, tidy, orderly
kĕmudian afterwards, after
kĕna strike, suffer from, must (106, 172)
kĕnal recognise, know (a person)
kĕnapa why
kĕnyang satisfied (after eating)
kĕpada/kĕ to (29, 43)
kĕpala head (of body), leader
kĕping numerical coefficient; piece, fragment
kĕra long-tailed monkey
kĕrajaan (see raja)
kĕrana because, on account of
kĕrani clerk

kĕras hard, stiff
kĕrbau water-buffalo
kĕreta car, vehicle
kĕring dry
kĕrja to work, job
kĕrjasama co-operation
kĕrtas paper
kĕrusi chair
kĕtam crab; carpenter's plane
kĕtawa/tĕrtawa to laugh (155)
kĕtika when, the time when
kĕtua chief, head of
khabar news
Khamis Thursday
khidmat obedient, duty
kilang factory, mill
kipas fan, propeller
kira count, reckon (125)
kiri the left
kirim send
kita we (inclusive) (21)
kolam pool, pond
kosong zero; vacant, empty
kota town, fort (137)
kotak carton, box
kotor dirty
kuak bellow, croak
kuasa power, authority
kuat powerful, strong (118)
kuih cake
kulit skin, leather, bark, shell
kumpul collect, congregate
kucing cat
kuning yellow
kura the spleen
kurang less, lacking (76, 121, 122)
kursus a course (of training)
kurus thin (of people)

L

labuh hanging down
  berlabuh to anchor, to
    dock
laci a drawer
lada pepper
ladang estate, dry field
lagak pose, swank
lagi again, more, even,
  additional (62, 63, 122, 147)
lahir to be born
lain different, other (147)
laki-laki male (of people)
laku saleable, in demand;
  act, behave (166)
  berlaku happen, behave
lalai careless, listless
lalang type of tall grass
lalu to pass, last (of dates)
  (155)
lama old (of things), a long
  time (31, 61)
lambai to wave
lambat slow, late
lampau excessive, past (155)
lampu a light, lamp
langgar knock, collide,
  infringe
lantai floor
lapan eight
lapang open, spacious, free
lapar hungry
lapur report
larang forbid, prohibit
laras numerical coefficient;
  barrel (of weapon)
lari run, flee
lat interval (151)
latih practise, train
laut sea
lawan oppose, fight,
  opponent

lawat visit
layar sail
  bĕrlayar to sail
lebar wide, broad
lĕbat thick (jungle, hair *etc.*)
  heavy (rain)
lĕbih more (76, 121, 122)
lĕkas quickly, fast
lĕlaki (see laki-laki)
lĕmah weak
lĕmbu cattle
lĕmbut soft
lĕpas free, after, past
  sĕlĕpas after
lewat late
libat involve
lihat to see
lima five
limau citrus fruit
lompat jump
luar outside, external
luas wide, extensive (115)
lubang hole, hollow
luka wound, hurt
lulus pass (examination),
  approve
lumba a race, contest
lupa forget
lurus straight

M

maaf excuse, pardon
mabuk intoxicated
macam like, sort, type
  (121)
mahal expensive (66)
mahkamah law-court
mahu to want (129)
main to play
makan eat, consume
makin the more, increasing
  (164)

malam night (68)
  sĕmalam yesterday, a night
malang unfortunate
malas lazy
malu ashamed, shy
mana which, where (27)
mandi bathe
manis sweet
manusia mankind, human
marah angry
mari come! here (6)
masa period, time
  sĕmasa while
masak to cook, boil (water);
  ripe
masam sour
masih still, yet
masuk enter
mata eye
  mata-mata police
matahari the sun
mati dead, expired (80)
memang indeed, of course
mĕnang to win
mĕngaku (see **aku**)
mĕninggal (see **tinggal**)
mĕntĕri minister
mĕnyĕbĕrang (see **sĕbĕrang**)
merah red, brown
mĕrbahaya dangerous
mĕreka they; to invent
  (23)
mĕrokok (see **rokok**)
mĕsjid mosque
mĕsti must, have to
mĕsyuarat meeting,
  conference
milik possess
minggu week
minta request, ask for,
  please (152)
minum to drink

minyak oil, grease, petrol,
  fat (111)
miskin destitute, poor
monyet monkey
muda young, light (of
  colour), unripe
muka face
mula beginning (134)
  mula-mula at first
mulut mouth
murah cheap
murid pupil
mustahak essential,
  important

N

naik rise, go up, go aboard,
  by (of transport)
nakal naughty
nama name
nampak see, catch sight of
  nampaknya it seems,
    apparently (116, 153)
nanas pineapple
nanti wait, by and by
  (107, 108)
nasi cooked rice, food
nasihat advice
nĕgara the state, national
  (120)
nĕgĕri country, a state (120)
nganga gape
niaga (see **bĕrniaga**)
nilai value, worth
nipis thin (of objects)
nyamuk mosquito
nyata clear, apparent

O

oleh by, on account of
orang person, people,
  somebody (57, 139)

P

pada   at, on (69)
padam   extinguish
padang   field (73)
padi   rice plant
pagar   fence
pagi   morning
pahat   chisel
pakai   use, wear, put on
  (clothes)
paksa   compel
paku   nail
paling   extremely, the most
palsu   false, counterfeit
panas   hot
pandai   clever, skilled,
  accomplished (50)
pandu   guide, drive
panjang   long
panggil   call, invite
panggung   cinema, theatre
pangkal   beginning, start
pangkat   rank, status
pantai   shore, coast
parah   severe (of wounds)
parang   chopper, machete
parit   ditch, drain
pasal   concerning, because
  (154)
pasang   to fix, to light, rising
  (of tide) (84)
pasar   market
pasir   sand
pasukan   team, unit (military),
  force (police)
patah   snapped, broken
patung   puppet, statue
payah   difficult, hard
payung   umbrella, parachute
pĕcah   smashed, broken
pĕdas   hot (as of spices)
pĕgawai   officer, an official

pĕjabat   office
pĕkan   market-town
pĕlan-pĕlan   slowly, quietly
pĕlanduk   mouse-deer
pĕluru   bullet, ammunition,
  missile
pĕnat   tired
pendek   short
pĕngaruh   influence
pĕnghulu   chief (government-
  appointed)
pĕnjara   prison
pĕngurus   manager
pĕnuh   full
pĕrahu   boat, prow
pĕrcaya   believe, trust
pĕrĕmpuan   woman, female
pĕrgi   to go, away (32, 40,
  55)
pĕriksa   examine, inspect,
  search
pĕrintah   command, govern
pĕriman   civilian
  (preman)
pĕrkakas   equipment, kit,
  tools
pĕrlahan-lahan   (see
  pĕlan-pĕlan)
pĕrnah   ever, at times (145)
pĕrsatuan   (see satu)
pĕrtama   first
pĕrut   stomach
pĕta   a map
pĕtang   afternoon, evening
pĕti   box, crate
pijak   tread on
pikir   think
pilih   choose
pindah   transfer, move
pinggang   waist
pinjam   borrow
pipis   grind, mash

209

pipit sparrow
pintu door, gate
pisang banana
pisau knife
pokok tree; base, root
pondok shed
potong cut
puas satisfied, have enough of
puasa a fast
pucuk numerical coefficient; a shoot, sprout
pukul hit, beat, o'clock (71)
pula then, -ever, too, next, instead (157)
pulang return (135)
pulau island
puluh ten(s)
pun even, also (144)
punya possess (79)
pusing turn, go round
putus severed, snapped; decide

R
Rabu Wednesday
raja ruler, prince
  kĕrajaan government
rakan pal, friend
rakit raft, dinghy
ramai many, crowd (165)
rambut hair
rambutan a red, hairy fruit
ranting twig
rapat close, tight
rasa feel, taste (153)
ratus hundred
raya public, great, main
rebus boil in water
rehat rest, break
rĕndah low, short (stature), humble

ribu thousand
rimba primary (of jungle)
ringan light, slight
ringgit dollar
rokok cigarette
  mĕrokok to smoke cigarettes
rompak rob
rosak damaged, broken down
rotan rattan
roti bread
rumah house, building
rumput grass
rupa appearance, looks (116, 153)

S
sahaja/saja only, just
sakit ill
salah wrong, guilty
salak to bark
sama same, with, equally (7, 121, 148)
samar disguise
sambil while, at the same time
sampah rubbish, trash
sampai arrive, till, as far as
sana yonder, over there
sangat extremely, very, too (83)
sapu wipe, sweep
sarung sheath, envelope, skirt (127)
satu/sĕ one (58, 148)
  pĕrsatuan association
  kĕsatuan union
saudagar merchant
saudara relation, cousin, a form of address
sawah padi paddy-field

210

saya   I, me, my (8, 34)
sayur   vegetable
sĕbab   reason, because
sĕbat   cane, whip
sĕbĕlum   (see belum)
sĕbĕrang   across
   mĕnyĕberang   to cross (98)
sĕbĕlas   eleven
sĕbut   mention
sĕdang   in the process of,
   while (159)
sĕdap   tasty, pleasant
sĕdar   aware
sĕdikit   a few, a little
   (sikit)
sĕjuk   cool, cold
sĕkam   chaff, rice-husk
sĕkarang   now (54)
sĕkĕjap   a second, a moment,
   a 'jiffy'
sĕkitar   in and around
sĕkolah   school
sĕlam   submerge, dive
sĕlamat   safe, secure
sĕlalu   always, often
Sĕlasa   Tuesday
sĕlĕpas   (see lepas)
sĕlimut   blanket
sĕluar   trousers
sĕmak   undergrowth
sĕmalam   (see malam)
sĕmasa   (see masa)
sĕmbahyang   pray, perform
   prayers
sĕmbilan   nine
sĕmbunyi   to hide
sĕmĕntara   while, during
sĕmpat   have time to, able
sĕmpit   narrow
sĕmua   all (148)
sĕmut   ant
sĕnang   at ease, free, easily

sĕnapang   rifle
sĕndiri   oneself, own (150)
sĕngaja   deliberately
sĕnjata   weapon
sĕntuh   touch
sĕpĕrti   like
sĕrah   submit, hand over
sĕrang   attack
sĕrbu   to rush
sĕsat   astray, lost
siang   day, day-time
siap   ready, prepared
sifat   characteristic, quality
sihat   healthy, well
sikit   (see sedikit)
sila   please, cross-legged
   (9, 152)
silap   error, slip
simpan   store, keep, put
   away
simpang   road-junction
sini   here (10)
siram   sprinkle
situ   there
songkok   the oval Malay
   hat
suami   husband
subur   fertile, health (of
   plants)
sudah/'dah   has already, is
   now (52, 54, 61, 108)
suka   to like
suku   quarter (1/4) (74)
sungai   river
sungguh   genuinely, really
   (181)
sungguhpun   although
sulit   confidential, secret
suluh   torch
supaya   so that, to
surat   letter, document
suruh   order, tell

211

susah difficult, trouble, worry
susu milk
susun stack, arrange
syarikat a firm, company

T

tadbir administer
tahan last out, endure;
  detain, arrest, stop
tahu know (facts), know
  how to
tahun year
tajam sharp
takkan it's unlikely that
takut frightened, afraid
talam tray
tali rope, string
tambah increase
tambang fare (on transport)
tanah earth, land
tanam plant, bury, invest
tanda sign, mark
tanduk horns
tangan hand, arm
tangga ladder, steps, stairs
tanggung bear, support
tanggungjawab responsibility
tangis weep
tangkap catch, arrest
tangki tank (as for petrol)
tanya ask, enquire
tari dance
tarik drag, pull
tarikh date
taruh put, place
taun cholera
tawa (see ketawa)
tebal thick, dense
tĕgal because
tĕgap well-built, sturdy
tĕkan to press
tĕlur egg

tembak to shoot, fire
tĕmpat place, place where
  (88)
tĕmpurung coconut shell
tĕngah middle, in the process
  of (159)
tengok look at, watch
tĕntu sure, certain, bound to
  (108, 155)
tĕpi edge
tĕrang clear, bright
tĕrbang to fly
tĕriak shout, scream
tĕrima receive
tĕrjĕmah translate (155)
tĕrlampau (see lampau)
tĕrlalu (see lalu)
tĕrus straight, continue,
  immediately
tĕtapi/'tapi but
(tiada = (1) tidak (2)
  tidak ada)
tiang pole, post
tiap-tiap every, each
tiba arrive
tiba-tiba suddenly
tidak/tak no, not (19, 102)
tinggal to live; remaining,
  left
  mĕninggal die, pass away
  (4, 80)
tinggi high, tall
tingkap window
tipu cheat, deceive
tiup to blow
tolak push, reject
tolong to help; please (152)
tong bin, barrel
tongkat walking-stick
topi hat
tua old (of people);
  dark (of colour)

212

tuala   towel
tuan   form of address, Mr (2)
tuduh   accuse
tugas   task, duty
tujuh   seven
tulis   write
tukang   skilled worker (103)
tukar   change, exchange
tulang   bone
tumbuh   flourish, grow
tumpul   blunt
tunai   cash
tunggu   wait for
tunjuk   show, demonstrate
turun   descend, alight from
turut   follow, join in
   mĕnurut   according to
tutup   shut, close, cover

U
ubat   medicine, remedy
udang   prawn, shrimp
udara   air, atmosphere
ular   snake

ulu   (see hulu)
umur   age
undang-undang   law,
   regulation (113)
untuk   in order to, for;
   share, portion
untung   profit, lucky

W
wabak   epidemic
wajib   obligatory, essential
waktu   time, time when,
   while
wang   money
wanita   woman
warna   colour
wayang   a show, performance

Y
ya   yes (24)
yang   which, who (93, 94,
   119, 121)
yu   shark

Grammatical Index

Since Malay words do not fit easily into the matrices of English grammar, students will find that the English terms are loosely used at times. Some terms, such as 'juxtaposition', seemingly more suited to literary composition are included because such devices assume greater importance where there are no mechanical rules for indicating conjugation, declension and gender.

For reasons of space, this index is necessarily selective. Where numerous examples abound in the exercises then only a brief description is considered here.

The numbers used refer to lesson notes, unless attention is being drawn to a particular type of sentence in this way:

p 38 C 22 = (sentence 22 of exercise C on page 38).

215

mĕ-i/kan (167); mĕ, ke-i/kan (168); me, per-i/
kan (169); pĕ-an (171); pĕr-an (170)
other affixes: sĕni, wan, wati (p 157)

appellatives, names	(12, 87, 112, 174); **kawan** and **saudara** are also used like personal pronouns.
articles	definite (25); indefinite (25, 57, 58)
be, (verb)	copula understood (14, 26); locative, **ada** (36); become/happen (90); **adalah** is sometimes used as a copula to stress the complement; **ialah**, which is, actually, stressed pronominal repetition of a noun antecedent, acts as 'be' in sentences containing some degree of definition:

Kangaroo ialah sĕjĕnis binatang yang ganjil.
The kangaroo is a peculiar kind of animal.

clauses, subordinate	adjectival: restrictive introduced by **yang** or **tĕmpat**, or the relative is omitted; non-restrictive traditionally not used, the clause being made another main clause, or apposition being employed. However, there is increasing use of **siapa yang** and **yang mana** to introduce nonrestrictive clauses, and cases are to be found where writers employ commas to distinguish between restrictive and non-restrictive.
	noun: all the usual interrogatives may introduce but particular attention is drawn to **adakah** (whether), **bahawa** (that, in reported speech), **waktu** (when), **sĕbabnya** (why), **yang** (that, the fact, that) **tĕmpat** (where), **ĕntah** (175). See also 153.
	adverbial: conjunctives to introduce various types are: comparison **macam/saya** (equal), **dari** (unequal); concession—**sungguhpun, walaupun, sĕkalipun**; condition—**jika, kalau, kalau-kalau**; degree—**sĕbĕrapa** (148); place—**di mana, di mana-mana**; purpose—**untuk, supaya, nak, takut kalau**; reason—**sĕbab, pasal**; result—**sampai/hingga** (introduced by **bĕgitu**+adjective/adverb); time — **bila, apabila, bila-bila, bila saja, sĕbĕlum, sĕsudah, sĕlĕpas, sĕbaik-baik, sĕmasa, sĕmĕnjak**
coefficients, numerical	See *number and quantity*
command, exhortation, obligation, request	**Bĕr** is the only prefix used in imperatives, and adverbs are used as imperatives (**Cĕpatlah!**— *Quickly!*); **nanti** balancing imperatives (107);

216

imperative with **lah** (41); **mari** (6); **marilah kita** (lesson 4); **jangan** (22); **jangan**+passive (p 97 D); **mahu/nak**+passive (129); indirect command (p 60 C3); **tak usahlah, tak ▮▮ahlah** (p 134 G); **patut, harus** (p 145 F); ▮a, minta, sila, tolong (9, 152), harap (176); ▮k, eloklah (96); biar, biarkan (158)
In officialese **hĕndaklah** co▮▮only replaces **mĕsti**:

Orang ramai hĕndakla▮ mĕnĕntukan ...
The public are to en▮▮e that ...

217

The relative pronoun is not governed by prepositions in Malay. Use a relative adverb or rephrase the clause in such cases.

pronouns   personal: saya (8); kami/kita (21); dia orang (23)

	familiar	*polite*	*plural*	*other*
1st person	aku (ku)	saya	kita	beta (*by ruler*)
			kami	patik (*to ruler*)
2nd person	ěngkau (kau)	awak		anda (*adverts*)
	kamu (mu)			
3rd person		dia (ia)	mereka	běliau (*newspapers*)

If required, **orang** or **sěmua** may indicate the 2nd person plural (**kamu orang, awak sěmua**).
Names, titles, and words, indicating a relationship are frequently used as personal pronouns.
interrogative: **siapa, apa**; relative: **yang**; emphatic: **sěndiri**; reflexive: **diri**; indefinite: **siapa, siapa-siapa, barang, apa, apa-apa, orang** (see also **lah**, 100); possessive: **punya** (79)

reduplication   (140, 141, 162, p 157)

responses   short affirmative and negative (37, 53)

subjunctive   There are no changes in verb form to make explicit the subjunctive. The English subjunctive is in translation most commonly expressed through use of **lah, barangkali, boleh jadi, nanti, těntu, kalau, takut kalau, kalau-kalau,** and **supaya**. Since context is all-important, there is no simple method of transposing the English subjunctive into Malay. The following are simply examples of possible subjunctives:

Kalau saya kaya nanti   *If I were to become rich*
Kalaulah saya kaya! — *If only I were rich!*

stress   Because of the word economy characteristic of spoken Malay, emphasis, juxtaposition, and established word order are essential safeguards against ambiguity. The notes under these headings should be seen together as interdependent elements of Malay idiom.
word order (26); **lah** and **kah** (41); **bukan** (91) and **ada** (179); **děngan** (110); **lěbih . . . lagi** (122); **bělum . . . lagi** (72); **juga** in time phrases (130); **saja** (139); **pun** (141); reduplication (140, 141); **sěndiri** (150); **mě** prefix (161)
(There is also tautological use of some synonyms: **masih . . . lagi; hanya . . . saja.**)

tense	implied or understood (13)
	When not apparent from the context, tense is indicated by abverbs and abverbial phrases of time or by words classed as tense-indicators in the lesson notes. Performing sometimes the rôle of our continuous tense forms are: **lagi, masih, sĕdang/tĕngah** (159), **makin** (164), and the prefix **tĕr** (155, state).
	Indicating future and past timing of the verb are: **hĕndak/nak** (28), **akan** (159), **nanti** (107), **dĕkat nak** (117); and **belum** (39), **dulu** (48), **tĕlah/sudah** (52). Concerned with completion of the verb are: **habis, bĕlum, tĕlah/sudah**, and the prefix **tĕr** (155).
time	of clock (72)
transitive verb	(101)
word order	interrogatives (15); stress (26); **mana** (27); adjectives of quantity (44, 47); **cukup**, adverb (47); **hendak** (28); numerical coefficients (57); **sĕ** (58); **batu** (60); fractions (74); **bukan** (91); **juga** (130); passive agent (138); **takkan** (180); **sungguh/ bĕnạr**
	See also *adjectives, adverbs, demonstratives, juxtaposition*, and *stress*.

SANSKRIT

Michael Coulson

This course in Sanskrit has been devised to enable the student to read Indian classics in the original. The carefully-graded chapters explain Sanskrit grammar and style with exceptional clarity. Exercises, most of which use only sentences taken directly from Sanskrit authors, enable the student to check his progress.

This is not only a primer, but also a work of scholarship, for the book contains much new material on Sanskrit syntax and usage. Its explanation of how to use Sanskrit commentaries is especially useful. The text also includes an appendix on prosody, extensive vocabularies both into and out of Sanskrit, and full keys to the main exercises.

Michael Coulson was head of the Department of Sanskrit at Edinburgh University.

UNITED KINGDOM	£2.95
AUSTRALIA	$9.45
NEW ZEALAND	$9.30
CANADA	$9.95

*recommended but not obligatory

ISBN 0 340 05982 6

TEACH YOURSELF BOOKS

☐ 20380 3	**Indonesian** J. B. Kwee	£1.40
☐ 05800 5	**Japanese** C. J. Dunn and S. Yanada	£1.25
☐ 12464 4	**Punjabi** C. Shackle	50p
☐ 05982 6	**Sanskrit** Michael Coulson	£2.95

All these books are available at your local bookshop or newsagent, or can be ordered direct from the publisher. Just tick the titles you want and fill in the form below.

Prices and availability subject to change without notice.

TEACH YOURSELF BOOKS, P.O. Box 11, Falmouth, Cornwall.

Please send cheque or postal order, and allow the following for postage and packing:

U.K. – One book 22p plus 10p per copy for each additional book ordered, up to a maximum of 82p.

B.F.P.O. and EIRE – 22p for the first book plus 10p per copy for the next 6 books, thereafter 4p per book.

OTHER OVERSEAS CUSTOMERS – 30p for the first book and 10p per copy for each additional book.

Name ....

Address ....

....

....